W9-BYK-800

REVISED EDITION

# FIRESEEDS

*Of Spiritual Awakening*

*dan HAYES*
AUTHOR

FOREWORD BY
MARK GAUTHIER

Written by Dan Hayes

Published by Cru Press

Cru Press is the publishing division of the Campus Ministry of Campus Crusade for Christ.

Campus Crusade for Christ
100 Lake Hart Drive 2500
Orlando, FL 32832

Book and Cover Design:
Aaron Martin *www.iamaaronmartin.com*

Manuscript Revision:
Rick James

Copy Editing:
Eric Stanford *www.editresource.com*

Proofing:
Avery James

To order, go to
*www.crupress.com*
1-800-827-2788

ISBN number: 1-57334-063-4

# FIRESEEDS

*Of Spiritual Awakening*

*dan HAYES*

AUTHOR

# ACKNOWLEDGMENTS

John Donne said, "No man is an island." Certainly that is true when it comes to writing a book. No man writes one by himself. Therefore, I would like to offer my sincere thanks to some who have helped in the endeavor.

Roger Randall and the Campus Crusade for Christ national campus team helped me discern the needs of college students and offered many helpful suggestions. Ney Bailey spurred me on when the going got rough. Judy Steward spent many hours working on the original manuscript. Claude E. Robertson Jr. has helped me by organizing, editing, and typing the revised edition.

Thousands of college and university students have testified personally in the last ten years to the validity of the truths contained in this book and have, by their frequent critiques and insights, made many improvements in this edition.

My wife, Charlotte, and children—Janie, Danny, and Cindy—have exhibited the sort of love and patience that were necessary to allow this book to be written. Without all these men and women (and many more who played larger roles than I probably realized), this book and the benefits it has produced would never have been possible.

# NOTES ON THE REVISION

*As this book has had a great* influence on my prayer and expectancy over the years, it has been a privilege to work on the revised manuscript. The revisions to *Fireseeds* fall into four general categories.

First, we sought to widen the focus of the book from the revivals and campuses of the U.S. to those of the world. This was at times a daunting task, the challenge lying in the absence of written histories, not an absence of spiritual activity.

Second, we included examples of more current movements of God's Spirit, as a great deal has happened in the last two decades relating to prayer and revival.

Third, where appropriate, we also made note of the role of women in these revivals, since their contribution is sometimes overlooked.

And, last, we concluded the book with an additional chapter that provides anyone and everyone with the opportunity to be filled with the Spirit and experience renewal in their walk with the Lord. We cannot control when God brings revival, but we can control whether we are filled and walking with His Spirit.

My excitement for this book stems from my belief that the ideas it contains are even more significant now than when it was first written.

In 1747 Jonathan Edwards wrote a small book to encourage prayer, entitled *A Humble Attempt*. It was his hope that the book would further fuel the Great Awakening in which he was involved. It didn't, at least not significantly. Instead, due to a 1789 reprinting, the book found its audience and spurred another revival (the Second Great Awakening) a full generation after it was written.

In much the same way, I believe we are the generation that God ultimately intended this book for, and that is the heart and faith behind this revision and reprint.

Sincerely,<br>
Rick James<br>
Publisher, Cru Press

CONTENTS

# CONTENTS

# FOREWORD

*Accounts of the First and Second Great* Awakenings, and the movements that were birthed by them, have always inspired me. The interest was born in me during my time in ministry in Boston. Perhaps it was walking the same roads that men like Jonathan Edwards traveled that did it. Perhaps it was reading the many inscriptions etched into the stone of the churches in New England that testified to the transformation wrought by Edwards' call to prayer and fully surrendered lives. Of course there were the excursions to Williams College in western Massachusetts where the Student Volunteer Movement had its roots in an impromptu prayer meeting. But most profoundly, my great interest in all these movements of God was established by the experience of working daily with the college students of New England and recognizing in them their great potential, and envisioning how the Lord could use students again.

*Fireseeds* is a book of stories—stories of how God has worked in and through generations past. All over the globe and for thousands of years, God has been at work in His people of every tongue, tribe and nation for His glory. Many of those inspiring stories are recounted here. But *Fireseeds* is more than stories, as powerful as they are. Within this book you will find a compelling vision for how God can transform your life, your campus, and your world.

The first time I read this book, God used it to move me to greater surrender and more fervent prayer. He wooed me into a bigger vision for how He wanted to work in and through my life. And as He worked through this book in the lives of others around me, it translated into radical change in my community and on our campuses.

This book has been reprinted and updated because it contains a message for this generation. This message is a call to prayer, to surrender and to action that I believe God will use to fuel movements among the students of the world.

It will be these movements, characterized by students who seek God with all their hearts, who call on Him to change their realities, and who step out in faith with the Gospel, that will ultimately and radically transform our world.

I leave you with the prayer of Habakkuk in his book, chapter 3, verse 2: "Lord, I have heard of your fame; I stand in awe of your deeds, O Lord. Renew them in our day, in our time make them known; in wrath remember mercy."

Mark Gauthier
National Director, U.S. Campus Ministry

# INTRODUCTION

*Dr. Charles Malik, one of the architects* of the United Nations, asserted in a speech at Wheaton College that "once [a person] realizes that Jesus Christ would find Himself less at home on the campuses of the great universities of Europe and America than almost anywhere else, he will be profoundly disturbed, and he will inquire what can be done to recapture the great universities for Jesus Christ, the universities which would not have come into being in the first place without Him."[1]

That is what this book is about: recapturing colleges and universities—not through political action but through campus spiritual awakening.* There are available to Christian collegians more joy, more power, more challenge, and more significance than they have ever imagined.

God is beginning to draw a spiritual force of students from all corners of the world, a movement that will, by God's grace, obliterate the apathy, purposelessness, and spiritual malaise that have afflicted our campuses for years.

Spiritual awakening can come to our colleges and universities, and it may come soon. This book is written to help us get on board, to get caught in the joyous jet stream of God's Spirit as He sweeps across and through the campuses of the world.

In these pages can be found the motivation, perspective, methods, and results of massive spiritual stirrings in our residence halls, fraternities, sororities, athletic teams, and classes.

My prayer is that we might be stirred, motivated, and instructed to lay the foundations for spiritual revolution in the home and halls of academia. If we expect it, follow the principles outlined here, and don't quit, we will see it happen.

*It has happened before and God can bring it again in an even more powerful action of His Spirit, sweeping movements everywhere into the torrent of spiritual awakening. May we not miss the chance to cooperate with Him in helping university communities know personally the very Incarnation of Truth Himself, Jesus Christ.

# LET'S TURN THE COLLEGE CAMPUS RIGHT SIDE UP

*"God's concern is worldwide. How the church has responded to that mandate is also clear in the light of history. All too frequently the Church has fallen into lethargy in relation to its world-wide obligations. But God does not leave Himself without a witness. Whether it be a Nicolas Von Zinzendorf, a Samuel Mills, a C. T. Studd, a Robert Wilder, a John Mott, a Jim Elliot or a hundred others who could be named, God singles out a man to prophesy to His church. And with remarkable frequency that man has been a student."*
*– David Howard*[1]

*Out of the 17 million college students* in the U.S. (90 million worldwide), a growing number of freshmen would identify themselves as being Christians, by which they sincerely mean "Christ followers," not "Our family has a Christmas tree instead of a Hanukkah bush." Yet, however you want to quantify it, or whatever metric you use, this growing number has not translated into a growing influence for

Christ. On most campuses our heads rarely rise above sea level to be recognized as anything more than another club or subculture, listed in the student activities manual under "Christian Groups," sandwiched between "Chess Club" and "Cross-Country." It would be more accurate to say that we, who ought to be the salt of the earth, have instead become its vanilla extract.

As I move from campus to campus, I look for revolutionary Christians who will stand up and say they are committed to living for Christ, no matter what the cost and no matter what they might have to sacrifice. But it is hard to find such Christians. I've been to more worship services than I can count, and I've heard students voice vehement conviction in the lyrics of their praise. I just don't see the follow-through. And I've been in the follow-through business. When students said they wanted to go and serve Christ around the world, I've set up the trips and witnessed firsthand the discontinuity between the worshiping multitudes who claim "I'll sing your praises to the world" and the handful who actually get on a plane.

Well, it wouldn't take much effort to keep things on autopilot and continue to grind out mediocrity. But let's not. Instead, I want you to pause and honestly ask yourself: Is there revolutionary Christianity on my campus? Is there an immense amount of spiritual power being released where I attend college?

First Corinthians 4:20 has exploded like a bomb in my mental and spiritual life. It says, "The kingdom of God does not consist in words but in power" (NASB), meaning, unlike every other human club or activity, the Christian life is not defined by its terminology (saying or singing the right words), nor can it be reduced to a program (doing the right activities). The Christian life is primarily about spiritual transformation through spiritual power, manifested in spiritual community—a work of God's power, not ours.

In light of 1 Corinthians 4:20, here are the questions to

ask if you want to diagnose the spiritual vitality of your Christian group on campus: Is spiritual power being manifested in answered prayer? Is there spiritual power at work, leading others to Christ and energizing students to witness? Is there spiritual power to resist temptation and overcome evil? Is there spiritual power to move others for God and move God down to us through prayer? Is there spiritual power to disciple others in a way that is life changing? Is there spiritual power to love enemies, to pray for them, to do good for them, and to draw them to Christ? Is supernatural power being exerted?

On most campuses the honest answer to those questions would be that the evidence of supernatural, life-transforming power is severely lacking.

**Living with Impotence**

When we look at life on campus, what we see are students immersed in sexual relationships, enslaved to pornography, and obsessed with dating (appearance, exercise, clothes, and so on). That's not some finger-wagging accusation but simply a statement of fact; the majority of those engaged in this sexualized lifestyle lack the capacity to withdraw even if they desired to. Against this backdrop I wish I could say that Christians stand as shining beacons of purity, but you and I both know that's not true. The degree to which, and the percentage to which, Christians struggle with these issues are not remarkably different from those for nonbelievers. Not only is there missing power to fight such temptation, but our sexual dalliances drain us of the limited spiritual reserves we do have. Lust, sex, and pornography have diluted and neutralized our spiritual power.

When there is a lack of spiritual vitality, joy, and zeal, Christianity drifts toward legalism: adherents define themselves by what they don't do rather than by what they do and what they are—Christ followers. The result is that on many campuses we are not perceived as a radical community of transformed individuals but as the local "abstinence club," refraining from all activities fun and enjoyable and judges of those who participate.

Many are straddling the fence for Jesus Christ, with one foot in the world and one foot in the kingdom. One student volunteered, "I'm not sitting on the fence. I'm lying on top of it." We lack the spiritual power to immunize us to the heart disease of materialism, choking off our souls like arteries clogged with mayonnaise. We smuggle in the American dream, cleverly packaged in Christian/family verbiage to avoid guilt detection—going in quest of a Christian spouse, Christian house, Christian car (fish on the bumper), Christian computer (Bible verse screensaver), parental and peer approval, financial security, and travel. Dress it up in Sunday church clothes, but it's still the American dream: the pursuit of happiness ... materialism.

This may seem harsh, but as you look around, it seems Christians have done the one thing to Christianity that even Christ's enemies could not do. Christ's enemies scourged Him, mocked Him, beat Him, tried Him falsely, hung Him on a cross, jammed a crown of thorns on His head, stuck a spear in His side, and finally sealed Him in a stone-cold tomb. Centuries after His resurrection, His enemies denied that He ever existed. But with all this, we Christians have dealt Christ a more damaging blow. We have not killed Him, but we have made Him boring.

## Our Need for Power

I don't say any of this as an alarmist, pessimist, or cynic. Lamenting our witness, critiquing the Christian subculture, or berating our failures does none of us any good. In fact, I'm rather optimistic: I truly believe that we could have an impact for Christ beyond anything we have ever experienced. But the journey toward that destination must begin with truthful analysis. It does not begin with our Christian witness as we would like it to be, or wish it were, but as it is currently being lived out on campus—clearly with a lack of spiritual power.

Several million Christian college students around the world have a desperate need for power, holiness, and New Testament vitality to characterize their lives. The changing of these students' lives would have a profound impact on the millions who do not know Christ, no doubt resulting in the entrance of hundreds of thousands into the kingdom. We must ask, then, what is the solution to our spiritual impotence?

In reality there are a number of things. But the most comprehensive answer, the one I'm proposing in this book, is that what we need, what we really want and long to see, is revival and awakening on our campuses and in our lives—a holy fire bringing heaven down to earth. We long, as the prophet Habakkuk did, to see and experience God's power: "Lord, I have heard of your fame; I stand in awe of your deeds, O Lord. Renew them in our day, in our time make them known" (Habakkuk 3:2).

Would it not be amazing to see God renew His awesome deeds in our day? I'm not sure what that would look like, but—oh, God!—what I would give to see it. And deep within my heart, I honestly believe we are going to see it, if we will meet God's conditions for revival. I believe God wants to move across the world's six thousand-plus campuses, sweeping them up into a holy fire, causing believers to get off the fence and live passionately for Him and bringing multitudes of new believers into His kingdom. I think He wants to take the inverted university world and turn the entire system right side up.

But before delving deeper into the subject of campus revival, we need to answer two flagrant questions: What is revival? And why is the university so important?

### Why the Campus?

There is a tendency to think of campus ministry as a youth

group: a cozy support structure for Christians temporarily transposed from home and church. And while it certainly is a support structure, that's a little like saying that the most important application on a personal computer is the calculator.

Campus ministry was not the unique idea or vision of any individual. Rather, it is a ministry and mission strategy based on an observation that throughout recent history the university has been God's primary vehicle for expanding His kingdom and spreading the gospel to the world. Given that the university is highly secular, arrogant, and atheistic, one would assume that the gospel would have detoured the university altogether. It didn't. It barreled through like a truck, turning a gauntlet into a highway for God's global plan of redemption—so much for assumptions.

In his recent book *The American Evangelical Story*, church historian Douglas Sweeney demonstrates that modern biblical or evangelical Christianity is a river fed from four major sources (besides, obviously, the Scriptures).[2]

The first of these sources was the Reformation of the early sixteenth century, when reformers such as Luther, Zwingli, and Calvin jousted with the feudal decadence and doctrine of the medieval church. And where did this movement originate? The campus. It was mounted and mobilized from the universities of Wittenberg, Geneva, Zürich, and Toulouse (among others) before disbursing to the masses.

Then came the Puritans in the early seventeenth century. A spiritual reform movement that would proliferate their teaching and train their leaders through the establishment of colleges such as Yale, Harvard, and Dartmouth.

Harvard's original stated purpose for its students was "To be plainly instructed and consider well that the main end of your life and studies is to know God and Jesus Christ." One requirement of students was this: "Everyone shall so exercise himself in reading the Scriptures twice a day that he shall be able to give an account of his proficiency therein."

One of Yale's requirements for its students read as follows: "Seeing that God is the giver of all wisdom, every student, besides his private and secret prayer, will be present morning and evening for public prayer."

The third source was the Pietists of the mid seventeenth century. Though relatively unknown today, this spiritual renewal movement was birthed in the German universities of Leipzig, Württemburg, and Halle. It bequeathed to the Christian world the prayer movement (the Moravians), small-group Bible study, mass printing and distribution of the Bible, and modern missions. And let's throw in the conversion of John Wesley while were at it.

The last major source of modern evangelical faith is the awakenings and revivals of the eighteenth and nineteenth centuries. Like their distant grandchild, the Billy Graham crusades of the twentieth century, these meetings brought together believers from many denominations for the purpose of evangelism and spiritual renewal. These awakenings spread across the college campuses, and it was through student missionaries and organizations (such as the Student Volunteer Movement) that these revivals were exported to the world.

Do you see the centrality of the campus, the common thread that weaves through and stitches together God's redemptive movements in modern history? Well, just in case, let's consider two examples.

### *The Global Awakening and the Student Volunteer Movement*

In 1886 the first-ever Christian conference for college students was held at Mount Hermon, Massachusetts. On Friday evening, the last day of the conference, 250 students were given a challenge by Princeton senior Robert Wilder to consider taking the gospel to the world as foreign missionaries. One by one, students came forward to accept the challenge—a hundred students from schools such as Yale, Harvard, Dartmouth, and Cornell. As a symbol of their commitment, students signed a pledge, which simply read, "We the undersigned, declare ourselves willing and desirous, God permitting, to go to the unevangelized portions of the world."

Seeing God's hand at work, Wilder spent the next year feverishly traveling to over 150 campuses, giving the same challenge, and seeing an additional 2,100 sign the pledge. And this was only the beginning. For over fifty years, graduating seniors would pour from the Student Volunteer Movement to the far corners of the earth—a total of 20,500 missionaries, the largest single missionary endeavor in the history of the church.[3]

In 1948 the Student Volunteer Movement splintered. It had become liberal in its theology, and its evangelistic core, feeling increasingly unwelcome, was forced out. They joined up with a newly formed college ministry and began holding yearly mission conferences in Urbana, Illinois. The group is known as InterVarsity, and it was soon joined by Campus Crusade for Christ and other campus ministries—a whole new missionary enterprise once again springing from the campus and flowing out to the world.

### *Wesley, Whitefield, and the First Great Awakening*

It was at Oxford University, in the early 1730s, that John and Charles Wesley, along with two other students, began to meet together three or four evenings a week to pray, fast, study Scripture, and discuss their spiritual lives. Over the next few years the community grew, running in size between ten and fifteen students and notably attended by George Whitefield. The group became known on campus as the Holy Club, which carried with it the same sardonic connotations the label would carry today.

While there is much more to the story, we'll fast-forward to New Year's Day of 1739. John and Charles Wesley, George Whitefield, several other members of the Holy Club, and about sixty other like-minded believers held a "love feast," which may or may not have been a corny name even for back then. Later Wesley gave this account of what followed:

> About three in the morning, as we were continuing in prayer, the power of God came mightily upon us, insomuch that many cried out for exceeding joy, and many fell to the ground (overcome by the power of God). As soon as we recovered a little from the awe and amazement at the presence of His majesty, we broke out with one voice, "We praise Thee, O God; we acknowledge thee to be Lord."[4]

It was on this evening that God gave these men the deep assurance that He was going to do something beyond all measure and expectation. A week later, at the age of twenty-two, Whitefield was ordained, and shortly after he gave his first sermon outdoors in Kingswood, England (a rather barbaric mining town). His first message was preached to two hundred people. The next day, five thousand returned. The day after, twenty thousand mobbed to hear him. At times the entire mass wept with conviction.[5] "White gutters made by tears plentifully fell down their black cheeks as they came from the coal pits."[6] The movement of God's Spirit had begun, and the world would never be as it was before.

Let's forget for a minute about Charles Wesley and the eight thousand hymns he composed that led the planet in worship for a couple centuries and just focus on the ministries of John Wesley and George Whitefield.

Wesley started the Methodist movement, which became the evangelistic pulse of America. When he died, there were already 120,000 committed members (now 20 million). He preached to millions and saw thousands come to Christ. If you wonder how that's humanly possible, it's because he preached an estimated 46,000 sermons, traveling 226,000 miles on horseback. Oh, and he wrote four hundred books and pamphlets, usually in transit.

George Whitefield, on the other hand, preached a mere 18,000 sermons—a real slacker! But Whitefield was the pioneer of outdoor preaching (it was previously unheard of to give a sermon outside a church), and being blessed with a megaphone for a voice, he was able to make up the 28,000-sermon surplus of his friend John Wesley, with crowds that swelled as high as 30,000. It is estimated that he preached the gospel to some two million listeners.

They were stoned, punched, and screamed at, and they traveled to exhaustion, and yet everywhere they went, revival followed. Along with Jonathan Edwards, these men *were* the First Great Awakening—humanly speaking, that is. And it began as a Bible study at Oxford University.

### *A Chosen Vessel*

In hindsight we could posit any number of reasons why God has used the campus as His vehicle for accelerating the spread of the gospel. Perhaps it's due to the zeal and radical nature of college students, evident in student uprisings and protests. Or perhaps it is the unique community that exists on campus, where students can meet day or night for prayer and fellowship. And then there is the viral campus culture that causes ideas, trends, messages, and fads to spread like germs from one campus to the next. Or it could be because the university represents the most influential percentage of the population. (Though the university comprises only 1 percent of the world's population, almost every military, political, religious, athletic, and cultural leader will arise from the student population.)

Whatever the reason, we clearly observe the importance of the college campus in God's global plans and surmise that if revival is to break out again, there is a great likelihood that it will be on the campus, as it has been historically, and that the results of such a revival today would be nothing short of the fulfillment of the Great Commission.

### What Is Revival?

I can't remember the exact image that came to my mind the first time I heard the word "revival," but I'm pretty sure it involved a banjo or a snake handler or a faith healer or something like that. This is not revival, though it may assume the name "revival meeting." Perhaps the following eyewitness account of the Pyeng Yang, Korea, revival of 1907 would be the best way to introduce us to revival.

> The room was full of God's presence ... a feeling of God's nearness impossible to describe. The whole audience began to pray. ... It was not many, but one, born of one Spirit, lifted to one Father above. ... God came to us in Pyeng Yang that night. ... Man after man would arise, confess his sin, break down and weep. Some threw themselves full length on the floor; hundreds stood with arms outstretched towards heaven. Every man forgot each other. Each was face to face with God.
>
> Everywhere the story was told the same Spirit flowed forth and spread. All through the city men were going from house to house, confessing to individuals they had injured, returning stolen property and money. The whole city was stirred.[7]

Charles Finney, an evangelist of the nineteenth century who was responsible for helping much of America find revival, said, "Revival is nothing more than renewed zeal to obey God." It is renewed desire to be obedient to the God who made us and who always makes plans for our welfare. Individuals are changed and begin to move from selfishness to selflessness, from self-centeredness to love, from anger to patience, and from turmoil to inner peace. But while this happens all the time to individuals, I am going to be using *revival* in a corporate sense, as in the "Pyeng Yang Revival." For *revival* also means a moving of God among great masses of people so that multitudes are turned quickly to renewed zeal for obeying Him.

Theologian J. I. Packer puts it this way: "Revival, I define as a work of God by His Spirit through His word, bringing the spiritually dead to living faith in Christ and renewing the inner life of Christians who have grown slack and sleepy. In revival, God makes all things new, giving new power ... and new spiritual awareness to those whose hearts and consciences have been blind, hard, and cold."[8]

Strictly defined, *revival* means a movement of God's Spirit through which multitudes of believers are renewed (revived) in their zeal and commitment to the Lord, while awakening is when nonbelievers move from death to life (conversion). As both are often concurrent during powerful movements of God, I will be using the terms interchangeably. And while we often speak of revival as a "great work" or "outpouring" of God's Spirit (because the Holy Spirit is the vehicle of our experience), we should never lose sight of this definition provided by David Bryant, lest we be moved from Christ-centered worship:

> From whatever angle we view it, therefore, revival is fundamentally one thing: Revival is Christ. That's because God can do nothing greater for His church than to reawaken us to the sufficiency, supremacy, and destiny of the Lord Jesus. Jesus exhausts for us all we can ever know about God. He encompasses everything we hope to receive from God, everything we hope to become for Him.[9]

Revivals are mentioned throughout the Scripture, and there have been many sprinkled over the history of the church. This book will review some of those historic revivals, but to set a trajectory for how revival might occur on our campuses today, I will give primary attention to campus revivals and the students who (humanly speaking) brought them about. But I will also focus here because students as well as the campus were the overwhelming impetus for much of what God did in these revivals, whether as the sparks who ignited them or as the missionaries who spread them.

Starting in the early 1700s, and moving through the 1800s into the early 1900s, there have been several powerful movements of God's Spirit (revivals and awakenings) that have swept through the college campuses. The result of these movements was renewal among believers: self-destructiveness was changed to wholeness, apathy to zeal, impotence to power, hate to love, indifference to passion, and carnality to spirituality.

The result among unbelievers was equally startling. In some cases one third to one half of the students of a university were affected, giving their hearts and lives publicly to Jesus Christ and going on to become fruitful disciples.

Many of the universities involved in these revivals are well known. Thousands were converted and discipled at schools such as Princeton, Yale, Harvard, Baylor, Emory, Cornell, Northwestern, and the universities of North Carolina and Illinois. These later made a tremendous impact upon society for good and for God.

For example, at Princeton University in 1875, a Christian student group known as the Philadelphia Society joined with the YMCA (which at that time was committed to evangelism and discipleship), with the following objectives:

1. The importance of seeking the salvation of students for their own sake and their influence as educated men

2. The importance of securing their salvation while in college
3. The value of united work and prayer

These objectives were to be achieved by the following:

1. Diligent study of the word of God
2. Prayer
3. Personal work (one-to-one evangelism)
4. Efficient organization[10]

Through this effort, the famous nineteenth-century evangelist Dwight L. Moody was persuaded to conduct a series of evangelistic meetings on the campus of Princeton, during which nearly one third of the student body indicated that they had received Christ. Among those working with the Princeton YMCA were some of the most outstanding campus leaders of that generation. One such student evangelist eventually became president of Princeton University. Later still, he became better known as T. Woodrow Wilson, the twenty-eighth president of the United States.

Though we lack exposure to our spiritual history through secular textbooks, these experiences have been common in the history of colleges and universities. Believers were stirred for God and thereby changed. Unbelievers were so stunned by these movings of God's Spirit and the transformation in the lives of believers that they came in droves to give their lives to Christ, becoming part of great spiritual movements on their campus. Christian society swelled, mission movements advanced, morality on campus and in society changed, professors were converted, great leaders emerged, and major segments in the life of this country, as well as the world, were deeply affected.

### A Fifty-Year Wait?

As we'll be touching on several different revivals and awakenings, it might be helpful to have a basic time line of the revivals as well as the countries that were impacted.

> Great Awakening (1726–56): affecting Germany, the U.S., Wales, England, and Scotland
>
> Second Great Awakening (1776–1810): affecting the U.S., Canada, Scotland, Wales, England, Finland, and Norway
>
> Transatlantic Revival (1813–46): affecting Germany, Switzerland, Holland, France, Norway, Sweden, the U.S., Scotland, Wales, England, South America, and the Pacific Islands
>
> Layman's Prayer Revival (1857–95): affecting the U.S., Canada, Scotland, Wales, England, and South Africa
>
> Global Revival (1900–39): affecting the U.S., Wales, England, Brazil, Canada, Chile, Scandinavia, India, Ethiopia, East Africa, Korea, Norway, and China
>
> Evangelical Awakenings (mid twentieth century): Canada, the U.S., Taiwan, and the British Isles[11]

It's generally agreed that the last worldwide revival occurred over one hundred years ago, in the Global Revival, whose apex was the years 1904 to 1907. Here are a few snapshots of that spiritual tsunami that arose in Wales and swept across the globe:

> As the revival leaped from Wales to England an estimated two million people received Christ.
>
> When it arrived at Norway, the churches were so packed that they had to ordain lay- persons in order to serve Communion to the masses.
>
> The revival moved from Europe, to Africa, to India, to China, to Korea, and then to the U.S.
>
> In Atlantic City, New Jersey, out of a population of sixty thousand, it was said that "not even fifty" refused to come to the Lord Jesus Christ.
>
> In Paducah, Kentucky, the First Baptist Church added one thousand new converts as the pastor died, reportedly from exhaustion.
>
> In Denver the mayor declared a day of prayer, and by ten in the morning the churches were filled and another twelve thousand packed downtown theaters.
>
> It is estimated that twenty million people came to Christ in the U.S alone.[12]

As the revival spread, virtually every campus in America was touched, as were campuses in Wales (where the revival began), England (Oxford and Cambridge), Ireland (Queens in Belfast), Scotland (Edinburgh University), Germany (the University at Halle), China (Tungchow and Weihsien, where 196 out of 200 students professed faith in Christ), Korea (Pyongyang), India (Nellore, Ongole, and Kottayam College), South Africa (Lovedale), as well as campuses in Australia, New Zealand, Chile, Brazil, and beyond. And, as a result of what God was doing on the campuses, as many as fifteen thousand college students went overseas as missionaries from the U.S. alone.

This quote from an eyewitness at Linfield College in the U.S. may help you to get your mind around how powerfully God was at work on the campuses around the world: "[I] saw something ... never witnessed before, the president and all of the faculty on their knees together praying for the unsaved students under their care."[13] It is doubtful that any of us have witnessed such a thing or such an outpouring of God's power. But we could.

Many historians place the most recent spiritual outpouring in the midst of the twentieth century, though it was more a resurgence than a revival, lacking in magnitude and drama. Among notable events, this time period saw the Christian population in China grow by millions; an uninvited evangelist (Thomas Hicks) arrive in Argentina and end up holding one of the largest evangelistic campaigns in church history (two million attending); the launching of the Billy Graham Crusade, Youth for Christ, Navigators, and InterVarsity's first mission conferences (Urbana). There was also revival on the campuses of Seattle Pacific, Northwest, Baylor, Houghton, and other colleges. And, perhaps, most significant of all, was the Forest Home College Briefing Conference, a national event for youth and college ministers held in June 1947.

At the Forest Home College Briefing Conference the evening's main speaker, Henrietta Mears, gave an impassioned plea for total commitment and availability to Christ. Several men were so moved by her words that they asked to meet in her cabin later for prayer. Mears's biographer would describe the ensuing prayer meeting in these words:

> As they knelt they were overcome by a sense of helplessness and inadequacy. They prayed on into the late hours of the night. There was much

> weeping and crying out to the Lord. At times no one prayed as God spoke to them.
>
> Then the fire fell. However it can be explained. God answered their prayer with a vision. They saw before them the college campuses of the world teeming with unsaved students, who held in their hand the power to change the world. The college campuses—they were the key to world leadership, to world revival.[14]

One of the men attending that prayer time was Bill Bright, a Christian for all of a few months. Dr. Bright would go on to found Campus Crusade for Christ in response to this powerful revelation. And God has used the ministry of Campus Crusade to expose billions to the gospel of Jesus Christ around the world.

While the movement of God in the mid twentieth century may not be accorded the status of a full revival (I wonder who makes such decisions), and while these revivals have differed in magnitude, the observable pattern of these awakenings seems to be an outpouring every forty or fifty years in any given location/country—seemingly timed contractions or labor pains of the kingdom to come. And for those of you doing the math, that would mean we are overdue (though God is never obliged to do anything).

Indeed, collegiate revival could well occur in our day. In fact, as the missionary statesman Dr. James Stewart noted, you and I may be the fireseeds:

> If we could but show the world that being a follower of Christ is no tame, humdrum, sheltered monotony but the most exciting experience the human spirit can know, then those who are standing outside the church looking askance at Christ would come crowding

> into our churches to pay Him allegiance and we might well see the greatest revival since Pentecost.

Joining with hundreds of thousands of students on campuses around the world, we could play a significant role in seeing the campus transformed and with it the world, for the fifty-year-old slogan of Campus Crusade for Christ is every bit as true today: "Reach the campus today, reach the world tomorrow"—the campus being the highway of the Great Commission.

Charles Finney said, "One way that we may know that revival is coming is when it is desperately needed."[15] I think we can settle on the fact that revival is desperately needed only because the lexicon holds no stronger term than *desperately*.

**Turning Campuses Right Side Up**

This book is intended to help you as a student or faculty or staff member to become that fireseed for spiritual transformation and revival on your campus. True, you are only one person, but as we will see, that is of little consequence to God. By grabbing hold of the truths in this book, you can be used by God to influence thousands for Jesus Christ. You can help turn the campus right side up for the Savior.

Pause and ask God to make you available to be one of those people who will spark a revival on your campus. You may have great natural abilities or virtually none at all—this is not the issue. It is not your ability that God is looking for but your availability. Before reading any further, tell the Lord that you desire to be available to Him, to be used to seed a campus awakening. Believe Him for something supernatural. Offer to Him your mustard seed of faith.

# AWAKENED AT SIXTEEN; AWAKENER AT TWENTY-SIX

*"Though Josiah had these obstacles as a hindrance, there was one great obstacle which he did not have to overcome. He was not confirmed in sin. There is nothing so hardening to the heart, and so blinding to the eyes, and so searing to the conscience as sin. "Those who seek me early shall find me." Men who seek late in life, if they truly seek, will find, but it will not be such easy work for them as it is for the young."*
*– Ernest Baker*[1]

*I have often heard this sentiment expressed,* in one form or another, from Christian college students: "How can we really make a difference? We're young. We don't have any resources. We don't have time; we're just studying and working to get through school." Even if it's never articulated, college students live with a pervasive sense or mindset that college is "life interrupted"—a time to have fun, a period of preparation for life, a time to acquire the tools to make a mark, just not the time to leave one.

Yet, from the perspective of God's redemptive plans, college could be the time of our greatest impact, the time to leave our greatest mark. When God has moved powerfully in human history, He has typically called on young men and women to accomplish His mission, to further His purposes, and to interject into history those awakenings that have changed its course. Mentally page through the Bible: think of Samuel, David, Daniel, Esther, Mary, Ruth, Joseph, and others. These were mostly teenagers when God intervened in their lives and began to use them. Without young men and women availing themselves to God, many of the great movements of Scripture and history would not have occurred.

Let's look at one of those movements and one of those young men in Scripture—Josiah—and see what principles we can draw about who God uses and the way He works in and through them. If we can lay hold of these principles and faithfully follow them, we can profoundly impact our campuses for Christ, and much of the skepticism and Christian apathy that now exist will be changed into heartfelt searching—and finding—of God and His Son, Jesus Christ.

### The Worst of Times

Second Chronicles 33 and 34 describe the worst and the best of times in Judah, Israel's southern kingdom. It had been ruled by a succession of both good and evil kings. In chapter 33 we see two of the worst of the worst: Manasseh and Amon.

Manasseh ruled for fifty-five years, and he had the distinction of being one of the most despicable kings who ever ruled any nation in the world. God said about him, "He did evil in the sight of the LORD according to the abominations of the nations" (2 Chronicles 33:2, NASB). In other words, he was wicked like the kings of the godless nations around him.

Not content with his own wickedness, Manasseh spent most of his free time involving others in the creative process, encouraging their capacity for evil: "Manasseh misled Judah and the inhabitants of Jerusalem to do more evil than the nations whom the LORD destroyed before the sons of Israel" (2 Chronicles 33:9, NASB).

Among the baser things that he did in Israel was to perpetuate the practice of witchcraft, spiritism (2 Chronicles 33:6), and the worship of the gods Molech and Baal. He actually encouraged the people to sacrifice their own children on altars of fire—a national pastime that might have made even Mao or Stalin queasy.

When Manasseh died, his son Amon took over. Amon was much like his father, just less creative. Second Chronicles 33:22 says, "He did evil in the sight of the LORD as Manasseh his father had done, and Amon sacrificed to all the carved images which his father Manasseh had made, and he served them" (NASB). The only good thing you can say about Amon is that his rule was brief. After two years, his servants put him to death.

### Josiah the Boy King

Judah was now in a bad way. After fifty-seven years filled with witchcraft, murder, immorality, and all manner of pagan idolatry, the people had forgotten God and had grown intensely materialistic, jaded, and perverse. They were consumed by their own wants, desires, and passions and apathetic to any semblance of real spiritual life. Yet sometimes the darker the night, the brighter the morning. Into this scene enters the protagonist, Josiah the boy king.

There's a new sheriff in town, but he's only eight years old. Second Chronicles 34:1-3 tells us:

> *Josiah was eight years old when he* became king, and he reigned thirty-one years in Jerusalem. He did right in the sight of the LORD, and walked

> in the ways of his father David and did not turn aside to the right or to the left. For in the eighth year of his reign while he was still a youth, he began to seek the God of his father David; and in the twelfth year he began to purge Judah and Jerusalem of the high places, the Asherim, the carved images and the molten images. (NASB)

**Josiah the Praying Teenager**

What a contrast to his grandfather and to his father! Only eight years old when he started to reign, Josiah clearly had within him a heart for God from the very beginning. At age sixteen he began to seek God fervently and earnestly. The result of this was a deep intimacy with the Lord and a righteous heart that grieved over the practices of the palace around him and those of the nation that was named with God's own name. How many hours in the next four years must he have prayed and wept and thought and planned and studied until, gradually, ideas and directions came into focus? Though still young, he knew what was necessary and courageously stepped out in faith.

Josiah set out to eliminate idolatry from Judah and Jerusalem. He was like the sons of Issachar, who Scripture describes as men who "understood the times and knew what Israel should do" (1 Chronicles 12:32). Understanding "the times" and, as a result, knowing what God's people should do in response is the definition of spiritual leadership, and Josiah was a spiritual leader. He never said, "I know things are bad and I'm disgusted by the culture, but what can I do about it?" Now, granted, Josiah was king. But he was also a kid—a kid surrounded by older advisers who usually ran the administration and would have warned him that he should not get involved and that moral reform was equivalent to political (or more likely, actual) suicide. And as Josiah's father had been assassinated, there was nothing abstract about any of this. If nothing else, it would have been easy for Josiah to delay the effort—to put it off until he was a little older, a little more experienced, and had gained a little more respect.

But for Josiah, youth was neither an excuse nor a handicap. And, if I can engage in some speculation, I'm guessing he realized that God had placed him in a unique position to help accomplish the renewal of his nation and society. He knew he had the passion and vision, not having been scarred by years of habitual sin. As a young man, he had uninhibited freedom and energy, not burdened by responsibilities or worn down by years of shouldering them. And I think he suspected that there were others who felt as he did, other young men and women who shared his convictions and who, if rallied, would follow, forming an army that would accomplish Judah's cleansing.

The battle to liberate Israel from spiritual bondage took Josiah far from his home in Jerusalem. He traveled to the cities of Manasseh, Ephraim, Simeon, and Naphtali, tearing down altars, crushing carved images into powder, and chopping down the incense altars—basically, amputating the diseased appendages of spiritual apostasy. When the campaign was completed, he returned to Jerusalem.

It's an inspiring story, a spiritual version of *Braveheart*. This young man sought to take back his country for God and to destroy the things that brought Him dishonor ("They tore down the altars," 2 Chronicles 34:4, NASB). He led the people in an exodus out of sin, rallied them to return to God, and drove out the idolatry, apathy, and wickedness that had pervaded the nation. In the face of opposition, he burned white-hot with passion for God and for righteousness. This zeal not only drove him but also compelled others to follow.

In the space of about six years, all of Israel was outwardly cleansed of the idolatrous practices that had characterized the reigns of the two previous kings. Can you imagine? He turned the whole nation around in six short years—about as long as it takes some people to finish college!

Despite the thorough cleansing and whitewashing of Israel's exterior, the deeper problem of inward cleansing and renewal remained. You can legislate moral actions and outlaw immoral ones, but spirituality and righteousness can come only from inside a population and from within an individual. Josiah had made the right start and had accomplished more in a few short years than most people do in an entire lifetime, but how could the inward transformation of Israel be accomplished?

### Josiah the Righteous Young Man

As part of Josiah's spiritual reforms, he organized and raised money for the restoration of the temple in Jerusalem. This structure had been the heart and soul of Israel's worship and the nation itself, but (rather metaphorically) it had been allowed to fall into disrepair. While the restoration was underway, a discovery was made. Somewhere in the clutter and debris they found the lost Book of the Law given to Moses by the Lord. "While they were bringing out the money that had been taken into the temple of the LORD, Hilkiah the priest found the Book of the Law of the LORD that had been given through Moses" (2 Chronicles 34:14).

This was not like recovering a box of old love letters in the attic. Believed by most scholars to be the Book of Deuteronomy, this restatement of the Mosaic Law was intended to remind Israel not to forsake their God and to warn them of the consequences if they did—and they had lost it! Shoved down a crevice in the temple, out of sight and mind; this would appear to be the very definition of irony.

When Josiah was told of the discovery and "heard the words of the Law," he tore his clothes (2 Chronicles 34:19). In Scripture this is a mark of great sorrow, grief, and repentance. (I'd have to think that shredding your clothing would carry similar meaning today.) The act also stands as a symbol of renewed consciousness of the holiness, majesty, and presence of God. It dawned upon Josiah, with utter shock and outrage, that no one had even read this book for eighty years. No one had believed it, no one had followed it—it had simply been forgotten.

Josiah must have thought, *No wonder we've experienced such immorality, violence, and ungodliness in our country. No wonder the people are spiritually and morally bankrupt. We have not obeyed God. In fact, we have not even known what obeying God means.*

Josiah immediately took action. Second Chronicles 34:29-33 describes what he did and the long-term response of the people to this new exposure to the Word of God.

> Then the king sent and gathered all the elders of Judah and Jerusalem. And the king went up to the house of the Lord and all the men of Judah, the inhabitants of Jerusalem, the priests, the Levites and all the people, from the greatest to the least; and he read in their hearing all the words of the book of the covenant which was found in the house of the LORD. Then the king stood in his place and made a covenant before the LORD to walk after the Lord, and to keep His commandments and His testimonies and His statutes with all his heart and with all his soul, to perform the words of the covenant written in this book. Moreover, he made all who were present in Jerusalem and Benjamin to stand with him. So the inhabitants of Jerusalem did according to the covenant of God, the God of their fathers. Josiah removed all the abominations from all the lands belonging to the sons of Israel, and made all who were present in Israel to serve the Lord their God. Throughout his lifetime they did not turn from following the Lord God of their fathers. (NASB)

Obviously, finding the Book of the Law was not just good fortune. God had undertaken to solve the second part of Josiah's dilemma: how to produce the inward transformation that would fuel and sustain the outward cleansing he had accomplished in Judah. The solution was to provide the power of His Word, which cut like a scalpel to the heart of Josiah, his friends, and the entire nation.

### Revival of a Lifetime

The people turned to the Lord, and Scripture reports that they "did not turn from following the LORD God of their fathers" during Josiah's lifetime. No longer was their obedience merely external, motivated by fear and obligation to the king, and no longer did they follow Josiah alone. The people now came under the conviction of God's Word and desired to serve Him from the heart: the Word and Spirit fueling obedience to the Law and King.

The next chapter of 2 Chronicles tells us that the Passover was celebrated as it had not been celebrated in centuries. In fact, this was probably the greatest Passover in Israel's history, reflecting a genuine renewal that the nation had experienced on both individual and corporate levels. Awakening by God's Spirit had come!

What God did through this young leader was nothing short of incredible, yet it was certainly not unprecedented. What was different about Josiah? A closer examination reveals five roles that Josiah played, allowing him to influence a revival and provide spiritual leadership to the nation.

### Josiah the Prayer Warrior

Josiah was successful because he did not depend on either his personality (diplomacy) or position as king (legislature) to bring about spiritual transformation. He knew that only God could produce an awakening in his apostate nation, and so he prayed. When the Scripture says that Josiah "began to seek God at age sixteen," it means that he largely devoted himself to prayer.

But the question that lurks in the back of our minds is this: *Can the prayers of a few really change the course of an entire nation?* It is not so much a doubt as wondering if God still works in this same way outside the Scriptures. Revival in general, and this story of Samuel Mills in particular, illustrate that He most certainly does:

> As an entering freshman at Williams College [in 1806] Samuel Mills cut anything but an impressive figure. Mills was described by one of his roommates as having "an awkward figure and ungainly manner and an inelastic and croaking voice." ...
>
> Soon after his arrival he came into contact with a group of fellow Christians who were meeting weekly to pray for revival among the students of Williams College. Fearful of contempt and possible disruption from their peers, the group met in the countryside some distance from the college. Although he was but a freshman he was also twenty-three and because of his maturity and the depth and sincerity of his own religious life, Mills quickly became the leader of these students.
>
> The group continued to meet on a twice-weekly basis throughout the summer. One hot, sultry August afternoon, the skies began to darken and the accompanying thundershowers and lightning persuaded them to return to the shelter of the college buildings. Before they could reach the campus, however, the clouds began to disperse and they were able to continue their meeting under the shelter of a

> nearby haystack. After some discussion, Mills invited the students to join with him in offering their lives in the cause of foreign missions, so as to reach the under-privileged peoples of the world. "We can do this if we will," he said, revealing a determination differing from the expected "we will do this if we can."[2]

The impact of the resulting revival was so great that "not only Williams College, but also Yale, Amherst, Dartmouth, Princeton, to name a few, reported the conversion to God of a third to one half of their total student bodies."[3]

As with Josiah, it was the prayers of Samuel Mills and his friends that sparked an awakening at Williams College, spreading to all of New England. In addition, it launched one of the greatest foreign mission thrusts in the history of the church. The following story demonstrates that missionary impulse that flows from revival as well as the manner by which revival spreads from campus to campus and nation to nation.

> A Hawaiian student named Henry Obookiah, happened to be at Yale when the revival spread from Williams College to New Haven. It was at Yale that Obookiah came in contact with Mills who happened to be visiting the campus. As a result of their meeting, in 1820, a small party of student missionaries set off for Hawaii, then part of the Polynesian kingdom. Within fifteen years (1836) these young missionaries had planted seventeen churches among the islands, which, as it turned out, was only the preliminary work, for in 1837 the Hawaiian Great Awakening occurred, which saw the conversion of a fifth of the island's population (27,000 converts).[4]

Think about that: a revival in Hawaii tracing back to a handful of students at Williams College—and all because they were willing to pray.

### Josiah the Activist

Young Josiah was also effective in the awakening of his day because he took action concerning his convictions. Second Chronicles 34:3 reports that he began to seek the God of his father David, and he began to purge Judah and Jerusalem of the carved and molten images on the high places. Josiah was an activist, a radical, and a revolutionary. He knew that he could not do *everything*, but he knew that he could do *something*...and he did it. He also knew that by his example and leadership others would be motivated to take action. No doubt it was lonely being on the leading edge of moral and spiritual change, but others joined him as his example and passion drew many to the cause.

Taking a radical stand is never an easy thing to do, especially when the cause is unpopular and when you may be subject to ridicule from students, professors, friends, and family. But it is always worth the sacrifice. God is always worth the sacrifice.

I had a friend in college named Bruce. He and I had been Christians for about a year. We both had an English professor who was renowned on the campus as a skeptic toward things Christian. His classes numbered from three hundred to four hundred every semester, and he delighted in taking every opportunity he could to discredit the Bible and the gospel of Jesus Christ. Semester after semester, unknowing students would write down what he said as "truth" and find their Christian faith (if they had any) completely undermined. This professor was extremely intimidating and would make a point of ridiculing anyone who would dare to stand up for his or her faith. Consequently my approach was to decide, *I'm just going to keep quiet and try and suffer through this class and hope I don't get ridiculed.*

Bruce took a different tack. He decided he was going to take action and not allow his beliefs to be trampled upon without a struggle. One afternoon he approached this professor and questioned him concerning his statement about two allegedly contradictory sets of Ten Commandments in the Old Testament. Grudgingly, the professor pulled out a Bible from his shelf and opened it to show my friend "the error of his ways." After pausing for a few minutes to search for the two passages, he looked up with a surprised expression and said, "Well, what do you know? There are two sets of Ten Commandments in Scripture, and they don't contradict each other after all."

As far as I know, the professor never taught that falsehood again. Bruce was willing to stand up for his faith and be an activist, even when his grade might have been in jeopardy. This experience emboldened him, and finally me, to become more aggressive witnesses for Christ.

The people who have changed the world have not necessarily been the smartest or the richest or the most powerful. Instead, they have been those willing to take a stand, activists willing to sacrifice for their faith. In fact, when I think of the small steps Bruce and I took as students (steps that seemed so difficult to us at the time), it seems trivial compared to the courage, radical faith, and sacrifice of students in nations hostile to Christianity. One such story comes to us in a letter from the Henan Province, dated from 1982.

> When one girl of only fourteen, after being beaten, revived and continued witnessing, all kinds of people broke down, repented and believed in Jesus. Four young men were arrested and forced to kneel for three days without food or water, but even as they were being beaten, they continued praying, singing, and praising the Lord, until even their tormentors were convicted and believed the gospel.

The writer went on to say that in that province "the flame of the gospel spread everywhere."[5] Such stories clear up the mystery of how the illegal, underground church in China could go from one million members in 1951 (when all missionaries were deported) to ninety million five decades later. It serves as an example of how sacrifice, courage, and radical faith are being lived out in different parts of the world this very minute.

### Josiah the Preacher

We notice in the life of Josiah that he was willing to proclaim the truth of God's Word. Holding up the Scripture, he preached, proclaimed, and pleaded with the nation to return to the Lord. About a century ago, there was another young man (twenty-six years of age, to be exact) who was not afraid to call his contemporaries to seek after God. He was Evan Roberts of Wales. Roberts, a student at Newcastle Emlyn College, had a profound encounter with God in which he experienced the Spirit's cleansing and awakening as well as a profound burden for revival.

> For a long time I was much troubled in my soul and my heart by thinking over the failure of Christianity. ... But one night after I had been in great distress about this, I went to sleep, and at one o'clock suddenly I was awakened up out of my sleep, and I found myself with unspeakable joy and awe in the very presence of the Almighty God. And for the space of four hours I was privileged to speak face to face with him as a man speaks face to face with a friend. At five o'clock it seemed to me as if I again returned to earth. ... And it was not only that morning but every morning for three to four months ... and I knew that God was going to work in the land and not this land only, but the world.[6]

These nighttime prayer vigils were also accompanied by recurring visions in which Roberts felt God communicating to him that a hundred thousand souls would be saved in a revival about to sweep Wales. (The fact that it happened certainly seems to accredit the visions.)

Impassioned by his prayer and vision, and with the permission of his college principal, Roberts left his studies and went home to the village of Loughor to preach his first sermon. Apparently God had not given an accompanying vision to his pastor, who only reluctantly allowed Roberts to preach after the Wednesday night service to any who might choose to stay and listen. And so his first message was preached to a crowd of only seventeen and consisted of four simple points: confess any known sin to God and put right any wrong done to man; put away any doubtful habit; obey the Holy Spirit promptly; and confess faith in Christ openly. Roberts described the event: "At first they did not seem inclined to listen: but I went on and at last the power of the Spirit came down."[7]

The Spirit did indeed come down. Two women were overpowered by God's Spirit and began shouting. Roberts himself was overcome with awe, as people started yelling, "No more, Lord Jesus, or I die." Others cried for mercy, wept, sang, and praised God. This, together with "the sight of many who had fainted or lay prostate on the ground in an agony of conviction," was (according to historian Eifion Evans) "as unbelievable as it was unprecedented."[8]

From that meeting and that college student, word spread throughout Wales and so did the awakening. Church historian J. Edwin Orr reported that within three months a hundred thousand converts had been added to the churches of Wales.

> Welsh newspapers printed the names of those being born into the kingdom. Roads to the Chapels were lined with people. Colleges closed

> down and students marched singing and praising God on their way to prayer meetings. Prayer brigades formed: one town boasted a get-out-of-bed prayer brigade where they would pray all night for God to rouse others out of their sleep, convict them of sin and save their souls. And indeed there were reports of people climbing out of their beds in the middle of the night, searching out a prayer meeting and crying out for the Lord Jesus to save them.[9]

Alcoholism dropped by 50 percent. Crime plummeted so much that some judges were presented with white gloves, meaning there were no crimes to try. There was even a work slowdown in the coal mines because so many workers became converted and ceased using profanity. How exactly would that cause a slowdown in mines? "The horses are terribly puzzled. A manager said to me, 'The haulers are some of the very lowest. They have driven the horses by obscenity and kicks. Now they can hardly persuade the horses to start working because there is no obscenity and no kicks.'"[10]

And all of this was simply the beginning. From Wales the 1904–07 Global Awakening jumped to England, Europe, the U.S., and then to countries all over the world.

Roberts was not afraid to stand up and proclaim the truth. The Spirit of God took the simple words of this godly college student, turned a whole nation right side up for righteousness, and began a spiritual awakening that circled the globe within the next five years, bringing millions to Christ.

### Josiah the Confessor

Josiah was a man of prayer as well as an activist, a humble servant who honestly confessed his sins and the sins of his people. Upon hearing of the lost Book of the Law—

outrageously shelved for eighty years—not only did Josiah personally repent, but also he stood in the gap for an entire nation that was in grave danger of falling under divine judgment (2 Chronicles 34:19, 21). He confessed his sin and the sins of the people and then exposed them to the Word of God so that they might personally repent, confess, receive cleansing, and avert God's judgment.

Confession means agreeing with God that our sins are wrong, that they are forgiven through Christ's death, and that they are to be turned from (repentance). When we think of confession, we typically think of 1 John 1:9, the prominent New Testament passage on subject: "If we confess our sins, He is faithful and righteous to forgive us our sins and to cleanse us from all unrighteousness" (NASB). But there is a biblical corollary to confession that is critical to revival. James 5:16 says, "Confess your sins to each other and pray for each other so that you may be healed." While the focus of confession to God is on cleansing (1 John 1:9), the emphasis of confession to each other is on getting well, being "healed" (James 5:16). And that is what we see happening in revival.

Josiah did not try to hide his sin or disguise it behind a spiritual veneer. He did not try to blame others, rationalize it, or excuse it in any way. Rather, he sought out and embraced the very Word and Spirit that would convict and expose his sin. Of all the eclectic means and places that revival manifests, confession is one of only a few common denominators. We see confession at the outset of the 1904–07 Global Awakening in Wales, sparked by Evan Roberts: "It soon broke out when one of the proudest members of that assembly fell on her knees in agonizing prayer and unrestrainedly confessed her sin ... others followed rapidly with such spontaneity as to cause bewilderment."[11]

We witness confession as that awakening jumped the Atlantic to the campuses in America:

> For three weeks ... teachers and students were lying upon their faces. ... Awful confessions were made. ... It began at twelve o'clock noon and went on until the next morning. Some tried to get away and not confess but they had to come back and go through with it ... when the confessions were over the mighty presence of God filled the place. We walked on tiptoe the atmosphere was so holy.[12]

And we see confession as the Global Awakening reached Korea on the other side of the world: "Conviction of sin swept the audience. The service commenced at seven o'clock Sunday evening and didn't end until two o'clock Monday morning, yet during all that time dozens were standing weeping, awaiting their turn to confess."[13]

And confession is the required action for all who would experience God's power in their lives and become the vessels of spiritual awakening and revival.

### Josiah the Summoner of People

Josiah not only led the spiritual charge toward renewal, but he also persuaded others to join him in the cause. He was a mobilizer as well as a leader. "The king went up to the house of the LORD and all the men of Judah, the inhabitants of Jerusalem, the priests, the Levites, and all the people, from the greatest to the least; and he read in their hearing all the words of the book of the covenant which was found in the house of the LORD" (2 Chronicles 34:30, NASB).

Josiah did not merely impart information or hand out marching orders. He read to the people from the Scriptures so that they might yield their lives to God. He called them to service in the kingdom, pleading with them to surrender their hearts to the Lord and to be His vessels of righteousness, holiness, and love. Josiah alone could not possibly do the work that God had given him to accomplish;

tens, hundreds, and thousands of others would need to embrace the Lord as well as the mission. And so Josiah summoned an army.

Summoning an army sounds daunting, but through the working of God's Spirit prompting the heart and prodding the will, we can do that. In fact, we have to do that. None of us is strong enough, spiritual enough, talented enough, or smart enough to be the sole channel of blessing for our campus or our community. We must call others to join with us.

And as others join with us, they too must become mobilizers, calling still others to be a part. By a few calling a few, who in turn call a few more, a great movement quickly builds. In fact, exponential growth defines a spiritual movement—I tell two people, and each of them tells two people, and so on, and so on. Such a movement can permeate every segment of campus, as a multitude of leaders reach the communities to which they have the greatest relational ties.

At Berry College (a private secular college in Rome, Georgia) an awakening occurred in the mid 1980s because two students summoned others. With little organized Christian activity on campus, these two men became concerned about the welfare of their fellow students. After reading this book, they decided to call others to prayer and to join with them in their efforts to see revival. By their own testimonies, nearly 10 percent of the student body was in small-group Bible studies within two years, and Christian meetings had quadrupled in size.

Think of it! This happened because two students decided to pray and summon others to be involved.

## Spiritual Leadership

Here's the point. Spiritual awakening frequently starts with a few men and women who are willing to go out on a limb for Jesus Christ, praying fervently for spiritual awakening, courageously living out their convictions, honestly confessing their sins and the sins of their campus and community, and fearlessly exposing others to the Word of God. And then they call others to the same challenge and task with which they themselves have been burdened. We become spiritual leaders when we step into these roles, as Josiah did, for these are the activities that define spiritual leadership.

Think back on Evan Roberts. He was only twenty-six years old; a mere seventeen people heard his first sermon; he had not finished his college degree; and he was not an accomplished preacher. Yet he was willing to pray, to preach, to be an activist, to confess, and to call others to join with him. God used him and the others he reached to bring a hundred thousand people to the kingdom of Christ and change the moral climate of his country.

It's important to note that spiritual leadership can and does look different depending on the time, personality, and person. There is an important backstory to the Wales revival led by Evan Roberts. The earliest spark to that revival occurred six months before Roberts gave his first sermon.

The Reverend Joseph Jenkins was holding a prayer meeting for the youth of Cardiganshire, futilely prompting the teenagers to share something—anything—concerning their spiritual lives. Into the awkwardness and silence a young girl named Florrie Evans spoke. Evans, a recent convert, stood and with a trembling voice gave this testimony: "If no one else will, then I must say that I love the Lord Jesus with all my heart." Journalist W. T. Stead recorded the following: "The pathos and the passion of the avowal acted like an electric shock upon the congregation. One after another rose and made full surrender, and the news spread like wildfire from place to place that the Revival had broken out, and that souls were being ingathered to the Lord."[14]

Roberts and Evans provide us an example, and encouragement, that any of us, and all of us, can be spiritual leaders initiating revival and awakening. The apostle Paul said to Timothy, "Let no one look down on your youthfulness" (1 Timothy 4:12, NASB). And historically it may be more accurate, not to say that "God can even use young people," but to say that "God usually uses young people" to spark revival. Let us never hide behind our own youth or inexperience. The time for spiritual awakening is now, and we can be the ones who will ignite it.

# FIVE PREREQUISITES TO REVIVAL

> *"The appearance of revivals owes nothing to chance; they are a witness to God's sovereignty. ... We are able to see a regularity in their appearance and, within certain limits, to anticipate their coming. ... First of all, we perceive that they come when preparations have been made, when the times are ripe."*
> *–James Burns*[1]

*As we consider revival and awakening on* our campuses, the question we must ask is, what is my part in seeing revival take place, and what is God's part? In seeking an answer, there are two things to keep in mind. First, God is the only source of revival. He brings it; He establishes it; He conserves it. The second thing to remember is that God often waits in bringing revival until we have exercised our own faith and obedience. We cannot do His part, but we can fulfill ours. G. Campbell Morgan once said, "We cannot organize revival, but we can set our sails to catch the wind from heaven when God chooses to blow upon His people once again."[2]

As we study revivals, we discover five prerequisites that help set our sails toward the wind from heaven. If we meet these, quite possibly God will be pleased to pour out spiritual blessings on our campuses, our countries, and our world.

Though these prerequisites are found throughout Scripture, they are particularly encapsulated in the summary text on spiritual awakening: 2 Chronicles 7:13-14. "If I shut up the heavens so that there is no rain, or if I command the locusts to devour the land, or if I send pestilence among My people, and My people who are called by My name humble themselves and pray and seek My face and turn from their wicked ways, then I will hear from heaven, will forgive their sin and will heal their land" (NASB).

The foundational requisites for revival in this passage are the following:

1. God's people must recognize that there is a desperate need for spiritual awakening.
2. God's people must humble themselves before Him.
3. God's people must confess their sin and repent.
4. God's people must continually and earnestly pray.
5. God's people must call others to join with them to meet these prerequisites.

Let's look in depth at the first of these prerequisites.

## God's People Must Recognize the Need for Spiritual Awakening

The context of 2 Chronicles 7:13-14 is important. These are words given by God to Solomon at the apex of Israel's history. In a sense, Israel was already in a time of spiritual awakening. After centuries of Israel's worship services being conducted in a portable tent, Solomon was at last holding the ribbon-cutting ceremony for the newly completed temple. Solomon was revered throughout much of the world for his wisdom. Israel's political and military strength were at their height and there was no obvious spiritual declension in the land. Yet, if they were in a time of spiritual blessing, why did God speak so forebodingly about pestilence, locusts, and drought ("If I shut up the heavens so that there is no rain, or if I command the locusts to devour the land, or if I send pestilence among my people ...")?

The reason is that God knows that human beings do not do well in prosperity, whether spiritual or material. As John Wesley pointed out, spiritual prosperity brings diligence, diligence brings economic abundance, economic abundance produces laziness and greed, laziness and greed produce spiritual decline, and spiritual decline brings about God's judgment, necessitating another awakening.

What God seems to have been saying to Israel is that it would become necessary once again to get their attention concerning their spiritual condition when the prosperity cycle had run its course. Verse 13 tells us three ways (out of the many possibilities) that He would do that: through drought, disease, and locust infestation. These manifestations are renderings (amazingly enough) of His grace. Through compassionate discipline, God will help His people meet the first prerequisite for revival: recognizing and experiencing their desperate need for spiritual awakening. And sadly, the only things that seem to get our attention are those that cause us pain. "Pain," C. S. Lewis said, "is God's megaphone to rouse a deaf world."

Though God may first send prophets, preachers, and His Word to warn us, quite frequently it takes tragic consequences to really get our attention. And if that doesn't work ... well, then you might expect a swarm of locusts. Without the recognition of our need and spiritual poverty, we will go on our way, down paths to ever-greater harm.

If you polled a thousand Christian students on campus

today regarding apathy, spiritual breakdown, lack of purpose, and moral corrosion, asking, "Do you think we need an awakening today?" there's no doubt that most would answer, "Of course we do." But objective assent is not what God is asking for.

Admitting that there's a problem or that something ought to be done is entirely different from being gripped by the problem and propelled to action. People addicted to nicotine might know that they need to quit smoking, but they might be roused to action only when they receive a diagnosis of lung disease.

When a handful of committed Christians begin to feel a sense of urgency and desperation about the declining state of affairs and then experience a growing burden to do something about it, you have the seeds of spiritual awakening on your campus.

### Modern Plagues

What leads to that burden and sense of urgency? Following 2 Chronicles 7:13, it is often moral and spiritual plagues that reach epidemic proportions in our society, on our campus, and—most painfully—in our personal lives.

As we are not physically Israel, there is certainly a point at which the analogy breaks down. For example, most of the plagues we face today are, more or less, the natural consequences of sin or of living in a sinful and broken world. While God certainly allows these consequences, this is quite different from His causative discipline of Israel. And, more typically, the plagues we face are of the moral, intellectual, and spiritual varieties (though I should probably first check my yard for insect infestation before glossing over the literal).

With that said, we dare not miss the parallels either. So what might be some of those physical, moral, intellectual, and spiritual plagues whose causalities have now swelled into the millions? Consider the following: drug and alcohol abuse, AIDS, pornography, eating disorders, sexual addictions, divorce, child and spouse abuse, abortion, self-loathing, unbridled materialism, depression and anxiety disorders, hatred and violence, prejudice, atheism and godlessness, war and genocide, natural disasters, despair, meaninglessness and suicide.

You and I, as Christians, are not immune to suffering personally from anything on the preceding list. And at some point—yes, in our Christian life—almost all of us will be oppressed or enslaved to something: rage, eating disorders, lust, pornography, depression, and so forth. It is during these times that we experience firsthand the pain and suffering that attend these spiritual plagues. We feel the shame, hopelessness, and lack of power. We suffer the effects and consequences. And then, finally, we come to the end of ourselves and cry out for God to intervene, realizing our need for the Spirit's empowerment, transformation, and personal spiritual renewal.

Whether we are burdened by what is happening on the broader societal level or are personally afflicted, oppression is what breeds revolutionaries, or at least it can. We can choose to stay oppressed and impoverished, lower the trajectory of our prayers, acquiesce to life as it is, accept our circumstances, bow to determinism, and embrace an anemic version of Christianity. Or we can humble ourselves, rise up, and cry out. It is choosing the latter course that causes the winds of revival to begin to blow.

## Burdened for Change

Josiah, Samuel Mills, and Evan Roberts were all overwhelmed with the need for change and for a turnaround in their situations. This is the first step, the initial prerequisite to revival. If a person really sees the need for revival, then he or she will be motivated to do something about it, beginning to pray and taking the first steps of faith.

In John 2:13-22 we find the story of Jesus' cleansing of the temple. Upon seeing people selling animals and changing money in the temple, Jesus made a scourge of cords, drove them out of the temple, poured out their money, overturned the tables, and then said, "Get these out of here! How dare you turn my Father's house into a market!"

Jesus was outraged, consumed by zeal to stop the denigration of the temple. He did not do as we often do. He did not passively wring His hands and lament the deplorable conditions. "What a horrible situation! What an absolute mess we have going on in the temple! Someone should clean that up. I mean, I would, but that's not my job, and I'm just too busy doing other things. Besides, I might offend someone if I said something, and I don't want to seem judgmental or narrow-minded."

Jesus not only saw the need but also did something about it. The editorial comment that John makes after this event sums it up: "His disciples remembered that it was written, 'ZEAL FOR YOUR HOUSE WILL CONSUME ME' " (John 2:17, NASB). The King James Version says, "The zeal of thine house hath eaten me up." Jesus was "eaten up" with the need to do something about the problem. What consumes the Christians on your campus? What grips you? What is eating you up?

Have you fully realized that the need on your campus, and in your life and the lives of students around you, is so appallingly great that, apart from God manifesting Himself in grace and power, no appreciable change will occur? Have you and your Christian friends felt the burden for awakening in such a way that you will begin to pray and gather others to pray? Is there anything that grips you so strongly that, if God does not do it, you will become physically ill? As management expert Bobb Biehl asks, "What makes you weep and pound the table?"

The zeal and fervency that the Lord Himself can and must produce in us are needed so that we will be willing to pay whatever price is required to bring revival and awakening to our campus. For example, Evan Roberts, before seeing revival break out in Wales, prayed through the night, not just on one occasion, but for months, as he felt a growing burden for God to bring revival. "And it was not only that morning [that he prayed from one o'clock until to five o'clock] but every morning for three to four months. ... And I knew that God was going to work in the land and not this land only, but the world."[3]

Think about that. Praying through the night, every night ... for months. Roberts was clearly "eaten up" about the need for a spiritual awakening.

As large as the burden must be to launch three months of prayer, imagine a burden large enough to propel thirty years of it. This is exactly what led to the 1860 revival in Cape Town, South Africa.

In the 1830s, Scottish missionary to South Africa, the Reverend Andrew Murray Sr., had a longing to see God work powerfully in Cape Town and devoted every Friday evening to praying for revival. Eventually other local ministers joined Murray in his Friday evening prayer, as did his son, the beloved Christian writer Andrew Murray Jr. (After attending seminary, Murray Jr. followed his father into the ministry and mission work of South Africa.) They continued to pray, year in and year out, and in 1860, almost thirty years after the initial burden, God began to move. This quote, from eyewitness Reverend J. C. DeVries, who was leading the meeting, allows us to see the moment when thirty years of prayer came to fruition:

> On Sunday evening there were gathered in a little hall some sixty young people. I was leader of the meeting, which began with a hymn and a lesson from God's Word, after which I prayed. Three or four others gave out a verse of a hymn and prayed, as was the custom. Then a colored girl of about 15 years of age, in service with a

> nearby farmer, rose at the back of the hall and asked if she too might propose a hymn. At first I hesitated, not knowing what the meeting would think, but better thoughts prevailed, and I replied, "Yes." She gave out her hymn-verse and prayed in moving tones. While she was praying, we heard, as it were, a sound in the distance, which came nearer and nearer, until the hall seemed to be shaken. ... The whole meeting began to pray, the majority in audible voice, but some in whispers. Nevertheless, the noise made by the concourse was deafening. A feeling which I cannot describe took possession of me. Even now ... years after these occurrences, the events of that never-to-be-forgotten night pass before my mind's eye like a soul-stirring panorama.[4]

It's hard to miss the irony that God used the testimony of a fifteen-year-old native South African girl to spark the revival in Cape Town.

It's often surprising to see who God chooses to use, who He burdens, and who responds to that burden. The Lewis revivals of 1948 to 1952 are a great illustration of this.

The Lewis Islands are off the west coast of Scotland. In the mid twentieth century these islands were swept by an awakening in which the unlikely fireseeds were two sisters, Peggy and Christine Smith, ages eighty-four and eighty-two! Peggy was blind and Christine was bent over with arthritis. They led the revival from their cottage, being too old and sick to travel to the church.

> In November 1949, this gracious movement began on the island of Lewis. Two old women, one of them 84 years of age and the other 82 (one of them stone blind), were greatly burdened because of the appalling state of their

> own parish. It was true that not a single young person attended public worship. Not a single young man or young woman went to the church. And those two women were greatly concerned, and they made it a special matter of prayer.
>
> A verse gripped them: "For I will pour water upon him that is thirsty, and floods upon the dry ground" (Isaiah 44:3a). They were so burdened that both of them decided to spend time in prayer twice a week. On Tuesday they got on their knees at ten o'clock in the evening, and remained on their knees until three or four o'clock in the morning—two old women in a very humble cottage.[5]

The sisters, anticipating the revival, had appealed for a full-time minister to preside over the churches. Through an intensely intimate prayer life, the sisters knew the revival was coming; they knew God was going to send the Reverend Duncan Campbell to pastor it; they knew his name before he arrived; they knew where he was supposed to preach; they knew the seven future elders of the church (who were yet to be converted); and when they instructed Campbell in where to find those elders so that he could convert them, they become cranky with his reluctance. "Mr. Campbell if you were living as near to God as you ought to be, he would reveal his secrets to you also."[6]

The sisters' ceaseless prayer extended for several months, until the revival exploded. Kathie Walters, in *Bright and Shining Revival*, gives this description of the outbreak:

> The first meeting was held in the old parish church. Many people had gathered in a great expectancy but nothing exceptional happened....

On the second night buses came from the four corners of the island, crowding into the church. Seven men were being driven to the meeting in a butcher's truck when suddenly the Spirit of God fell on them in great conviction and all were saved before they reached the church building! As the preacher preached his message, tremendous conviction swept down. ... Tears rolled down the faces of the people and men and women cried out for mercy from every corner of the church. So deep was their distress that some of their cries could be heard outside in the road.

The meeting closed when the people began to move out. As the last person was leaving a young man began to pray under a tremendous burden of intercession. He prayed for three quarters of an hour and as he continued to pray people kept gathering outside until there were twice as many outside as there had been inside. When the young man stopped praying the people streamed back into the church again and the meeting continued until 4 am. The moment the people took their seats, the Spirit, in great conviction began to sweep through the church, and hardened sinners began to weep and confess their sins.

As the meeting was closing someone excitedly hurried to the preacher, "Come with me! There's a crowd of people outside the police station; they are weeping and in great distress. We don't know what's wrong with them but they are calling for someone to come and pray with them."

> The minister described the scene outside the police station; "I saw a sight I never thought possible. Something I shall never forget. Under a starlit sky, men and women were kneeling everywhere, by the roadside, outside the cottages, even behind the peat stacks, crying for God to have mercy on them."
>
> Nearly 600 people, making their way to the church, suddenly experienced the power of God falling upon them in great conviction, and like Paul on the road to Damascus, fell to their knees in repentance.[7]

Revival had come in power, and for five weeks it swept across that one parish before it moved on to other towns. Revivals follow a birthing process and someone must always assume the labor pains. In the Lewis Revival it was two octogenarians named Peggy and Christine Smith. On your campus that person could be you.

**Burden for the Campus**

It is always someone, or a small group of individuals, who assume the burden. In the fall of 1984, on the campus of UCLA, it happened to be eight young men.

That year I spoke at a large weekend conference for university students in California. More than five hundred attended, representing over thirty colleges and universities. Many of these campuses had twenty, thirty, or even one hundred students in attendance. But UCLA, the location of the first ministry of Campus Crusade for Christ and an important link in the university system of California, had only eight students attending—all men. It was a dismal number for a student body of over thirty thousand.

Some of the UCLA students came and asked what I thought could be done differently. They had tried many things in their ministry to encourage students to get committed. More would come to the meetings, but these eight were the only students truly committed.

I asked if they had yet come to the point where they realized that the only real hope for both their campus and the ministry was to see God sovereignly and supernaturally stir them up in spiritual awakening.

Each one of them replied that he had.

I then suggested that they begin to meet the other criteria for spiritual renewal and refuse to quit until God had blessed them in a significant way.

In a time of prayer together, they admitted their need and admitted that they had not been fervent in laying the foundation for spiritual awakening. They also asked for God's enablement in the days to come.

Shortly after I spoke at this conference, our third child was born. In the midst of the adjustment this brought in the next eight months, I periodically recalled the men at UCLA but gave them little focused attention in either my prayers or my thoughts.

The next summer I was teaching a Bible class and one of the students was from UCLA. In talking with him one day, he asked me the following question: "Well, I guess it is pretty interesting what happened at our school, isn't it?"

Since I had heard nothing, I asked him to tell me more.

The story he told me was remarkable. It was apparent that God had intervened.

After such low commitment prior to the fall conference, the students began to take seriously the admonition to meet God's criteria. So those eight men began to meet daily to pray for revival. They decided that, no matter how long it took, they were not going to quit.

Within a few weeks, not only did the meeting size begin to grow, but students also began to talk spontaneously about their own lack of commitment to Christ and their desire to change. This produced fertile ground for the next conference on the agenda, the California Christmas conference. After taking only eight students to the fall conference, the movement now took forty-five to the Christmas conference (more than a fivefold increase).

Upon their return to campus for the winter quarter, individuals began to pray each week in large numbers, in a group they called Hour of Power, a prayer time strictly for revival on campus. Students crowded to get involved in discipleship and evangelism. The average weekly meeting now numbered 175. And when an InterVarsity traveling evangelist came to the campus in February, the Campus Crusade for Christ students banded together and did one-on-one evangelism among the large crowds he drew. Hundreds of students heard the gospel that week!

In the spring quarter they decided to have another weekend conference. Instead of eight students coming, over a hundred attended this one and hearts were changed in deep and powerful ways. When the Campus Crusade staff left for their summer mission assignments, the entire ministry was turned over to students for the remainder of the quarter. This resulted in even greater commitment to the ministry.

Eight months following the weekend fall conference, the Campus Crusade movement sent over forty students to summer mission projects. While they were unable to get more than eight students to come to a weekend conference in the fall, they saw five times that number give up their summers to serve Jesus Christ. Truly, some sort of awakening had started.

As I tracked the ministry at UCLA the next year, I discovered that God did still more in their prayer meetings and in the ministry. A giant outdoor prayer meeting involving all the Christian groups on campus was so significant that the front page of the student newspaper, *The Daily Bruin*, carried a photograph and a large article about the work God was doing on that campus. When I asked students what God had done to change things, their immediate response was to look at me in surprise and say, "Obviously, it was prayer and our willingness to meet God's criteria that allowed Him to work in such a great way on our campus." (When I asked a Campus Crusade for Christ staff member some years later what had caused that awakening to dwindle after the third year, he ironically said, "No question about it. We began to overorganize God's work.")

God did an amazing work at UCLA, and we must not lose sight of this central fact: it most assuredly would not have occurred if the eight students had not met the first of God's prerequisites—that they be gripped with a need to do something about the spiritual condition of their ministry and their campus.

Before discussing the second prerequisite for revival and awakening, let me suggest three action points. First, take a piece of paper and list at least fifteen reasons why you believe your campus needs spiritual awakening and why your ministry needs revival. Keep it in a place where you will see it daily. Second, make it your daily prayer that God would burden you and your friends with the need for awakening on your campus. Third, talk to others about this need, bring others into praying for it, and hold each other accountable to pray.

By doing these simple yet profound things, you are taking the first step toward spiritual awakening on your campus.

# HUMILITY AND ITS ROLE IN REVIVAL

37. *Resolved, to inquire every night, as I am going to bed, wherein I have been negligent, —what sin I have committed, —and wherein I have denied myself; —also at the end of every week, month and year.*
48. *Resolved, constantly, with the utmost niceness and diligence, and the strictest scrutiny, to be looking into the state of my soul, that I may know whether I have truly an interest in Christ or not; that when I come to die, I may not have any negligence respecting this to repent of.*
65. *Resolved, Very much to exercise myself ...with the greatest openness of which I am capable, to declare my ways before God, and lay open my soul to Him, all of my sins, temptations, difficulties, sorrows, hopes, desires, and everything, and every circumstance.*
*– From the seventy "Resolutions" of Jonathan Edwards, 1723*[1]

*According to Wikipedia, there was a nun* in the twelfth century named Saint Humility. She took the name Humility upon entering the monastery and was later canonized. It seems to me that there would be a lot of pressure in taking on the name Humility, like a guy changing his last name to Stud. But apparently she locked herself in a cell and didn't speak to anyone for twelve years—only prayed—so I think she may have pulled it off. If I could do that, I'd tell everyone and probably write a book on it: *Perfect Humility and How I Attained It*. Which I guess answers the question why I have never changed my last name from Hayes to Humility. *Humility* is a word we attach to many attributes, such as introspection, meekness, low self-esteem, graciousness, self-effacement—many or most of which are far from the word's definition. But define it we must, for a study of history and the Word of God makes it clear that without it revival cannot occur. Thus humility is the second prerequisite for spiritual awakening.

### The Definition of Humility

Let's start by clarifying. Humility is not thinking less of yourself than you ought to. It is not low self-esteem. In the symmetry of human virtues it is parallel to truth. It is a wholly accurate appraisal of yourself comprised of (at least) the following attitudes:

> Submission to God and legitimate authority
>
> Recognition of the virtues and talents that others possess, particularly those that surpass one's own, and giving due honor and, when required, obeisance
>
> Recognition of the limits of one's talents, ability, or authority, and not reaching for that which is beyond one's grasp

Low self-esteem, negative self-image, and self-loathing do not qualify as humility, because they assess our value falsely. That is, they assess it as less than others would and as less than what we truly are. They move as far from the plumb line of truth as pride does, just in the opposite direction. As pride makes it impossible to be truly humble, so does a negative self-image. How can I humbly submit to another person if I think that person is actually superior to me ("Of course I'll listen to you; you're better than I am"). But if we perceive ourselves accurately and as equals, then it will take humility to give deference to someone else's point of view.

In this vein Dr. Howard Hendricks, professor at Dallas Theological Seminary, tells the story of a student who came to him and said, "Professor, pray that I might be nothing."

Dr. Hendricks replied, "No, I won't pray that you'll be nothing. You take that by faith. What I will pray for is that you will believe God to use you because of how significant a person you are because of Christ's work on your behalf."

Packaged between the lines of Dr. Hendricks statement is a great deal of truth worth expounding, for the foundational attitude of humility is comprised of at least these theorems: (1) I am deeply flawed and sinful, yet I am loved and valued by God. (2) I cannot earn God's favor but have received it as a gift. (3) I have been cleansed and forgiven for all of my sins and am a child of God. (4) God has given me certain gifts and abilities that I willingly surrender to His service. (5) I desperately need God's resources (strength, wisdom, empowerment, and so on) to accomplish whatever He has called me to do, think, live, and be. (6) I am part of the body of Christ and must depend on and value the gifts and abilities of others. This is the perspective of humility, viewing our spiritual condition as it is wrapped up in Christ.

Oh, and let's clear up one last misconception: as humility does not equate to low self-esteem, neither does it equate to a personality type. No one is naturally humble. Some personalities may seem more humble than others (quiet, shy, introverted), but this is not an accurate gauge of the heart. Humility is not natural for anyone, but it is possible for all of us who know Jesus Christ to see this quality become more and more a part of our lives. Jesus is truth and therefore we have a relationship with the truth and this should increasingly lead us to greater humility, that is, truer and truer thoughts about ourselves.

### Humility and Revival

In the context of revival and spiritual awakening, humility is seeing with great acuteness the glory and power of God and our subordinate, dependent relationship to Him. We see ourselves as creatures and see God as the Creator. We see ourselves as unworthy while at the same time having been made worthy in Christ. We understand ourselves to be weak and yet strong in Him. We see our inconsistencies, but we see them as spaces through which God's grace can flow. Humility is the lens through which we see and experience the paradoxical nature of the Christian life: Christ in us.

Having seen the need for spiritual awakening, humility bows our head before the Lord. Individually and corporately, we admit that we cannot make spiritual awakening happen but trust that God can.

Humility acknowledges not only our need for God but also our need for others. We submit ourselves to fellowship, prayer, and laboring with other believers who may think differently than we do. It means that, although our doctrines might not all be in the same slots, we are willing to focus on the same end: seeing our campus ablaze for God. In every age and time it has been this sort of humility that has ignited believers and allowed them to become channels of the Holy Spirit, drawing thousands of Christians and non-Christians to the foot of the cross and then thrusting them out into the world to exalt His name.

Isaiah 57:15 illustrates humbling ourselves before the

Lord and how it produces revival:

*This is what the high and lofty One says—*
*he who lives forever, whose name is holy:*
*"I live in a high and holy place,*
*but also with him who is contrite and lowly in spirit,*
*to revive the spirit of the lowly*
*and to revive the heart of the contrite."*

Note here that the Lord says He dwells in two places. First, He dwells in a high and holy place. He is lofty; He is exalted. He is the Creator and we are the created. We bow before Him because He alone is worthy of our trust, love, and homage. We praise Him as majestic, as awesome, as great. He is separated from us by loftiness and grandeur. However, God has a second dwelling place. According to this passage, He also dwells with the contrite (humble) and lowly of heart. He lives next to, with, and in those who are humble of heart. His presence and availability here are real to those who admit their need.

The moment we recognize Him as high, lofty, and holy and then act accordingly (humbly acknowledging our creaturely status, weakness, and need), He transfers His dwelling place from transcendence to immanence. He is right next to us, in us, and with us, closer than any relative or friend. All of His mighty presence and power becomes our present possession when we yield ourselves to Him. Jesus Christ, the One whose heart burns for revival more than any other, now becomes our daily resource to produce revival and awakening in our situation. To those who humble themselves, God promises "to revive the spirit of the lowly and to revive the heart."

The converse of this is that God does not revive the proud. We have usurped God's place and cut ourselves off from His power if we, and other Christians on campus, say, "With a new strategy, a little more hard work, materials, leaders, and money, we'll accomplish the job." We could stay on our knees until they fuse to the floor, but we would never see revival because we are not humbling ourselves. God brings awakening only to those of us who say, "Lord, we can't, but You can."

### A Humble Example

This has been a significant amount of description for a virtue that is best demonstrated, not discussed. There have been many humble servants whom God has used as channels of revival, but none who have inspired a passion for humility among Christians more than David Brainerd. (You probably thought I was going to say Saint Humility, but alas, humility is tested and developed in the company of humans, not cloistered from them.)

What is immediately attractive about Brainerd is that he was expelled from Yale in his junior year for commenting about one of his tutors, "[The man] has no more grace than this chair." (Unless the word "chair" was profanity in the eighteenth century, this punishment seems a little harsh.) Upon leaving Yale, he trained for the ministry, and in 1742 (at the age of twenty-four) he was licensed to preach and devoted himself to missionary work among the Native Americans, spending most of his short ministry (a little less than five years) with the Delaware Indians of Pennsylvania and New Jersey.

As humility is a disposition of the heart, it is difficult to examine, but Brainerd's journal, which was preserved and later published by Jonathan Edwards, affords us a glimpse into the soul of the man and the revival that broke out as a result of his ministry. In the entries leading up to the revival we witness as good a picture as we're likely to find of a heart humbled before the Lord.

> *Friday, April 1, 1743*. I rode to Kaunaumeek, near twenty miles from Stockbridge, where

the Indians live with whom I am concerned, and there lodged on a little heap of straw. I was greatly exercised with inward trials and distresses all day; and in the evening, my heart was sunk. … Oh that God would help me!"

*Thursday, April 7.* Appeared to myself exceedingly ignorant, weak, helpless, unworthy, and altogether unequal to my work. Towards night, I had the exercise of faith in prayer, and some assistance in writing. Oh that God would keep me near him!

*Friday, April 8.* Was exceedingly pressed under a sense of my *pride*, *selfishness*, *bitterness*, *and* [divisive] *spirit*, in times past, while I attempted to promote the cause of God. Its vile nature and dreadful consequences appeared in such odious colours to me, that my very heart was pained. I saw how poor souls stumbled over it into everlasting destruction.

*Wednesday, April 13.* My heart was overwhelmed within me: I verily thought I was the meanest, vilest, most helpless, guilty, ignorant, benighted creature living. And yet I knew what God had done for my soul.

*Tuesday, May 10.* Was in the same state, as to my mind, that I have been in for some time; extremely pressed with a sense of guilt, pollution, and blindness: Oh! the *pride*, *selfishness*, *hypocrisy*, *ignorance*, *bitterness*, [*divisiveness*], and *the want of love*, *candour*, *meekness*, and *gentleness*, that have attended my attempts to promote religion and virtue … alas,

> what corrupt mixtures attended my best duties!"
>
> *Tuesday*. Oh that God would humble me deeply in the dust before Him. I deserve hell every day for not loving my Lord more, who has, I trust, loved me and given himself for me. Every time I am enabled to exercise any grace renewedly [sic], I am renewedly [sic] indebted to the God of all grace for His special assistance. Where then is boasting? Surely it is excluded when we think how we are dependant on God for the being and every act of grace.
>
> *Lord's Day*. In the afternoon I still felt barren when I began to preach, and after half an hour I seemed to myself to know nothing and to have nothing to say to the Indians; but soon after I found in myself a spirit of love, and warmth, and power to address the poor Indians.

The revival built through June of 1745, coming to a remarkable crescendo in August.

> *Friday, June 12*. I know not that ever God helped me to preach in a more close and distinguished manner; and yet I was so sensible of my defects in preaching that I could not be proud of my performance.
>
> *June 22*. Preached to the Indians again. Their numbers, which at first consisted of about seven or eight persons, was now increased to thirty. There was a solemn attention among them ... some began to feel their misery and perishing state, and appeared concerned for a deliverance from it.

*August 6*. There was about fifty-five persons in all. They seemed eager of hearing; but there appeared nothing very remarkable, except their attention, till near the close of my discourse. Then divine truths were attended with surprising influence ... there were scarce three in forty that could refrain from tears and bitter cries. They all seemed in an agony of soul to gain an interest in Christ ... the more I invited them to come and partake of his life, the more their distress was aggravated, because they felt themselves unable to come.

*August 7*. Preached to the Indians from Isaiah 53:3-10. Most were affected and many in great distress for their souls; and some few could neither go nor stand but lay flat on the ground, as if pierced at heart, crying incessantly for mercy. It was remarkable that as fast as they came from remote places the Spirit of God seemed to seize them with concern for their souls.

*August 8*. Their number was now about sixty-five persons. ... The power of God seemed to descend upon the assembly like a "mighty rushing wind." ... I stood amazed at the influence that seized the audience almost universally, and could compare it to nothing more aptly than the irresistible force of a mighty torrent or swelling deluge ... almost all persons of all ages were bowed down with concern together and scarce one was able to withstand the shock of the surprising operation.

*August 9*. The cry of these was soon heard by

> others, who, though scattered, immediately gathered round. I then proceeded in the same strain of gospel invitation, till they all except two or three, melted into tears and cries and seemed in the greatest distress to find and secure an interest in the great Redeemer. For so great was their concern, that almost everyone was praying and crying for himself ... *Guttummaukalummeh, Guttummaukalummeh that is*, "have mercy on us, have mercy on us."[2]

The accounts of the revival continue on in his journal, the entries ending in 1747, when at the age of twenty-nine Brainerd died of tuberculosis. In fact, he carried on a great deal of his ministry in various degrees of illness, which further added to his brokenness and dependence ("Sept 8: coughing up blood in almost the whole of the journey"; "Sept. 10: Was extremely overdone with heat and showers this day and coughed up a considerable quantity of blood").[3] As you read his journal, it is apparent that Brainerd's physical illness and emotional disposition were not ideal for the challenges of pioneering ministry. Clearly it was his humility that qualified him to partake in the ministry as well as revival.

### Women in Revival

It would be hard to find anyone who approached the ministry with greater humility than David Brainerd, except perhaps a whole class of individuals: women.

In the histories of revivals women are often mentioned only in passing or in a brief byline. For example, we can read in great depth of James McQuilkin and the hundred thousand people who came to Christ through his preaching in the Great Layman's Prayer Revival of the mid nineteenth century. But as you trace it back, McQuilkin was a degenerate unbeliever whose life revolved around gambling and cock fighting, until he invited into his house a Baptist missionary going door-to-door—a woman we know only by the name of Mrs. Colville. To derail the evangelistic conversation, McQuilkin asked Mrs. Colville if she was a Calvinist, to which she bluntly replied, "I do not care to talk on mere points of doctrine. I would rather speak of the experience of salvation in the soul. If one were to tell me what he knows of the state of his heart towards God, I think I could tell him whether he knows the Lord Jesus savingly." In response McQuilkin became deeply convicted of his sin and she was able to share the gospel with him.[4] No Mrs. Colville, no James McQuilken.

We read about that same revival (the Great Layman's Prayer Revival) as it reached South Africa and spread through the ministry of Andrew Murray Jr. and others. But we barely catch in the accounts the revival's true flashpoint in South Africa:

> One Sunday evening, during the youth fellowship meeting, an African servant girl arose and asked permission to sing a verse and pray. The Holy Spirit fell upon the group as she prayed. In the distance there came a sound like approaching thunder. It surrounded the hall, and the building began to shake. Instantly everyone burst into prayer.[5]

In fact, Murray, who had been out of the room, came in and demanded, "I am your minister sent by God. Silence!"[6] They ignored him (praise God) and kept praying. Amazingly, we don't even know the African girl's name, but it was her psalm that launched the revival.

Or consider the accounts of the Global Revival of 1905–07. A truncated history relates that the student evangelist Evan Roberts launched the revival in Wales, when the full account shows (as noted in chapter two) that it had in fact sparked months earlier in the testimony of a young woman (Florrie Evans) who simply stood and said, "I love the Lord Jesus with all my heart."[7]

A primary vehicle of that same Global Revival spreading to India was the unceasing prayer of Pandita Ramabai and the revival that sparked in Mukti, her home for orphans, widows, and famine victims.[8]

The list goes on and becomes even more impressive if you include the effects of prayer and discipleship of godly mothers such as Susanna Wesley (mother of John Wesley). And yet it is not fair to the godliness of these women to say that it is history that humbled them (though it certainly did), giving them only a few sentences of recognition. Rather they willfully embraced humility and were content outside of the spotlight, so long as Christ enjoyed it.

If we are looking to find the greatest examples of humility, it is to the women of revival that we should turn our attention and be awed by hearts that repudiated fame, title, position, and prominence—servants of the kingdom who in God's economy are the greatest.

## Humbling Ourselves

As a virtue, humility grows over time, through the process of walking with Christ. By growing in our knowledge of Him, through adversity and trials, through obedience, through sin and restoration, and through maturing and wisdom, we come more and more to the truth of who and what we are.

And yet there are means by which we can put the growth process on steroids—at least temporarily. In deliberate ways we can humble ourselves before the Lord.

### *Fasting*

One of those ways is through fasting. Dr. Bill Bright, founder of Campus Crusade for Christ, who devoted much of the last years of his life to prayer and fasting, had this to say about the discipline:

> Down through the years, godly people who have done mighty things for God have testified to the necessity of prayer and fasting. The roll call of other great Christian leaders who determined to make prayer with fasting a part of their lives reads like a Hall of Fame: Martin Luther, John Calvin, John Knox, Jonathan Edwards, Matthew Henry, Charles Finney, Andrew Murray, D. Martyn Lloyd-Jones and many others. Fasting is a primary means of restoration. By humbling our souls, fasting releases the Holy Spirit to do His special work of revival in us.[9]

Far from just putting out a theory, Dr. Bright participated in several forty-day fasts, during which he sought to humble himself and pray for revival, calling other godly leaders and ministries to join him in the endeavor.

Fasting creates a habit of reliance in our lives. Hunger, which normally arises every five or six hours (or in my case, every two or three), becomes acute every five or six minutes. When we are fasting, hunger becomes a trigger mechanism prompting us to turn to God for empowerment. All day long we call out to God for strength, endurance, self-control, and wisdom.

Fasting makes us weak, and when we are weak, we are more humble. Fasting gives us a firm grip on our smallness, finitude, and lack of power—as opposed to coffee, which makes us feel fast, smart, and competent.

It is also a plea for help, a red flare sent up from the soul for a specific reason or cause. When we are in distress and desperate for God, we fast. But with this caution: we are not attempting to manipulate God or make Him care for us more than He does—holding our breath until we're blue to get our way. Rather, we spend our passion and desire for deliverance by choosing fasting instead of manipulating, blaming, whining, or turning to sin for comfort.

In short, fasting provides a teaching aid in humbling ourselves before God.

*Naked before God*

The great reformer Martin Luther was asked when he came to faith. His response was that it was while he was on the toilet. Now, Luther had no aversion to crudeness, so it's quite possible that this was the actual location (thanks for that image, Martin). But scholars generally agree that he was using a metaphor for humility, one popular in the Middle Ages: "sitting on the toilet." And if you think about it, it's a darn good metaphor for humility, for if there is ever a time or place where you are completely humbled, it is sitting on the toilet. There are no pretenses, no facades, no pride, no image management. The toilet is ground zero for humanity; at that moment you really are what you are.

On a regular basis, and certainly in preparation for revival, it's important to visit that restroom and strip yourself naked before God. What I'm describing is not simply confession of sin but also an acknowledgement of your weaknesses, your hidden motivations, fears, insecurities, comparisons, arrogant thoughts, and ugliest fantasies. Lay the whole sordid mess before God, declaring, "This is who I am, God." Take an hour or two and pull away somewhere and just lay yourself naked before God. And when you're done, thank Him for His love and mercy in Jesus Christ, and thank Him for fully accepting you in light of all you are. Having laid yourself bare, wallow in the grace that is yours and trust Him anew for mighty works.

While not an everyday event, this is also not a once-a-year spring cleaning. This is an ongoing habit of humbling ourselves.

*Public Confession*

As confession, public and otherwise, will be the subject of the next chapter, I will only touch on it here. But typically public confession (to another person or to an entire group) has been the spark that ignites the flame of revival, and it's easy to see why: it not only removes the hindrance of sin but also requires a profound degree of humility to make such a public acknowledgment. In public confession we are concurrently humbling ourselves, confessing, and often repenting as well.

### *God's Humbling Hand*

Alcoholics Anonymous has popularized the saying "You will either humble yourself or you will be humiliated." In humbling ourselves we are not simply left to our own spiritual ingenuity. With a Fatherly love, God will also provide circumstances that humble us, and we need to embrace them instead of running from them or quickly moving to image management and saving face.

Having become quite a sensation in America, in 1873 evangelist D. L. Moody began a three-year evangelistic tour in the British Isles. One night, as he spoke to the students of Cambridge University, seven young men committed their lives to Christ and missions. Later known as the Cambridge Seven, these men pioneered missions in China and used their hefty fame and influence on campuses in the U.S. to propel the Great Commission.

This evangelistic lecture at Cambridge was a pivotal event in Christian missions. But what is often ignored is that Moody had only a seventh-grade education and felt terribly inadequate about this speaking engagement. Far from dispelling his insecurities, he rudely encountered his worst fear, as many of the Cambridge students ridiculed him, finding him extremely ... well, uneducated.[10] It's doubtful that the coinciding of the Spirit's power and Moody's humbling was an accident, but instead it was a profound example of the principle "When I am weak, then I am strong" (2 Corinthians 12:10).

But for an example of humility clothed in God's power, we do not have to leave our own century to find a man who humbled himself before the Lord and as a result became the fireseed of revival.

**Billy Graham**

Billy Graham has spoken and preached to more people than any man who has ever lived—a fact that you wouldn't think could coexist with humility. But it has in the life of Dr. Graham. During fifty years of personal ministry, he has maintained godliness, holiness, and Christian standards of integrity even in the face of attacks and defections by others. Though he has received many honors and had a number of opportunities for financial reward, he has consistently followed the calling of God to win men and women to Jesus Christ until the Lord returns.

One incident in Billy Graham's life illustrates the nature of humility and its results. In 1945 Billy was almost thirty years old, already an evangelist and president of Northwestern College in Minneapolis. He had, however, no national recognition, nor did he seem destined for any. He was obscure outside of what was considered the fundamentalist subculture.

At this same time an outstanding young Canadian evangelist named Charles Templeton was beginning to have serious doubts concerning the authenticity and reliability of the Scriptures. He went to graduate school in an attempt to resolve his doubts, but they only grew more intense. He and Graham often discussed these concerns, and soon he began to challenge Billy's commitment to the authority of Scripture and suggested that he should rethink his position on the Bible.

In 1949, at a conference center named Forest Home in southern California, Billy was deeply hurt to hear of a remark by Templeton implying that Graham's ministry would be curtailed, and he would never do anything significant for God, if he continued to believe, trust, and preach the authority of the Bible. In his biography of Billy Graham, John Pollack describes this time of struggling before the Lord:

After supper, instead of attending the evening service, he retired to his log cabin and read again the Bible passages concerning its authority. He recalled someone saying that the prophets used such phrases as "the Word of God came to us" or "Thus saith the Lord" more than 2,000 times. He meditated on the attitude of Christ, who fulfilled the Law and the prophets: He loved the Scriptures, quoted from them constantly and never once intimated that they might be wrong.

Billy went out in the forest and wandered up the mountain, praying as he walked, "Lord, what shall I do? What shall be the direction of my life?" He had reached what he believed to be a crisis.

He saw that intellect alone could not resolve the question of authority. He must go beyond intellect. He thought of the faith he used constantly in daily life: he did not know how a train, or a plane, or a car worked, but he rode them. He did not know why a brown cow could eat green grass and yield white milk, but he drank milk. Was it only in the things of the spirit that such faith was wrong?

Graham later described his own thoughts: "So I went back and I got my Bible and I went out in the moonlight. And I got to a stump and put the Bible on the stump, and I knelt down, and I said, 'Oh God: I cannot prove certain things, I cannot answer some of the questions Chuck Templeton is raising, and some of the other people are raising, but I accept this book by faith as the Word of God.'"[11]

What had Graham done? In humble faith he had placed his doubts and questions in the hands of his Creator. He humbly admitted that he did not have every answer, but he could trust God for them. What followed can only be attributed to the God who revives the heart of the contrite.

Two months later Billy Graham launched what was then an experimental evangelistic tent crusade in Los Angeles. It exceeded all expectations and hopes. So many thousands of people were converted, and so many multitudes of Christians were revived, that the crusade committee extended the campaign from three to eight weeks. Such attendance at a Christian meeting was unprecedented, as were the numbers of conversions. Many Hollywood personalities and even underworld figures were converted. Many gave public witness to the change in their lives.

The final service drew nine thousand people. This was by far the largest evangelistic crusade in America in over three decades!

He had been largely unknown to the American public prior to this time. Now *Time* and *Newsweek* both wrote about the "new" evangelist, Billy Graham. The Associated Press carried dispatches about him across the nation. Graham's ministry suddenly accelerated around the world. William Randolph Hearst, owner of a vast newspaper empire (which included the *Los Angeles Times*), issued his famous instruction to his reporters: "Puff Graham!" The work of God became something that the secular press would write about, a phenomenon that had not been true in America for years.

Why did this happen? It happened because one man, William Franklin Graham Jr., was willing to humble himself before God at great risk of failure, to look foolish and be pitied by his more learned contemporaries. He yielded everything (including his doubts) to the Lord of the universe. He decided to let God fulfill His promises to "dwell with the humble and contrite of heart" and to "revive the spirit of the lowly and revive the heart of the contrite" (Isaiah 57:15).

Graham's life is an example of impact stemming from humility. Could a great impact be made on your campus? Can you and a small group of other believers yield your rights, your possessions, your future, and perhaps even your doubts and prostrate yourselves before the God of the universe? Take the risk. Tell Him that, though you are weak, He is strong. And while you are unable, He is able—able to produce a spiritual explosion on your campus that will start a movement that will last for decades.

To feel the need for God like this is wonderful. You do not need to have all the answers. In fact, it may be better to know that you have fears, doubts, and questions. Joe Brown, senior pastor of Hickory Grove Baptist Church in Charlotte, North Carolina, said, "I don't find in the Bible where Jesus condemned people for asking too many questions. I do find where he condemned people for thinking they had all the answers."[12] Nor does He condemn people for having too little faith, only not exercising the amount they have.

If you have questions and know you do not have all the answers, take a few minutes now to meditate on Isaiah 57:15 and consider its implications for you and your campus.

> *This is what the high and lofty One says—*
> *he who lives forever, whose name is holy:*
> *"I live in a high and holy place,*
> *but also with him who is contrite and lowly*
> *in spirit,*
> *to revive the spirit of the lowly*
> *and to revive the heart of the contrite.*

Tell God that you are willing to lay everything before Him: your life, your future, your studies, your money, your ministry, your doubts and fears, and what others think about you. Ask Him to fulfill His promise to revive you. Then expect miracles to happen.

# CONFESSION AND REPENTANCE

*"A revival always includes conviction of sin on the part of the church. Back-slidden professors cannot wake up and begin right away in the service of God without deep searchings of heart. The fountains of sin need to be broken up. In a true Revival, Christians are always brought under such conviction; they see their sins in such a light that often they find it impossible to maintain a hope of their acceptance with God. It does not always go to that extent, but there are always, in a genuine Revival, deep convictions of sin, and often cases of abandoning all hope."*
*– Charles G. Finney*[1]

*The third prerequisite for revival is confession* and repentance. Second Chronicles 7:13-14—our cornerstone passage on revival—states, "If my people, who are called by my name, will humble themselves and pray and seek my face and turn from their wicked ways, then will I hear from heaven and will forgive their sin and will heal their land." We turn now to the important caveat: "... and turn from their wicked ways." This is the hinge upon which the door of revival swings open. Without this, our prayerful knocking will be in vain.

While we've had to blow the dust off some of our previous examples, the ink is still pretty fresh on this one, reminding us that revival is not just something God did in the past but also something He is doing today. The following is the account of the 1995 Wheaton College Revival, in which confession and repentance played a significant role:

> On Sunday evening, March 19, 1995, two students from Howard Payne University in Brownwood, Texas, spoke during a weekly student-led worship service at Wheaton.
>
> The two students "shared what God had done in their lives" during recent times of revival at their campus and at other schools, said Wheaton professor, Tim Beougher.
>
> After they spoke, there was no exhortation or manipulation, the professor said. "There was no attempt to try and force a repeat experience of what had happened at Howard Payne."
>
> But, "immediately students began to come up to the microphone and confess sin," Beougher said. "The confession was deep. It was painful. God really did a work of breaking people."
>
> The service had begun at 7:30 p.m. Sunday. It did not end until 6 a.m. Monday.
>
> Normally, about 400 students attend the service. That Sunday, about 700 came. It was difficult

to know how many attended because many who were there left and went back to get their roommates and friends.

The "beautiful thing" was that when a person would confess sin, 20 to 50 students would gather around the person and pray for him. "There was a real spirit of love and acceptance," Beougher said. "You could not point a finger at anyone else," because "all of us there had been stripped bare before the throne of God."

When the students broke up at 6 a.m., they agreed to meet again Monday night, March 20. They started at 9:30 that night and attendance climbed to more than a thousand. The seats of Pierce Chapel were filled, and students stood two and three deep along the walls.

As on Sunday night, the service began with praise and worship. Then came more "deep confession."

Students were given an opportunity to throw away things "that were hindering your walk with God or that might trip you up in the future." Many went back to their rooms and returned with secular music discs, pornography, alcohol, credit cards and other items. One student even brought a rose, apparently symbolic of an unhealthy relationship. The meeting lasted until 2 a.m.

The next night, about 1,350 students gathered in the church's 1,500-seat sanctuary. After a time of praise and worship, confession of sin followed again. ...

> On Thursday, it was time to celebrate. The students, 1,500 of them, held a "praise and worship service that raised the roof," the professor said. "It was glorious. ... It was a foretaste of what heaven is going to be like."[2]

Sin is the great curse of our existence. The sin of Adam and Eve, and the fall of humankind, meant the human race needed redemption from the pit into which it had fallen. Sin necessitated that the sin bearer, Jesus Christ, take our sins on Himself in order that we might be restored to fellowship with God.

### The Hindrance of Sin

Even for forgiven Christians, sin continues as a hindrance to God's power and plan for our lives. Actually, it does more then just hinder the flow; it puts an elephant on the air hose. It renders Christians fruitless and impotent. It blocks God's good intentions for each of us and steals, kills, and destroys the good that might have been (John 10:10).

Sin takes many different forms, but on campus its form has changed little over the centuries. Historian J. Edwin Orr described the campus climate in 1790, prior to the Second Great Awakening.

> In 1790 America had won its independence, but it had lost something as well. In the wake of the Revolutionary War, French infidelity, deism, and the generally unsettled condition of society had driven the moral and spiritual climate of the colonies to an all-time low. Drunkenness was epidemic; profanity was of the most vile kind; bank robberies were a daily occurrence; and for the first time in the history of the American settlement women were afraid to go out at night for fear of being assaulted. Conditions on

> campus were no better. A poll taken at Harvard revealed not one believer in the whole student body. At Princeton, where a similar survey showed there to be only two Christians on campus, when the dean opened the Chapel Bible to read, a pack of playing cards fell out, someone having cut a rectangle from each page to fit the deck. Conditions on campus had degenerated to the point that all but five at Princeton were part of the "filthy speech" movement of that day. While students there developed the art of obscene conversation, at Williams College they held a mock communion, and at Dartmouth students put on an "anti-church" play. In New Jersey the radical leader of the deist students led a mob to the Raritan Valley Presbyterian Church where they burned the Bible in a public bonfire. Christians were so few on the average campus and were so intimidated by the non-Christians that they met in secret. They even kept their minutes in code so no one could find out about their clandestine fellowship.[3]

It's easy to think that revival can't happen today because things have grown so much worse, but clearly that isn't the case. Give or take a laptop or cell phone, it might as well be 1790. As Solomon said, "What has been will be again, what has been done will be done again; there is nothing new under the sun" (Ecclesiastes 1:9). Without revival and God's supernatural intervention, like a black hole, sin's gravity extinguishes all light and inexorably pulls every campus down into the same mire of spiritual rebellion. And that rebellion looks pretty much the same in the twenty-first century as it did in the eighteenth century—or eighth century for that matter.

For we Christians, it is easy to be appalled by the grosser

manifestations of sin that surround us on campus, even thinking ourselves immune or innocent because we would never consider doing *that* (whatever "that" might be). But it's important to understand that sin runs far deeper than just the more obvious acts of rebellion. Romans 3:23 states, "All have sinned and fall short of the glory of God." That "all" refers not only to those who are flagrantly sinful but also to those of us who are more subtle and socially acceptable in our rebellion; it refers, in part, to a category we'll call "Christian sin."

Coldheartedness, apathy, criticism, backbiting, bitterness, pride, lust, jealousy, cynicism, prayerlessness, and caring more about the approval of others than the approval of God are just as sinful and sometimes more difficult to detect and mend as flagrant sins. Such a list could go on and on. In fact, it does go on and on and includes compromise with evil, cheating, lying (even little "white" lies), materialism, unrestrained anger against a brother or sister in Christ, uncaring attitudes toward the lost, lack of giving to the poor and needy, lack of respect to parents and authority, and general indifference to spiritual issues. The list could also include racism, gossip, crudeness, laziness, selfishness, and various other conscience-troubling issues. These all qualify as sin, short-circuiting God's mighty power in our lives and polluting our souls. But before God can bring revival and spiritual awakening, we who are burdened for it and are humbled before Him must be cleansed and empowered.

And that is why every revival preludes with confession and repentance from sin, as demonstrated by this account of the Hebrides Revival (1949–52) in Scotland, as reported by J. Oswald Sanders.

> Around 1950, there was a powerful movement of the Spirit in the Hebrides. The awakening did not just happen. For some months a number

> of men met three nights a week for prayer; they often spent hours. The weeks passed and nothing happened until one morning at about two o'clock. A young man read Psalms 24, verses 3 to 5, "Who may stand in his holy place? He who has clean hands and a pure heart, who has not lifted up his soul to falsehood and has not sworn deceitfully. These shall receive a blessing from the Lord."
>
> He closed the Bible and, looking at his companions on their knees before God, he cried: "Brethren, it is just so much humbug to be waiting thus night after night, month after month, if we ourselves are not right with God. I must ask myself, is my heart pure, are my hands clean," and at that moment something happened. God swept into that prayer group and at that wonderful moment, seven Elders discovered what they evidently had not discovered before, that revival must be related to Holiness. ... They found themselves in the searching power of the presence of God and discovered things about themselves they had never suspected. That the blood of Calvary heals and cleanses. ... These men found themselves lifted to the realm of the supernatural. These men knew that revival had come.[4]

Proverbs 28:13 says that, "He who conceals his sins does not prosper, but whoever confesses and renounces them finds mercy." This verse specifically warns that we should not attempt to cover our transgressions. Concealing them is hypocrisy and leads to disaster in our Christian lives. Rather, we are called to confess and forsake them. Religious words (*repentance*, for example) are notoriously vague and as shifty as Jell-O. So we will need to look carefully at both confession and repentance to provide some definition and draw some distinctions.

### Confession: Agreeing with God

The literal meaning of the word *confession* is to "agree with" or to "say the same thing as," and in its biblical context it means that we are to agree with God about our sin. First, we are *agreeing* with God that we have sinned. This stands opposed to rationalizing (lessening the crime), justifying (arguing that there was no crime), denying (pretending there was no crime), and blaming (pinning the crime on someone else).

Second, we are *agreeing* with God that Christ died for that sin and that it was forgiven at the cross. He died for all our sins, even the ones we'll commit ten years from now. We agree that He has paid the price, and we accept this by faith. This stands opposed to guilt, berating ourselves, and self-loathing (this is really assuming the punishment ourselves through self-inflicted suffering).

Confession also involves the exercise of faith, specifically in God's Word and what He has said concerning our forgiveness. First John 1:9 tells us, "If we confess our sins, he is faithful and just and will forgive us our sins and purify us from all unrighteousness." This is a promise from God and is the truth about our confessed sin. To experience it, we must choose to trust it, rely upon it, and have faith in it (reckon it to be true). Then—and only then—does it becomes operative in our lives.

Confession means that I bring each individual sin before God. I acknowledge it as wrong and thank Him that it is forgiven. I do not seek to hide it. Rather, I bring it into His light and the light of His Word.

Let me give you an example. At the height of the radical student movement in 1970 an event occurred at Asbury College in Kentucky. This was a spiritual awakening that showed the power of confession, as a typically fifty-minute chapel service lasted 185 hours nonstop.

> It began when a few concerned students began to meet to pray for spiritual awakening. On February 3, Asbury students went to a normal 10 a.m. chapel service. As sometimes happened, the dean did not give a message but instead asked students to share testimonies.
>
> Those who came forward were unusually fervent in telling what God was doing in their lives. One senior said, "I am not believing that I am standing here telling you what God has done for me. I have wasted my time in college up to now, but Christ has met me, and I am different. Last night the Holy Spirit flooded in and filled my life and now for the first time ever, I am excited about being a Christian." As the end of the chapel hour approached, the bell sounded for classes to begin, but went unheeded.
>
> Students confessed sins such as cheating, stealing, bitterness and drug use. The editor of the school newspaper had skipped chapel, but when he heard what was going on he came and hid in the corner. Eventually the Holy Spirit touched him: "I knew things in my life were a lie. ... I was a sick and miserably lonely young man. Yet I sat there for two hours refusing to do anything. ... There came that critical moment when I was forced to admit that my self sufficiency was failing me and I needed to be dependent upon Jesus Christ. I prayed at the altar for an hour and a half undergoing a spiritual revitalization."[5]

Sometimes sins need to be confessed publicly (as in the case of the student newspaper editor). And as we noted in the last chapter, what makes public confession so powerful is that it combines two of the prerequisites for revival (humility and confession) and, short of uploading it to the Internet, there are few things more humbling than confessing our sin to an audience.

But sometimes sins are best confessed only to the Lord. As J. Edwin Orr says, the amount of public confession should be "just enough to enlist the prayers of people right with God. The public confession of secret private sins might be dangerous."[6] We don't want to release the burden of our sin at the expense of a weaker brother or sister who might be hurt or tempted by what we've shared. Revival is never an excuse to dispose of discretion, for voyeurism is a part of everyone's sin nature.

### Repentance: Change Your Thinking

While the two are often clumped together, repentance is not the same thing as confession. Nor does repentance mean feeling sorry about our sin, though repentance certainly can be accompanied by sorrow. Recall Proverbs 28:13: "Whoever confesses and renounces them [sins] finds mercy." Indeed, godly sorrow for sin may produce repentance, but sorrow itself is not repentance.

Repentance comes from the Greek word *metanoia* and means to change or transform (*metamorphosis*) our thinking. Implied is a change of action, a change of direction. It involves forsaking sin. Theoretically, I could confess my sin and feel sorry for it but not forsake it, and as I have at times done this, there is really nothing theoretical about it. When people repent of their sin, they cannot go on consciously committing it without remorse.

Repentance brings results that affect what we do. Students stop getting drunk. Racial attitudes are changed. People live with greater compassion. Sexual immoralities cease. Members of the opposite sex treat each other with respect. Cheating ends; theft stops; and backbiting and unjust criticism become things of the past. Lives and situations dramatically change in times of genuine repentance.

Yet it needs to be emphasized that repentance is not a guarantee against failing or falling, nor is it a resolve or pledge to never sin in such a way again. It is a decision to move in the opposite direction from that sin, to never stop fighting against it, to do all in one's power to resist it, to never accept or tolerate its presence, and to always pursue holiness in that area. It is a decision to vigilantly fight until victory, not a vow to never suffer defeat—a commitment to wage a war, not win a battle (for such a commitment is not within our power to make). This is a critical distinction.

Living in sin is like living in a house with termites and never giving them a second thought but acquiescing to their shared occupancy of the home. Repentance is making a decision and commitment that the termites (a specific area of sin) must go. A commitment, that even if it takes years to be rid of them, and reliance on the most powerful pesticides (confession, accountability, fasting, the Spirit's empowerment, and so forth): you will never stop fighting to get rid of them, and you will never return to a state of peaceful coexistence with their living in your house (life).

Repentance is often fueled by conviction, a sensation of guilt aroused by the Holy Spirit in us, pricking the heart and throbbing the conscience like a migraine. What is so radically different about revival is the power in which people experience conviction. Any revival could serve as an example, but as we have not yet considered the revivals of Northern Ireland, let us turn there. Once again it was college-aged individuals—four of them—who provided the combustion.

> Four young men, converts from Conner, gave
> their testimony in a crowded service in the First

> Presbyterian Church. Several thousand were present. Suddenly a number of people began to call out to God for mercy.
>
> That night many of the people could not sleep. Some wept in their homes for hours. Others cursed and swore in anger. Monday night again there was a united service in the First Presbyterian Church. The building was overcrowded but the ministers spoke calmly. "The meeting felt still as a grave; the stillness was fearful. Those who were present will never forget it. At length the silence was broken by unearthly cries, uttered simultaneously by several in different parts of the church." In a few minutes the vestry was filled with people "who lay in mental agony and absolute bodily prostration."[7]

Here is one account among hundreds of those who attended the service:

> A well-educated merchant ... suddenly saw hell opened before his eyes, and an irresistible power seemed to force him headlong into it. He looked around and said to himself, "I know where I am. This is the church where I usually worship. I am under a delusion." But as he looked down, there was hell.
>
> He arose from his seat and seized the back of the pew in front of him. The smoke from hell seemed to rise in his face. He shuddered and his heart cried out, "My sins! My sins! I am lost!" He staggered out of the building and went home. Had anyone asked me, where are you going? I

> would have answered, in calm despair, "I am going to hell."
>
> Upon reaching his room, for several hours he called to God for mercy. Then God's promises came to his mind. He joyously seized them, and "a heavenly radiance" spread over his soul. He arose a Christian. He raced out into the night across town and knocked on his business partner's door. When the door opened, he called out, "I have found Christ and have come to tell you!" They prayed together, and three days later his partner was converted.[8]

And one final account:

> In some instances those prostrated while seemingly oblivious to all else showed wonderful anointed memory. One pastor told of a girl who lay with fixed eyes turned to heaven for four hours. She quoted over a hundred scriptures all related and applied to her own case. She repeated sermons and exhortations that the pastor had preached over previous months, quoting large sections of these verbatim. Afterward the pastor questioned her, but she could not remember the sermons or quote those Scripture passages as she had done when gripped by the Holy Spirit.[9]

Of course, we see a milder form of this conviction and repentance all the time as people come to Christ, but revival deepens the experience, intensifying conviction and fueling "deep tissue" repentance.

J. Edwin Orr provides us this endnote on the Northern Ireland revivals of the late nineteenth century, further supporting the centrality of the campus and students to revival. Not only was this revival started by the testimonies of the four young men, but also it was spread to other countries through the conduit of students. "As usual in such movements, the student awakening developed a missionary trend. In fifteen years the Missionary Union of Great Britain and Ireland had sent more than a thousand of its choicest graduates to the mission field, a third of them to India."[10]

**Restitution: Making Repayment**

After confession and repentance of sin, restitution sometimes needs to be made. *Restitution* simply means "repayment." If I have sinned against someone by word or deed, I may need to ask for his or her forgiveness or make some sort of repayment for what I have done. This is one of the hardest corollaries of confession and repentance. For example, even after I've confessed and repented, I may need to tell my professor if I have cheated on a test. It may cost me a lot. It may cost me my place in college, or it may cost me a grade in that course, but it will not cost me nearly as much as refusing to make restitution. If I have stolen, I need to repay. If I have assassinated someone's character, I must make it right with that person.

Restitution is a powerful concept. Dr. Stephen Olford illustrates its results:

> During a time of spiritual awakening in Africa, we are told that the police authorities were astounded at the genuine repentance and restitution that was made not only by converts, but by backsliders who were restored to the Lord. The Daily Dispatch of East London, South Africa, listed the following articles returned by repentant believers: 80 sheets, 25 blankets, 24 jackets, 34 trousers, 11 overcoats, 6 women's coats, 25 dresses, 27 skirts, 50 shirts,

> 22 bedspreads, 64 hats, 23 towels, 1 table, 4 chairs, 50 pillow slips, 15 scissors, 5 hair clippers, 9 wallets, 4 cameras, 4 wristwatches, 3 revolvers and ammunition, 30 tumblers and an assortment of jewelry, tools, cigarette lighters, crockery, cutlery, boots, shoes, pressure stoves, frying pans, lanterns, and safety razors.[11]

After I had spoken at a conference, a young professional woman came up and asked if I could help her solve a problem. She had garnered many honors during her university years and had been the outstanding student in her field of study. She was an officer in her sorority and in many clubs. She had already made many friends among the faculty and the administration. Her grade-point average was 4.0.

While she was taking an examination during the spring quarter of her sophomore year, her professor snatched the test paper from her in the middle of the session and instructed her to meet him in his office afterward. Startled, she complied.

At their meeting he said to her, "Young woman, you know why you are here—you know you were cheating on that exam. You have two choices: you can take an automatic F in the course, or because we have an honor code here, you can bring it before the honor council and appeal it. But I am sure you would not want to do that, because we both know you were cheating."

Her response was one of outrage. She replied, "I most certainly will appeal. I was not cheating. I will take it before the honor council." She stalked from the room, called her parents and the president of the university to protest this miscarriage of justice, and began to gather character references.

When the hearing was held, the professor presented his case for her cheating, and she presented hers. She was exonerated and received an A in the course.

In her junior year she encountered Campus Crusade for Christ, became a Christian, and grew to be very involved in the movement. The next year, she graduated from that university as the outstanding student in her major and then moved into her chosen profession.

Showing her sadness, she continued. "The only problem with this story is that I really was cheating on that exam. I couldn't admit it because I knew what it would mean to my reputation, my academic standing, and my parents and friends. Even after I became a Christian and God began to speak to me about setting this right, I didn't have the courage to do it."

I asked about the consequences she was experiencing as a result. She replied that whenever she sought to advance spiritually, it was as if Satan had her on a leash. He would jerk that leash and say, "Yes. Great Christian. You are really a spiritual giant. You made a professor in his first major teaching job look stupid, and you did not have the courage to admit your guilt. How can you ever move forward?"

She asked what I thought she should do. I repeated Dr. Orr's advice: public sin needs to be confessed publicly and private sin needs to be confessed privately. I asked her, "How public was it?"

Sheepishly, she replied, "How public was it? The president of the university was involved. My parents were involved. Faculty members were involved. Everybody knew about it."

Since her sin was very public, I suggested she needed to find those involved, confess, and make any restitution needed.

She said, "How could I do that? I might lose my degree, my academic standing. It even might affect my career."

I asked if she would rather have short-term pain now or long-term pain for the rest of her life.

She saw what I meant. I offered to pray for her, hold her

accountable, and call her if she wished. I also asked her to let me know about the progress she made.

Six to eight weeks later, I received a letter that included another letter. In her letter she described her efforts to get things right with those to whom she had lied at her university and how she had tracked down her former professor (who was now at another college). She also described how she had confessed to her parents and received their forgiveness. The second letter was the response from the wronged professor.

In his letter the professor responded with astonishment that she had contacted him after the intervening years and acknowledged that it had been difficult knowing that, despite her denial, she really had cheated. He then expressed his forgiveness to her. He added,

> I am deeply impressed with your willingness to admit that you cheated on the exam. That single act shows a significant depth of character that most people lack. I know that you spent many sleepless nights and anguished over writing the letter before finally doing so. The fact that you wrote is an indication of your moral fiber and your conviction as a Christian. I will always be impressed that you contacted me after all these years. Good luck with your career and with your future. Both are extremely promising.

When I called to ask how she was doing now, she replied, "I'm free. I'm really free."

In the years since, I have seen her on several occasions. Both her career and her life have moved forward with great fruitfulness. The lessons are obvious. Even when there is great personal cost and risk, the process of confession, repentance, and restitution is worth it.

Confession, repentance, and restitution—none of it is

easy. But if our campuses are to see spiritual awakening, we Christians must be cleansed. We cannot hold on to sin, short-circuiting God's mighty power. When we confess our sin and repent of it, we are cleansed vessels, available for the Holy Spirit to fill and use us. We are able to be confident in our walk with Christ, bold in our witness, and our prayers begin to be answered in greater abundance and fruitfulness.

If we do not confess and repent, the Holy Spirit is grieved and His power is quenched in our life. Now, the fire of God may still fall upon our campus, but we can be sure it won't be in response to our efforts.

You who are burdened for your campus, and for the work of God in your life and at your college or university, need to come before God. Confess the sins He lays on your heart and repent; make restitution when necessary; and be available to be filled with God's mighty power by faith. Calvary precedes Pentecost. It we want the Spirit to manifest Himself in resurrection power, the "crucifixion" that is repentance and restitution must come first.

Here is an exercise that has worked for thousands of students. Take a sheet of paper, a pencil, and your Bible. Ask the Holy Spirit to show you any areas of your life that are displeasing to Him. Take thirty minutes to an hour and make a list of those sins. Then tell the Lord that you acknowledge them as sin and by faith accept His forgiveness. In fact, write out 1 John 1:9 ("If we confess our sins, he is faithful and just and will forgive us our sins and purify us from all unrighteousness") across the list and tear up the paper. Those sins have been completely paid for, never to be remembered—unless you forget to throw out the paper. So do throw out the paper.

Now determine by His power to turn from those sins (resolve to move away from them, even if the exodus is at times marked by failures), and make restitution or public confession where necessary. (It may be tough, but it will be worth it.) If you were sincere when you did this, you will be a cleansed vessel ready to become a glowing spark of revival and awakening on your campus. You will also be ready for the fourth prerequisite of spiritual awakening—fervent prayer.

# THE SUPREME EXAMPLE OF PRAYER

*"The great people of the earth today are the people who pray. I do not mean those who talk about prayer, nor those who say they believe in prayer; but I mean those people who take time and pray. These are the people today who are doing the most for God; in winning souls; in solving problems; in awakening churches; in keeping the old earth sweet awhile longer. "*
*– S. D. Gordon*[1]

*"Throughout most awakenings, young people banded in prayer groups on their campuses have often been at the forefront of the whole movement, catalyzing concerted prayer in the church at large."*
*–J. Edwin Orr*[2]

*Some may ask, "If Jesus and the* Father are always at work in the world, as John 5:17 says, why do we need some special work, or revival, anyway?" Arthur Wallis tells this enlightening story from nature:

> There was once an ancient reservoir in the hills that supplied a village community with water. It was fed by a mountain stream and the overflow from the reservoir continued down the streambed to the valley below. There is nothing remarkable about this stream. It flowed on its quiet way without even disturbing the boulders that lay in its path or the footbridges that crossed it at various points. It seldom overflowed its steep bank or gave the villagers any trouble. One day, however, some large cracks appeared in one of the walls of the old reservoir and soon afterwards the wall collapsed and the waters burst forth down the hillside. They rooted up great trees; they carried along boulders like playthings; they destroyed houses and bridges and all that lay in their path. The streambed could not now contain the volume of water, which therefore flowed over the countryside, even inundating distant dwellings. What had before been ignored or taken for granted, now became an object of awe and wonder and fear. From far and near, people who in the usual way never went near the stream hastened to see this great sight.[3]

Like the gentle stream, God is always at work. But when He comes in exceeding power, like a raging torrent, this is revival. And nothing is the same. People who have never thought about God now think of no one else, talk of no one else, and concentrate on no one else, because His presence is so powerfully platooned in their midst. So powerful, in fact, that in the awakening of 1858, as ships drew within a hundred miles of the ports of American cities experiencing revival, they "seemed to come into a zone of the Spirit's influence. Ship after ship arrived with the same tale of sudden conviction and conversion. In one ship a captain and the entire crew of thirty men found Christ out at sea and entered the harbor rejoicing."[4] Imagine the scene, in New York Harbor, of a thousand men kneeling on the bottom deck of the battleship *North Carolina*, weeping and shouting for mercy.[5]

When I read the line from Wallis's nature analogy "From far and near, people who in the usual way never went near the stream hastened to see this great sight," I think of the First Great Awakening in the U.S. and this rather poetic eyewitness account of the evangelist George Whitefield arriving to preach in Middletown, Connecticut:

> We went down with the stream. I heard no man speak a word all the way, three miles, but everyone pressing forward in great haste, and when we got down to the old meetinghouse there was a great multitude—it was 3 or 4000 people assembled together. We got off from our horses and shook off the dust, and the ministers were then coming to the meetinghouse. I turned and looked towards the great river and saw ferry boats running swift, forward and backward, bringing back loads of people, the oars rowed nimble and quick. Everything, men, horses and boats, all seemed to be struggling for life.[6]

God desires to manifest Himself in power. He wants to come like that raging torrent, to overturn the things that stand in His way on the campus. We, as Christians, have a tremendous opportunity—and I'd say obligation—to prepare the way for such a movement.

Confession and repentance (including any needed restitution) are part of the vital preparation necessary for us to lay hold of God. But we are still lacking another important ingredient. Second Chronicles 7:14 says, "If my people ... will ... pray ..."

We need to pray. And I'm not talking about your typical Jesus-help-me-on-my-midterm prayers (not that that's wrong). John Piper once said, "Prayer is a war time walk-talkie and we don't understand why it doesn't work when you use it as a domestic intercom to ring the maid for another pillow." He was referring to fervent revival prayer—urgent pleas for people to come to Christ and for believers to experience life-altering renewal, as opposed to the selfish whines for a more comfortable life that so often characterize our petitions. Such prayer is the channel through which God's revival power flows. We must pour out our hearts in a fresh way for the salvation of our family and friends, our campus, and the world. This stimulates our faith and demonstrates to God that we are serious about our requests.

### The Prayer Life of Jesus

No vast spiritual movement has ever occurred without being preceded by palm-sweating, hand- clasping, fervent prayer. If you count the two thousand years of Christianity as such a movement, we find that this, too, was preceded by prayer—the three and a half years of fervent prayer by our Lord Jesus Christ.

A study of Jesus' personal prayer life started a radical change in my prayer habits. It added new power to my life and ministry. It also launched my burden for awakening. An examination of several aspects of Christ's prayer life will, I hope, motivate us to move forward in our praying so that we can see God's mighty work on our campus for His glory.

As we look at Jesus' prayer life, I will resist the urge to illustrate through revival accounts. While stories of past revivals provide a compelling reminder and testimony to the power of prayer, nothing could serve as a more sober rejoinder than the fact that Jesus—the all-powerful Son of God—humbly and incessantly prayed. While revival brings forth a stark contrast between the frailty and impotence of the one praying and the supernatural power that results, our study of Jesus' prayer life flips that contrast. Here we see the power and glory of the one praying and are amazed that He descends to His knees in such humble reliance. But descend He does.

Although Jesus was fully God, He was also fully human. As a man, He depended upon God the Father to meet His every need and to accomplish His earthly ministry. In fact, there is much evidence in Scripture to suggest that His prayers were the channels through which God's power flowed to Him and through Him, enabling Him to do mighty works.

By the time we reach the eleventh chapter of Luke, we see that the disciples had been following Jesus for over a year, listening to His teaching and observing His ministry and miracles. Wanting to experience similar results in their own lives as well as emulate their Teacher, they made a simple request. "One day Jesus was praying in a certain place. When he finished, one of his disciples said to him, 'Lord, teach us to pray, just as John taught his disciples' " (Luke 11:1). Interestingly, they did not ask about the mechanics of His miracles ("When You walk on water, Lord, where exactly do You store Your weight?"). Rather, they came to Him with the request "Lord, teach us to pray."

Though they had seen Jesus doing amazing things, they were perceptive enough to realize that the secret of Jesus' power, life, and ministry was the intimate prayer time He spent with His Father. And they realized that the only way they were going to experience similar results was to learn how He prayed.

Jesus was a master teacher of prayer—not just through His words but also through His life. And like the disciples, if we are to experience God's power, we need to learn from Jesus the importance of prayer. As we survey His ministry through the Gospels, we see a remarkable emphasis on prayer and we observe that Jesus' ministry began, was sustained, and ended in prayer.

**Beginning in Prayer**

We read in Luke 3:21, "When all the people were being baptized, Jesus was baptized too. And as he was praying, heaven was opened."

It is significant to note that Jesus was praying at the outset of His ministry. While He was praying, heaven itself was opened and (as we read later) the Holy Spirit descended upon Him and God the Father spoke audibly.

Following this event, Jesus was led out into the wilderness, where He prayed and fasted and was tempted by Satan. "Jesus, full of the Holy Spirit, returned from the Jordan and was led by the Spirit in the desert, where for forty days he was tempted by the devil. He ate nothing during those days, and at the end of them he was hungry" (Luke 4:1-2).

In preparation for His public ministry Jesus began with a forty-day fast, which—by the way—did not come with the disclaimer "Don't try this at home." (What would be wrong with trying an extended fast?) Interestingly, we see in His wilderness temptation the prerequisites of revival—humbling, seeking God's face, and praying. There is even a component of restitution. Though Jesus had no sin of His own to atone for, He did so for the sins of His people. As Israel had rebelled in their wilderness wandering, Jesus (the true Israel) amended the record, walking in perfect obedience to the Father's will.

On every apparent level (and I'm sure a hundred levels and layers that we will never comprehend), Jesus was laying the foundation for His ministry during this period of prayer and fasting. By the time we read these words commencing His public ministry—"From that moment on Jesus began to preach, 'Repent, for the kingdom of heaven is near'"(Matthew 4:17)—a great battle had already been fought and won through forty days of preparatory prayer and fasting in the wilderness.

As demonstrated by Jesus, all great works of God are launched through prayer.

## Continuing in Prayer

Jesus Christ began His ministry in prayer, and He persevered in prayer throughout His earthly life. This seemingly incidental passage in Luke 5:16—"Jesus often withdrew to lonely places and prayed"—confirms a lifestyle and habit of prayer. Prayer was not a haphazard or peripheral activity of our Lord but the very fabric of His life. One might wonder in what situations and circumstances Jesus found it necessary to pray. Here is a compressed list:

> He prayed in the morning, at the gateway of the day: "Very early in the morning, while it was still dark, Jesus got up, left the house and went off to a solitary place, where he prayed" (Mark 1:35). And He prayed in the evening when the day's labor was over (Mark 6:46).
>
> Prayer always preceded the seminal, transitional, and catalyzing moments of Jesus' ministry. It was while He was praying at His baptism that heaven was opened. This was the inauguration of His life and ministry.
>
> He prayed in the hour of His popularity—the time when so many are swept off their feet: "After the people saw the miraculous sign that Jesus did, they began to say, 'Surely this is the Prophet who is to come into the world.' Jesus, knowing that they intended to come and make him king by force, withdrew again to a mountain by himself" (John 6:14).
>
> He prayed through trials, struggles, and temptations. In the story of Jesus in the Garden of Gethsemane we read, "Going a little farther, he fell to the ground and prayed that if possible

the hour might pass from him" (Mark 14:35). He also commanded His disciples to pray during such times: "Watch and pray so that you will not fall into temptation" (Matthew 26:41).

He prayed for His disciples and others: "I have prayed for you, Simon, that your faith may not fail" (Luke 22:32).

He prayed before critical decisions. His selection of the twelve disciples was made only after a night of prayer: "Jesus went out to a mountainside to pray, and spent the night praying to God. When morning came, he called his disciples to him and chose twelve of them" (Luke 6:12-13). And it was only after a special time of prayer that He opened His heart to His disciples and confided in them about His approaching suffering and death.

It was while He was in the act of prayer that the majestic Transfiguration scene was enacted: "As he was praying, the appearance of his face changed, and his clothes became as bright as a flash of lightning" (Luke 9:29). Prayer was the cause; transfiguration was the effect. Is there a lesson here for us?

Great achievements were preceded by prayer. Many of Jesus' miracles followed after prayer: the feeding of the four thousand, the feeding of the five thousand, walking on water, the raising of Lazarus, and the healing of the possessed boy. Each of these miracles was linked with the prayers that preceded it.

> Great achievements were followed by prayer: "After he had dismissed them, he went up on a mountainside by himself to pray" (Matthew 14:23). When confronted with crises, we turn instinctively to prayer, but once the crisis is over, the task achieved, we tend to lean on our own abilities and wisdom. Jesus guarded against this evil by following such occasions with prayer.

In short, Jesus prayed all the time—and, no, I couldn't have just said that and spared you the list. You need to see that there was never a time when Jesus did not pray to meet the tasks, the pressures, the burdens, and the joys of His day. Prayer was the consuming passion of His life.

**Ending in Prayer**

Jesus began His ministry in prayer and sustained it in prayer. He also ended His ministry in prayer. On the night of His betrayal and capture, Jesus fortified Himself (as Luke 22 informs us) by going to the Garden of Gethsemane, falling on His knees, and spending an agonizing time of prayer with His Father. He warned the disciples, "Pray so that you [would] not fall into temptation" (Luke 22:40). Jesus knew the bitter reality of those words. Prayer was the antidote to temptation and sin, and He knew that capitulation to human weakness was best deterred by extended time with the Father.

Through the struggles and temptations of His final hours Jesus focused His eyes upon God the Father through ceaseless prayer. Even Jesus' final words on the cross were a prayer: "Jesus called out with a loud voice, 'Father, into your hands I commit my spirit.' When he had said this, he breathed his last" (Luke 23:46).

In the midst of such personal agony, how could Jesus manage to end His life in such a prayerful way? The answer is simple: because it was the practice of His life. Prayer had become habit and reflexive and therefore the most natural way to end His earthly life—the *only* way to end His earthly life.

### Praying Today

What is Jesus doing today? Hebrews 7:25 tells us, "He is able to save completely those who come to God through him, because he always lives to intercede for them." Jesus Christ is continually interceding for us in heaven today. He has not stopped. The habit of His earthbound life is the habit of His heavenly life. We are always on His mind, and He is always presenting us before the Father.

S. D. Gordon comments, "The Lord Jesus is still praying. Thirty years of living; thirty years of serving; one tremendous act of dying; nineteen hundred years of prayer."[7] And as Gordon said this around a century ago, and as Jesus' did not stop praying in the 1920s, we should amend that to "two thousand years of prayer."

His ministry began in prayer, continued in prayer, and ended in prayer, and He continues in intercession to this very hour. This is the example left to us by our Savior.

If we are to see awakening and see our campuses change for good and for God, we must learn to follow the example set by Jesus and become men and women of prayer.

If it is not currently your practice, begin to set aside at least twenty minutes a day for revival prayer. This can be in addition to or a part of your personal devotional life. You will want to boldly come before the Father, requesting transformation in your own life, the lives of your friends and family, and your campus. You will want to begin with specific requests for the salvation of people you know (friends, professors, students in your dorm or classes) and then move on to more broadly praying for the campus: dorms, athletic teams, teachers, the administration, and so forth.

It may be challenging to persist in this long in the beginning, but as you persevere, you will soon find that twenty minutes is barely any time at all. Then find someone else to pray with you. You might even find walking around the campus while praying to be a visionary experience. This joint prayer time could be the small beginning of a massive awakening.

# THE POWER OF FERVENT PRAYER

*"Through prayer, God has given us the privilege of being used by Him to help change the lives of men and nations. God has made available to us a vast reservoir of power, wisdom, and grace beyond words to define, if only we are willing to believe Him and claim His promises."*
*– Bill Bright*[1]

*"Whenever God is ready to do something new with His people, He always sets them to praying."*
*– J. Edwin Orr*[2]

*Prayer has always been the precursor to* revival. If we commit ourselves to prayer, there is no limit to what we can see God do. Genesis 32:26 gives us Jacob's instructive prayer to God: "I will not let you go unless you bless me." This is the kind of fervency and persistence that needs to characterize our prayers. Jacob was saying, "You can't make it rough enough for me to stop. I am holding on until You fulfill Your promises."

This is what Jesus was teaching about prayer when He encouraged His followers, "Ask and it will be given to you; seek and you will find; knock and the door will be opened to you" (Luke 11:9). Knocking—by definition—is persistent repetition.

This is extremely difficult for us to do. We are addicted to the short term, and with every advance in technology and convenience, and every new button added to our 'remotes', that habit intensifies. We pray a while. When no obvious answers are forthcoming, we become distracted or discouraged and quit. But lasting revival is the fruit of persistent prayer: weeks, months, sometimes years of petitioning God for a spiritual brushfire to break forth on our campuses, converting the lost, quickening believers, and drawing the focus of the entire campus to Jesus Christ.

### The Prayer of One Person

Consider the influence of just one person. James 5:16 states, "The prayer of a righteous man is powerful and effective." James goes on to support that idea with the example of Elijah. "Elijah was a man just like us. He prayed earnestly that it would not rain, and it did not rain on the land for three and a half years" (verse 17).

Like us, Elijah was a weak and sinful person, but he loved a great and powerful God. He prayed that it would not rain, so that the degenerate king of Israel, Ahab, would be brought to his knees before God.

God heard Elijah's prayer, and He answered specifically. For three and a half years there wasn't a drop of rain. In desperation the people turned to God, and Ahab himself finally admitted his need for divine intervention.

Elijah prayed again. This time he prayed it would begin to rain. And it poured. Through Elijah, James clearly makes the point that "the prayer of a righteous man is powerful and effective."

Do you believe this? Do you believe that your prayer has

the power to make it rain, both physically and spiritually? If so, even if no one joins with you, you need to begin praying for revival on your campus, persistently and expectantly.

Consider the following illustration by the great revivalist Charles Finney of what one person's prayer can accomplish. (I share with the addendum that Finney was more of a motivational preacher than a careful historian.)

> In a certain town there had been no revival for many years; the church was nearly extinct. The youth were all unconverted, and desolation reigned unbroken. There lived in a retired part of the town an aged man of so stammering a tongue that it was painful to hear him speak. On one Friday, as he was at work in his shop, alone, his mind became greatly exercised about the state of the church and of the impenitent.
>
> His agony became so great that he was induced to lay by his work, lock the shop door and spend the afternoon in prayer.
>
> He prevailed and on the Sabbath called on the minister and desired him to appoint a conference meeting. After some hesitation the minister consented, observing however that he feared that few would attend. When evening came, more assembled than could be accommodated in the house. All were silent for a time, until one sinner broke out in tears, and said, if anyone could pray, kindly would he pray for him? Another followed, and another, and so on, until it was found that persons from every quarter of the town were under deep conviction. And what was remarkable was that they all dated their conviction at the hour that

> the old man was praying in his shop. A powerful revival followed. Thus this old stammering man prevailed and as a prince had power with God.[3]

We are not talking about the need to be a spiritual giant. Rather, we are talking about ordinary people with a giant God who make an extraordinary effort to pray for awakening.

### Multiplying the Prayers of a Few

Ready for another true revival report? This one comes from the middle of the nineteenth century.

> Mr. Jeremiah C. Lanphier, a lay missionary in New York City, was greatly burdened for the salvation of souls. Almost daily in the lecture room of the old Dutch church on Fulton Street he would go alone to pray for a genuine revival.
>
> The going was slow. A few families came but often Lanphier would return to his room in the church consistory weary and discouraged. At such times he "spread out his sorrows before the Lord." And he never failed to draw new strength from his time of prayer.
>
> On September 23rd, 1857, Lanphier committed to invite others to join him, announcing a weekly prayer meeting with a simple placard on the church door which read, "Prayer meeting from 12 to 1 o'clock—stop 5, 10, or 20 minutes, or the whole hour as your time admits." It wasn't until 12:30 until he heard a step on the stairs. One man came in, then another and another until there were six. Nothing remarkable took place. After a few minutes

> of prayer the meeting was dismissed with the decision that another meeting would be held the following Wednesday. Twenty came to the next noon-hour meeting. The following Wednesday, forty. A week later it became a daily prayer meeting; the meeting room overflowed and simultaneous meetings were held in other auditoriums of the church building. The seats were all filled, passages and entrances were blocked and hundreds were turned away for lack of room as crowds swelled to 3,000, leading to the formation of prayer meetings throughout New York City.[4]

If one person praying for revival is good, two or more are better. The preceding account is of the Layman's Prayer Awakening of 1857 to 1858, and the dramatic break came when Jeremiah Lanphier went public with the meeting, calling others to join him in praying for revival. Jonathan Edwards, one of the premier channels of the First Great Awakening, said, "When God has something very great to accomplish for His church, it is His will that there should precede it the extraordinary prayers of His people."[5]

The Layman's Prayer Awakening soon spread from New York to Philadelphia as a few college and post-college men met for prayer. They became burdened for revival, and in November of 1857 they launched a daily prayer meeting as Lanphier had done in New York City. At first only a few attended, but they were not discouraged. They continued. Soon the room contained twenty, then thirty, forty, fifty, and finally sixty. The fervency of prayer increased. One could sense an explosion about to occur.

Four months after they began to pray, the revival began.

> At first, only the small room was occupied, with a few in attendance. Then it became

> overflowing, and the meeting moved to the main saloon, meetings starting there on the tenth of March. Twenty-five hundred seats were provided, and were filled to overflowing. The sponsors next removed a partition from the main floor space and platform; next, the floor platform and lower gallery, then floor platform and both galleries filled up; fully six thousand people gathered daily.
>
> For months on end each separate church was opened at least each evening. Some of them as often as three and five times a day and all were filled. Simple prayer, confession, exhortation and singing was all that happened, but it was so honest, so solemn, the silence so awful, the singing so overpowering, the meetings were unforgettable.
>
> In order to continue the work, which flooded churches with inquirers and converts, a big canvas tent was bought for $2,000 and opened for religious services on May 1, 1858. During the following four months, an aggregate of 150,000 attended the ministry under the canvas, many conversions resulting. The churches in Philadelphia reported 5,000 converts thus won.[6]

These numbers are even more amazing when you consider that the total population of Philadelphia was then at about 5 percent of its current size. Affected by the same revival and awakening, the adjacent state of New Jersey recorded over sixty thousand converts within a few weeks. At the same time, 40 percent of the students at Princeton were converted and 18 percent entered full-time Christian ministry.

Harvard historian Perry Miller chronicled the total number of converts to Christ (and added to the churches) in the U.S. during the Layman's Revival as one million, or 3.2 percent of the U.S. population. (An analogous number of converts today would be ten million.) Dr. Miller called this revival "the event of the century."[7]

The pray-ers were just ordinary people. Few have found their way into history books. Yet through their prayers they were responsible for thousands of converts and for multitudes of believers being set on fire for God. These percentages and numbers may seem mind-boggling in light of the spiritual apathy we witness on campus today, but we have to ask the rhetorical question repeated throughout the Scripture, "Is anything too hard for the Lord?" (Genesis 18:14). No, there is absolutely no reason why we should not expect something similar to happen among us today.

The people who prayed in Philadelphia caught the praying spirit of Christ. We can be infected like that today. Indeed, this infection is already spreading across our country and around the world.

## Models for Revival Prayer

In recent years I have received hundreds of reports from students all over the country detailing their burden for prayer and revival. And they have been putting their concern into action. Early in the morning, late at night, and at noontime, students on hundreds of campuses are praying for revival at their schools.

Leading demographer David Barrett reports that 170 million Christians worldwide are currently praying daily for a spiritual awakening and global evangelism. George Otis Jr. observes, "About seventy percent of all prayer toward completing the Great Commission has taken place since 1900. Of that, seventy percent has occurred since World War II. And seventy percent of that has come about in the 1990s alone!"[8] I'm curious how one would derive such a statistic, but I'm certain about the truth it represents: prayer and missions are definitely heating up.

How did this happen? What has begun the body of Christ praying? Well, besides this being a genuine work of the Spirit, the acceleration of prayer on our campuses and around the world seems to trace back to three significant historical impulses that continue to serve as models and inspiration. The first we've already studied: the great awakenings and revivals that were launched from Europe and America in the eighteenth, nineteenth, and early twentieth centuries. The second influence that deserves our attention is the passionate and persevering prayer in Korea that launched and sustained a revival and continues to this very hour. J. Oswald Sanders described the genesis of the revival that swept Korea in the early twentieth century.

> Some years ago a great revival swept over Korea, the fruits of which remain to the present day. This revival had been prayed down. Four missionaries of different denominations had agreed to meet together to pray daily at noon. At the end of one month a brother proposed that "as nothing had happened," the prayer meeting should be discontinued. "Let us each pray at home as we find it convenient," said he. The others, however, protested that they ought rather to spend more time in prayer each day, so they continued their daily prayer meetings for four months. Then suddenly the blessing began to be poured out.[9]

In less than two months more than two thousand unbelievers were converted. In one church it was announced that a daily prayer meeting would be held every morning at 4:30. The first day, four hundred people arrived long before the stated hour, eager to pray. The number rapidly increased to six hundred. Unbelievers came to see what was happening. They exclaimed in astonishment, "The living God is among you!"[10]

Commenting on this, Dr. Joon Gon Kim, respected Korean pastor and leader within Campus Crusade for Christ, said:

> In 1907, at Pyongyang, seven hundred people were dramatically filled with the Holy Spirit while attending a week-long Bible study conference. This conference is often referred to as the Korean Pentecost. The lives of those attending were changed. They began their new lives as fireseeds of prayer, founding a nationwide prayer movement which continues today. The fireseeds became witnesses for Christ, used mightily to start spiritual fires across our nation and into many corners of the world. Fireseeds traveled to China, Japan, and America. Anywhere Korean people assembled a spark seemed to ignite.[11]

Bill Bright wrote the following concerning Korea's heart and example of persevering prayer:

> In Korea ... we have helped to train over two million Christians who have gone from Korea to the ends of the earth with burning hearts. There is no place in the world where one finds a greater emphasis on prayer and fasting. God has honored that spirit, and today the influence of Dr. Kim and the Korean people embrace the world. ... Their zeal for Christ, their personal prayer life, their revival spirit prompts them wherever they go throughout the world to have a vital impact for the Savior.[12]

The Korean revival began in prayer, continued in prayer, and goes on now at an accelerated pace. Tomorrow morning at 4:00 a.m. (no, the a.m. is not a typo) millions of South Koreans will rise, dress, and go to homes and churches to pray. This has set, and continues to set, an example to the world of how to pray passionately and perseveringly for revival.

The third historical impulse is the eighteenth-century Moravian Pietists, led by Count Von Zinzendorf. This interdenominational community was comprised of Moravians (believers from the Czech region) as well as other persecuted refugees of the Protestant Wars who came to Zinzendorf's estate in Germany for asylum. This little community experienced a powerful revival, and within two weeks of the outpouring, twenty-four men and twenty-four women covenanted to pray "hourly intercessions," thus praying every hour around the clock. They were committed to see that "the fire must be kept burning on the altar continuously; it must not go out" (Leviticus 6:13). This prayer meeting would go nonstop for the next one hundred years and is seen by many as the spiritual power behind many of revivals of the eighteenth, nineteenth, and twentieth centuries.

The Moravians served as the example and inspiration for Peter Greig and the modern 24/7 prayer movement. After a visit to Herrnhut, the historic site of Zinzendorf's community, Greig figured, "If the Moravians could do a century of 24/7 prayer, we could at least try for a month in our church back home." So, in September of 1999, they began their experiment and found they couldn't stop praying after the month was up, continuing on until Christmas. Today there are thousands of prayer rooms in seventy countries and counting. They are mobilizing an army of revival pray-ers, willing to sacrifice, willing to persevere, willing to ... well, here, read Peter Greig's famous vision statement that galvanized the movement:

So this guy comes up to me and says "What's the vision? What's the big idea?" I open my mouth and words come out like this ... The vision?

The vision is JESUS—obsessively, dangerously, undeniably Jesus.

The vision is an army of young people. You see bones? I see an army. And they are FREE from materialism. They laugh at 9-5 little prisons. They could eat caviar on Monday and crusts on Tuesday. They wouldn't even notice. They know the meaning of the Matrix, the way the west was won. They are mobile like the wind, they belong to the nations. They need no passport. People write their addresses in pencil and wonder at their strange existence. They are free yet they are slaves of the hurting and dirty and dying. What is the vision? The vision is holiness that hurts the eyes. It makes children laugh and adults angry. It gave up the game of minimum integrity long ago to reach for the stars. It scorns the good and strains for the best. It is dangerously pure.

Light flickers from every secret motive, every private conversation. It loves people away from their suicide leaps, their Satan games. This is an army that will lay down its life for the cause. A million times a day its soldiers choose to lose that they might one day win the great "Well done" of faithful sons and daughters.

Such heroes are as radical on Monday morning as Sunday night. They don't need fame from names. Instead they grin quietly upwards and hear the crowds chanting again and again: "COME ON!"

And this is the sound of the underground. The whisper of history in the making. Foundations shaking. Revolutionaries dreaming once again. Mystery is scheming in whispers. Conspiracy is breathing ... This is the sound of the underground.

And the army is disciplined. Young people who beat their bodies into submission. Every soldier would take a bullet for his comrade at arms. The tattoo on their back boasts "For me to live is Christ and to die is gain." Sacrifice fuels the fire of victory in their upward eyes. Winners. Martyrs. Who can stop them? Can hormones hold them back? Can failure succeed? Can fear scare them or death kill them?

And the generation prays like a dying man with groans beyond talking, with warrior cries, euphoric tears and with great barrow loads of laughter! Waiting. Watching: 24—7—365.

Whatever it takes they will give: Breaking the rules. Shaking mediocrity from its cozy little hide. Laying down their rights and their precious little wrongs, laughing at labels, fasting essentials. The advertisers cannot mould them. Hollywood cannot hold them. Peer-pressure is powerless to shake their resolve at late night parties before the cockerel cries.

They are incredibly cool, dangerously attractive inside. On the outside? They hardly care. They wear clothes like costumes to communicate and celebrate but never to hide. Would they surrender their image or their popularity? They would lay down their very lives— swap seats with the man on death row—guilty as hell. A throne for an electric chair.

With blood and sweat and many tears, with sleepless nights and fruitless days, they pray as if it all depends on God and live as if it all depends on them. Their DNA chooses JESUS. (He breathes out, they breathe in.) Their subconscious sings. They had a blood transfusion with Jesus. Their words make demons scream in shopping centres. Don't you hear them coming? Herald the weirdos! Summon the losers and the freaks. Here come the frightened and forgotten with fire in their eyes. They walk tall and trees applaud, skyscrapers bow, mountains are dwarfed by these children of another dimension. Their prayers summon the hounds of heaven and invoke the ancient dream of Eden.

And this vision will be. It will come to pass; it will come easily; it will come soon. How do I know? Because this is the longing of creation itself, the groaning of the Spirit, the very dream of God. My tomorrow is his today. My distant hope is his 3D. And my feeble, whispered, faithless prayer invokes a thunderous, resounding, bone-shaking great "Amen!" from countless angels, from heroes of the faith, from Christ himself. And he is the original dreamer, the ultimate winner.

Guaranteed.[13]

## Calling Others to Pray

Revivals escalate. A few people are revived. They begin to pray for an awakening on their campus, in their church, upon their city. The more they pray, the greater the burden becomes. Since they cannot bear it alone, they need others to bear the burden with them.

So they call others to blend their hearts and prayers with them. God then touches these new participants, and they, too, are "set on fire." They then recruit others. Thus the numbers who are passionately praying increase.

Sooner or later, a critical mass of praying, fervent believers is gathered. Like a nuclear reaction (where molecules of radioactive material are continuously added until a certain mass is reached), when a certain number (known only to God) of fervently praying believers is reached, a spiritual explosion occurs. God then sends a sweeping movement to touch the campus, church, or city in order to revive believers and to arouse unbelievers so that they may be converted.

We see an example of this spiritual radiation and reaction in a revival that swept over India in the early part of the twentieth century. It began with a godly woman named Pandita Ramabai. In 1891 this brilliant Hindu social reformer was profoundly converted to Christ.

Ramabai had built a center/shelter/school in Pune, India (south of Bombay), for orphans, widows, and famine victims. She named it Mukti, meaning "salvation." For years she prayed and fasted for the salvation of the women at Mukti and for revival in India. In 1898 she traveled to a Christian conference in England and recruited every one of the four thousand attendees to pray for evangelization and revival in India and for her women at Mukti.

She produced a mission magazine called the *Mukti Prayer Bell*, through which she summoned believers all over the world to pray for God to move powerfully in India.

In September, 1901, Ramabai began a special prayer meeting for an outpouring of God's Spirit at her center in

Mukti, and as revival came, twelve hundred women were baptized in the course of two months. But her vision and burden went far beyond Mukti to the country of India itself. She organized her newly converted women in prayer circles (ten women in each) to pray daily for an outpouring of God's Spirit upon India, and she recruited friends and supporters to form similar prayer circles. Seeing the need for evangelism as well as prayer, Ramabai asked thirty of her women to give up their studies at the center to evangelize the local towns and villages.

As the thirty women prayed for God to empower them on their evangelistic mission, His Spirit powerfully manifested among them. "One of the thirty was so set aflame spiritually that the other girls saw a vision of fire engulfing her. One of the girls grabbed a pail of water to throw on her, only to discover that the fire, though visible, was not literal. It was the fire of the Spirit seen ... at Pentecost."[14]

As one witnessed described the scene: "One little girl of twelve is constantly laughing—her face, plain, even ugly, is beautiful and radiant. She does not know it. She is occupied with Jesus. You think you have looked on an angel face. Some claim to have seen the Lord—one, a blind girl. All speak of His coming again. One sang hymns composing them as she sang."[15]

The thirty women who had committed to witnessing in neighboring villages turned into seven hundred. Every day a group of sixty would go out, taking turns, while the others remained and prayed.

There is not space to describe how the revival continued to spread across India in the early twentieth century. (The "children's revival" of Khasia, where young children were so touched by God that they went door-to-door in nearby villages sharing Christ, is worthy of a book in itself.) The Methodists reported thirty-six thousand new members; the Presbyterians baptized eleven thousand in four years; the Lutherans, twenty-one thousand ... and the list goes on.[16]

In the Mukti revival, and in the example set by Pandita Ramabai, we witness the chain reaction of revival prayer as it grows from the burden of one into the mission of an army. The revival occurred because Pandita Ramabai saw her role extending beyond personal prayer to being a mobilizer of prayer—gathering the critical mass needed to start a chain reaction.

The place to begin, of course, is in your own devotional life. Pray daily for revival on your campus and in your dormitory or Greek house. Ask God for greater fervency and a spirit of persistence. After all, this is the basic meaning of 1 Thessalonians 5:17: "Pray without ceasing" (NASB).

Having begun your own prayer quest for revival, like Jeremiah Lanphier and Pandita Ramabai, the next step is to join with others to pray. If there is already a prayer group, great! Join that group and share with them your burden for revival. You might even share copies of this book with the group to encourage revival prayer.

If there is not a regular prayer meeting, following the courage and example of the godly individuals we've looked at, you be the one to call others to join you in prayer.

Besides a time of weekly prayer, I would suggest you designate and set up a prayer room on campus. This would be a place where anyone can go at any time to pray, a place where twenty-four-hour prayer can continue unabated if people are willing and committed. Be creative in setting up the environment of the room, having copies of visionary articles, prayer journals, books, music, lists of requests, and stories of answered prayer. Create an environment where, day or night, people can come and find a sanctuary to seek the Lord and pray for the needs of the ministry, the campus, and the world. Use this as the place to hold your weekly prayer times, and have a war room to set up prayer chains: 24/7 watches of prayer for the campus. As you pray, God will give you many creative ideas for mobilizing others and sustaining a prayer movement.

Let me close with the following exhortation from one of history's greatest students of revival, Leonard Ravenhill. It has pricked my prayer life for years, and I hope it will stimulate yours as well.

> The church has many organizers, but few agonizers; many who pay, but few who pray; many resters, but few wrestlers; many who are enterprising, but few who are interceding. People who are not praying are playing.
>
> Two prerequisites of dynamic Christian living are vision and passion. Both of these are generated by prayer. The ministry of preaching is open to a few. The ministry of praying is open to every child of God. ...
>
> Tithes may build the church, but tears will give it life. That is the difference between the modern church and the early church. Our emphasis is on paying, theirs was on praying. When we have paid, the place is taken. When they had prayed, the place was shaken (Acts 4:31).
>
> In the matter of effective praying, never have so many left so much to so few. Brethren, let us pray.[17]

# RESULTS OF SPIRITUAL AWAKENING ON CAMPUS

*"The really effective agency of religion in the life of the college was the revival ... which brought so many ... into church and into the ministry. Most college presidents and college faculties of this era felt that they or God ... had failed a collegiate generation, if once during its four years there did not occur a rousing revival."*
*– Frederick Rudolph*[1]

*Take a second and read (or reread)* the quote from Frederick Rudolph. Can you imagine the president of your college or university apologizing to the seniors at graduation because there had been no spiritual awakening on campus during their collegiate stay? Such might happen if we met the criteria for our part in laying awakening's foundation. Only God brings awakening. We cannot program His work. He has outlined our part in preparing a way. But when we do our part, a spiritual awakening could produce some predictable results.

The outworking of revival seems to fall into four areas:

1. Holiness of life for believers
2. Obedience to God and His Word
3. Increased power from God
4. A massive movement of God's Spirit in evangelism

Notice that these form the acrostic HOPE (holiness, obedience, power, evangelism). An examination of each of these areas follows.

### Holiness of Life

The *New York Herald*, referring to a revival at the University of Michigan in the 1850s, stated, "There has been at times a deep and solemn thoughtfulness among the students at the State University ... under the influence of the Holy Spirit ... banishing the last remains of skepticism."[2]

As Christians enter the channel of revivability through prayer, their moral lives improve. And when revival finally comes, it touches others who have not previously been burdened by the Holy Spirit for personal change.

The Spirit forcefully touches their sin, convincing them of their need to confess, repent, and make restitution. Individuals then lay aside their old habits and unholy lifestyles and walk in fellowship with Christ.

The Asbury College Revival of 1970 demonstrates this. We earlier discussed the prayer that led to awakening at Asbury. As the revival erupted, students began to give testimony to the changes Christ had produced in their lives. Then other students spontaneously began to rise, confess their sins, and ask for forgiveness. All classes were canceled and the chapel service continued unabated for 185 hours (nearly eight days!). Students found themselves ceasing immorality, drugs, drunkenness, cheating, and swearing. They got busy about serious Bible study, evangelism, honest work, and love for their neighbors. Perhaps the best way to picture it is through the diary of a student who journaled thoughts and observations sporadically as he sat amidst the outpouring beginning on February 3, 1970.

> Forgiveness—Expressions of hidden guilt and resentments. God is convicting His children.
>
> Two close friends are making their way to the altar. Fill their cups Lord.
>
> Two and one-half hours passed. Hands in the air—pointed toward God. A brother and a sister at the altar. Friends, couples, roommates at the altar.
>
> Three hours have passed. My roommate has found victory. He is urging other friends to rid themselves of the old trash and garbage that claim their lives. He says, "Shovel out the trash."
>
> Black people. White people. God's people.
>
> Hands in the air. A boy from California who says, "Praise God, I've kicked the habit." Applause.
>
> Five hours have passed. 2:55 p.m. Again, the song, "How Great Thou Art." A foreign student longs to go back to her island home in the Pacific and tell her people of our Lord.
>
> Six hours have passed. A poem from a student about the love of God. People still at the altar.
>
> A graduate of Asbury College prayed, "Forgive me. Forgive me." Conversion followed. Now twelve hours have passed since it all began.

> Intense prayers now that God would open the doors of Brazil to a couple who is called there to the mission field.
>
> Fourteen hours have passed. Midnight. A new day is about to dawn.
>
> After midnight. Running to the altar. We are in the presence of God. Awe—Wonder—Love—An unspeakable sense of His nearness ...
>
> 10:05 a.m. Seventy-two hours have passed. Revival has spread to other campuses. The revival is taking a national form.
>
> Teachers are witnessing to their faith in God.
>
> 106 hours have passed ... the revival goes on and on and on. Thirteen souls at the altar. 1,500—1,600 people present. People from many states.[3]

On many campuses Christian lives look little different from those of unbelievers. Even if they refrain from swearing or drinking, as is sometimes the case, their overall moral fabric and the love emanating from their lives is neither compelling nor noticeably different from the behavior of their non-Christian student counterparts. As a result, unbelievers write off Christ and His power. Never have we needed holiness more!

We would expect the results of revival on campus to have ramifications in, among other things, the sexual area: decreases in abortions, an increase in sexual abstinence, a lack of interest in pornography, the sanitizing of sexually crude innuendo and speech, the reduction of rapes and sexual perversion, and a renewed respect and love between the sexes. Other demonstrations of holiness on campus might include the closing of many campus bars; voluntary honor codes; a change in the tone and content of campus newspapers; a purifying and evangelistic transformation of personal Web pages; greater modesty in speech and dress; campus prayer meetings filled to overflowing; a decrease in suicide, depression, and other disorders; and a diminishing of cynical and sardonic humor and speech. In short, students would desire to change instead of being forced to; they would have a compelling vision for a life of purity and holiness.

### Obedience to God and His Word

The second major result of awakening on campus would be a renewed obedience to God and His Word. Revival is by nature a new submitting of ourselves to God. What we would see is students pouring over God's Word, the Scriptures becoming their most valuable text. Instead of ignoring God's promises and commands, students would be quoting them and stepping out in expectant faith upon them.

The new willingness to obey God that flows from spiritual renewal would also have a great impact on the needs and sufferings of others. Revivals almost always have clear, long-term effects on social problems. Before revival comes, believers are often self-absorbed, thinking little about the needs of others, particularly if others are invisible to their own social group. But as believers become revived and take the Word of God seriously, they discover many commands dealing with the poor, the hungry, the defenseless, the imprisoned, and the oppressed. In the past, revived believers established hospitals, orphanages, and halfway houses. They fought against slavery and child labor practices and oppression of the poor. Outreaches such as the Red Cross, the Salvation Army, and the abolition and temperance movements were direct overflows of revivals. James Montgomery Boice commented, "The best things that have ever happened in history have been as a result of that kind of movement, whether the Great Awakenings or the revivals of Wesley and Whitefield."[4]

Revival today could produce a new concern for the poor, persecuted, orphaned, widowed, war-torn, diseased, abused, and neglected people of the world. It could lead to greater humanitarian aid efforts abroad and concern for human rights violations everywhere. It could seek an end to human trafficking, unfair trade, AIDS, civil war, the sex industry, genocide, political and corporate corruption, and nuclear escalation.

Ethics without legalism could again have a place in the business, medical, and professional schools of our universities. Racism and prejudice (endemic in our society) would be honestly admitted. Wrongs would be confronted.

College students are the most idealistic demographic in the population. Awakening in the collegiate world could give eternal perspective to that idealism and generate new solutions to ancient problems both here and abroad.

### Increased Power from God

The Holy Spirit is the only One who brings revival to people, campuses, and nations. He is the power source for all that occurs. In 1 Corinthians 4:20 the apostle Paul states, "The kingdom of God is not a matter of talk but of power." Jesus, too, spoke of the Spirit's ministry in terms of power, saying, "You will receive power when the Holy Spirit comes on you" (Acts 1:8).

Because awakening causes believers to be more obedient, the Spirit can release greater power and influence. A. J. Gordon said, "God is ready to give you the power of His Spirit as soon as you are ready to obey Him."[5] This means the power to pray. It means power to forgive. It means power to love. It means power to change and power in the face of fear.

Josef Tson, leader of the spiritual revival in Romania in

the 1970s and 1980s, said that the secret to the revival was the courage to die and declared that what was hindering it "was our desire to survive." "Sometimes," said Tson, "the Lord wants you to stand up and die and through your death bring revival." As a courageous victim of numerous interrogations and beatings under the Romanian dictator Ceauşescu, Tson certainly knew what he spoke of. He preached this message of courage and sacrifice, and "the young people embraced it, declaring, 'We do not want the compromise of our parents. It is either or. Totally with Jesus or without Him.' " "It was at that moment," said Tson, "that revival came to Romania."[6]

This power will enable believers to stand firm and fight graciously and humbly (if necessary). It will enable them to witness boldly, and most of all it will be power to go the distance in the Lord's ministry. A good example of this comes from the testimony of a Chinese pastor renewed and revitalized during the Shantung Revival in China. (Shantung is a province of northeast China that was powerfully visited by God in the 1930s, affecting nearly every town and converting thousands.)

> I have been preaching for 30 years and have not been worth my salt. I was so lazy, I could not walk a mile and half to tell people about Jesus. Since the revival I go to prayer meeting at 5:00 in the mornings, go home and eat breakfast, take a little bread for lunch and walk 25 miles witnessing in villages, then come home and go to prayer meeting at night. The next morning I'm ready to go again. Dozens of villages surround us, and we have witnessed in all of them.[7]

I also think of the Student Volunteer Movement as an example of spiritual longevity. From its founding in 1888 until 1928, it is estimated that 20,500 students went as long-term foreign missionaries. This was the greatest missions movement of history. But when these missionaries signed on, they really signed on, many staying on the field for twenty, thirty, forty, even fifty years. They remained committed for life. Such is the result of the Holy Spirit's long-term power.

### A Great Movement of Evangelism

Revival never comes without producing a sweeping movement of evangelism, as the immediate results of the 1970 Asbury Revival attest.

> They began to take the message of this revival over the country to Christian schools nationwide. Nearly 40 colleges were either directly or indirectly affected. While covering this unusual "religious" happening, even a major network cameraman was touched. Hearing the confessions and testimonies and seeing the newly-changed lives of students, he put down his camera, walked to the altar of the college chapel, knelt, and gave his life to Jesus Christ. If the secular and the Christian campuses of America were to be awakened today, surely hundreds of such conversions would occur.[8]

Consider the Welsh Revival of 1905. In the space of three months, a hundred thousand people were converted, and eighty thousand of these were still in churches five years later. Winning people to Christ became the activity of every revived church member, not just that of a select few.

Evangelism was the focus of revival in the 1800s as well. In 1854 W. S. Tyler of Amherst College made a survey of awakenings in eleven northeastern colleges. He found that 34 percent of the students on those campuses had become Christians and nearly half of those converted were studying to become ministers. He asked for prayer for more awakenings and pleaded, "Why, we ask again, should not every year witness a revival in colleges, and every class ... receive a fresh anointing from on high? ... Why should any individual leave unconverted?"[9]

Evangelism and revival scholar Robert Coleman adds "a willingness for service" as a prerequisite for revival, stating that "we cannot expect God to pour out His blessing unless we are willing to become involved in some kind of redemptive service."[10] For example, a seminal event in the Shantung Revival in China came when a minister, Chiang Ki Yao, confessed his lack of evangelism and pledged to make restitution for it.

> "I am a murderer," he said. "The bandits here cause the death of only a few people, but I am the cause of the spiritual death of many. Now I am going to visit all the places where I have been before, confess my shortcomings, and present the Gospel to those people. This is my first task. I am a debtor to them and I must pay the debt." And wherever he went, the power of God went before him, and many of his former friends came to know Christ as a result.[11]

As the hindrances to the Spirit's empowerment are removed, there is a fresh motivation and freedom to share the gospel. As Erwin Lutzer, chronicler of the Canadian Revival of the 1970s, observed:

> During the revival God was, to use Augustine's phrase, "cutting loose the cords of the tongue," and Christians who had vowed that they would never open their mouths either publicly

> or privately for Christ found that they were speaking freely ... believers witnessed to their neighbors for the first time. ... Many believers never knew what God could do through them when their lives were free from sin.[12]

I cannot emphasize enough the importance of revival being channeled into evangelism and missions (which is the shepherding responsibility of the leadership). According to Jesus, the disciples were filled with the Spirit in order that they might be witnesses. "You will receive power when the Holy Spirit comes on you; and you will be my witnesses in Jerusalem, and in all Judea and Samaria, and to the ends of the earth" (Acts 1:8). And sure enough, we read the following things that happened when the Spirit descended upon the newborn church:

> "We gave you strict orders not to teach in this name," [the high priest] said [to the apostles]. "Yet you have filled Jerusalem with your teaching and are determined to make us guilty of this man's blood." (Acts 5:28)

> Day after day, in the temple courts and from house to house, they [the apostles] never stopped teaching and proclaiming the good news that Jesus is the Christ. (Acts 5:42)

Without any significant deviation, we see this same biblical pattern throughout the revivals of the previous three centuries. The great revival and "Pentecost in Japan" in October of 1900 was immediately followed the *tikyo dendo* (aggressive evangelism) campaign of May–June 1901.[13]

Pandita Ramabai's praying bands in India became an army of evangelists in the wake of the Mukti Revival. And as the Second Great Awakening blew through the college campuses, it swept up some twenty thousand missionaries, scattering them to the four corners of the world.

The reason I stress this is that, as wonderful as the current escalation of prayer is around the world, it is often channeled toward spreading the experience, humanitarian projects, pilgrimage, personal healing, and spiritual gifts. These are all fine and good, but even a cursory reading of the Book of Acts is enough to show that the biblical impulse of revival is predominately evangelistic. Revival brings zeal, and that zeal must be prayerfully channeled through the leadership or it is squandered, not on bad things instead of good but on good things instead of great. For the hope and survival of any nation, people, or person is the gospel of Jesus Christ—proclamation of the gospel and good works must go hand in hand.

J. Sidlow Baxter, who pastored in Edinburgh during a time of great spiritual awakening, was once asked by a friend of mine what it was like when revival came to his church. He replied, "I can only say that anywhere and everywhere you went God was in the atmosphere. People talked of no one but God; people thought of no one but God. People went to work as usual, but God was the focus of all their attention."

## Next Steps

"God was in the atmosphere": a great picture of what it would be like if awakening came to our campuses. That expectation alone seems worthy of the vast amount of prayer, humbling, and confessing that must precede it. There is much more that could be said about the results of revival. Actually, God may surprise us all. He is the God of the unexpected and is "able to do immeasurably more than all we ask or imagine, according to his power that is at work within us" (Ephesians 3:20). But one thing we can know for sure: when it does come, no one will be able to miss it. God's movement is going to be powerful; it is going to be sweeping; and it is going to be significant for virtually every student, administrator, and faculty member on campus.

Make a list of what you and your friends believe God could do on your campus when revival comes. Include names and places as God brings them to mind. Your list might include things like the dean of students becoming a witnessing Christian, a particular dormitory having five hundred or more in Bible studies every week, a certain person stopping his drunkenness or immorality, and so on.

I'd encourage you to craft it into a visionary document, much like Peter Greig did for the 24/7 prayer movement (reprinted in the previous chapter). Let it be the compass to your revival prayers. Ask God to act upon the things on your list and to expand your vision to believe Him for even greater things. Expect your campus to explode in spiritual awakening during your time there, and pursue everything within your means to bring that about.

# CONCLUSIONS

*"It is my sincere prayer that the burden which God has given me for spiritual awakening in our day may be the heart-cry for revival."*
*– Stephen F. Olford*[1]

*I believe that revival on campus is* not only needed but essential. I also believe that it is coming. If it does not come, I see little hope that the darkness on the colleges and universities of the world will be lifted at any time in the foreseeable future. If there is no revival, many will still be won to Christ and many will be discipled, but I do not see any way that the current influence of unbelief, atheism, apathy, and agnosticism can be mitigated apart from a sweeping movement of the Spirit of God.

But, as I said, I believe revival is coming. I think there is a tidal wave of dissatisfaction growing among Christian students today concerning the spiritual apathy and lethargy on campus. In fact, I think they are disgusted by it. I also see a growing movement of prayer for revival as well as attempts to meet God's prerequisites for it. Examples from past and current events indicate that the Spirit of God is doing something highly significant, perhaps something that has not happened since the last global awakening of the early twentieth century.

The movement of God's people, creating the environment for revival, is swelling. Each of us needs to be a part of this movement and not miss out on what God is doing, for there is a danger that apathy, materialism, unbelief, sexual immorality, and other snares will immobilize us. But the time for business as usual is over; its results are unacceptable. It is now time for some new beginnings. And committed and obedient believers can be a part of what God is already bringing to pass.

In 1747 Jonathan Edwards wrote a small book on prayer with an insanely long name: *A Humble Attempt to Promote Explicit agreement and Visible Union of God's people in Extraordinary Prayer, for the Revival of Religion and the Advancement of Christ's Kingdom on Earth, Pursuant to scripture promises and Prophecies Concerning the Last Times.* Assuming people could even finish the title, it was Edward's hope that the book would spur people on to revival prayer, and in the book he calls believers to a seven-year experiment of concerted prayer. He concluded the book with this reflection on patiently waiting upon God's time for revival:

> Let it be considered, whether it will not be a poor business, if our faith and patience is so short-winded, that we cannot be willing to wait upon God ... in seeking a mercy so infinitely vast. For my part, I sincerely wish and hope, that there may not be an end of extraordinary united prayer, among God's people, for the effusions of the blessed Spirit, when the seven years are ended, but that it will be continued, either in this method, or some other, by a new agreement, that will be entered into with greater

> engagedness. But, at the same time, I hope God's people, who unite in this agreement, will see some tokens for good before these seven years are out, that shall give them to see, God has not said to the seed of Jacob, Seek ye me in vain; and shall serve greatly to animate and encourage them to go on in united prayers for the advancement of Christ's kingdom, with increasing fervency. But whatever our hopes may be in this respect, we must be content to be ignorant of the times and seasons, which the Father hath put in his power; and must be willing that God should answer prayer, and fulfill his own glorious promises, in his own time.[2]

Some persevered in their prayers, but for the most part his plea went unheeded and his book was all but ignored, until forty years later when it was republished in England (1789). At that time it was embraced by a passionate prayer movement that used it as a manifesto for the Second Great Awakening. The book accomplished the purpose for which it was written, though Edwards did not live to see it, nor did many of the generation that he had originally called to prayer.

In the last twenty-five years, since I wrote the first edition of this book, there have been fits—starts and pauses—of concerted revival prayer (amid moments of great victory and power, to be sure). But as prayer movements emerged, and revival was not forthcoming, they waned and attempts were often aborted. Students didn't persevere.

But today is a different day, which is why I have revised this book. In recent years there has been a deluge of prayer movements all over the world. I have never witnessed anything like it: students everywhere embracing anew the long-term necessity of prayer, confession, and calling others to do the same.

Students are grasping that we are in a battle for the minds and souls of men and women. The stakes are not simply temporal but eternal. The destiny of the world, not simply our own concerns and comforts, is involved. The greatest hope of our globe is revived university students who are still unfettered by mortgages, mediocrity, or man-made distractions—students who will relentlessly serve Christ. Imagine spiritually led movements everywhere, men and women on every campus demanding that the universities of the world allow Jesus Christ on campus and allow Him to be Lord of all.

This book's purpose is to challenge you, to awaken you from the status quo, and to recruit you to be an insurgent for spiritual awakening, one who will pray and believe God to do something extraordinary on your campus. If you do, I believe your life will be significant beyond anything you could have ever hoped for, in terms of its spiritual impact.

As we move toward the coming awakening, there is no middle ground. We will either be fireseeds or we will melt back into the sea of spiritual mediocrity, the tepid waters in which most college students find themselves.

Let me invite you to become one of those revolutionaries who are praying, working, and expecting the Lord to revive believers on campus and awaken unbelievers to the glory of His name.

During the massing of German forces on the coast of France for an invasion of Great Britain in World War II, Winston Churchill made a speech that called on his fellow Britons to stave off disaster. His call on a temporal level is the same call I would like to give you on a spiritual level. Try to hear in these words the voice of God speaking to you about your part in the revival to come.

> What General Weygand called the Battle of France is over. I expect that the Battle of Britain is about to begin. Upon this battle depends

> the survival of Christian civilization. Upon it depends our own British life and the long continuity of our institutions and our empire. The whole fury and might of the enemy must very soon be turned on us. Hitler knows that he will have to break us in this island or lose the war. If we can stand up to him, all Europe may be free and the life of the world may move forward into broad sunlit uplands. But if we fail, then the whole world, including the United States, including all that we have known and cared for, will sink into the abyss of a new dark age made more sinister, and perhaps more protracted, by the lights of perverted science. Let us therefore brace ourselves to our duties, and so bear ourselves that, if the British Empire and its Commonwealth last for a thousand years, men will still say, "This was their finest hour."[2]

May this be your finest hour!

# AFTERWORD: SATISFIED?

> *"Without the Spirit of God, we can do nothing. We are as ships without wind. We are useless."*
> *– Charles Spurgeon*

> *"I believe it is impossible for any Christian to be effective either in his life or in his service unless he is filled with the Holy Spirit who is God's only provision for power."*
> *– Henrietta C. Mears*

*Revivals and awakenings are times of great* outpouring of God's Spirit. By definition they are excessive. It is like Christmas. And while the idea is appealing, Christmas doesn't happen every day. In fact, life would be quite bizarre, excessive, and unbalanced if it did.

If we attempt to make the excessive nature of revivals normative, it can lead to an imbalance in our life, our walk with God, and particularly our understanding of the Holy Spirit's ministry in us. Historically, it has at times done all of these. So, to gain all of the spiritual blessings of praying for, anticipating, and experiencing revival, while eliminating the negative side-effects of extremism, we want to review what the Spirit-filled life is.

### Believers Are All Indwelt by the Spirit

When you became a Christian, Christ indwelled you through the person of the Holy Spirit. I know neither the how nor the where, but I do know that the Holy Spirit's indwelling presence carries with it the assurance of our salvation. "Having believed, you were marked in him with a seal, the promised Holy Spirit, who is a deposit guaranteeing our inheritance until the redemption of those who are God's possession" (Ephesians 1:13-14).

We are now God's possession, and the Holy Spirit is, in effect, the down payment on His purchased property—that would be you. Like the idea expressed through the marriage ceremony, receiving Christ is a one-time decision. We don't awake each morning to a fresh need to say, "I do"; once was enough. Having received Christ, we became children of God. "To all who received him, to those who believed in his name, he gave the right to become children of God" (John 1:12).

In theory I could tell my parents that I no longer wished to be in their family, but I can never change the reality that I am their son. It's an established fact on the basis of my birth. I can sever our fellowship but not our relationship. And as there was not one thing we did to earn our salvation, so there is nothing we can ever do to lose it—we are eternally Christ's. But the Holy Spirit is more than simply an assurance of our salvation. It is through the Spirit that God enables and empowers us to live the Christian life.

### The Spirit Comes to Glorify Christ

As we experience the blessings of the Spirit, we can lose sight of Jesus—and we never want to do that. We need to remember that the Spirit works in us to glorify Christ.

"When he, the Spirit of truth, comes, he will guide you into all truth. He will not speak on his own; he will speak only what he hears, and he will tell you what is yet to come. He will bring glory to me by taking from what is mine and making it known to you" (John 16:13-14).

The Spirit-filled life is the Christ-centered, Christ-directed, life.

**Walking with the Spirit**

Walking is a process and not an event.[1] This is how the event of revival can throw off our thinking concerning the Spirit-filled life. Clearly there are events, moments in time, when God empowers us in a special way; that's what revival is. But the normative Christian life is predominantly a process, a walk. And the Spirit's influence in our lives is typically not an overwhelming, overpowering presence but a more subtle influence. If we get an overpowering experience—Score! Icing on the cake! Christmas morning! It's an additive, but not essential, blessing.

The normative Christian life is not an overpowering event but is daily seeking to do those things that increase the Spirit's influence and decrease the hindrances to that influence. So how, exactly, does the Holy Spirit exert control and influence over our lives, and what is our role in the process? Perhaps the most helpful passage in Scripture for answering these questions is this one in Paul's letter to the Ephesians:

> Be very careful ... how you live—not as unwise but as wise, making the most of every opportunity, because the days are evil. Therefore do not be foolish, but understand what the Lord's will is. Do not get drunk on wine, which leads to debauchery. Instead, be filled with the Spirit. Speak to one another with psalms, hymns and spiritual songs. Sing and make music in

> your heart to the Lord, always giving thanks to God the Father for everything, in the name of our Lord Jesus Christ. (Ephesians 5:15-20)

One is compelled to ask, "What does getting drunk on wine have to do with being filled with the Spirit?" Well, obviously they are opposite alternatives, but they must share some base of similarity, or else why couple them together? The link between them, or the similarity they share, is in the idea of influence. They are both foreign entities that, when internalized, influence our behavior.

In fact, this is not the only time Scripture places them side by side. In the coming of the Holy Spirit, it was suspected that the Spirit-filled believers "had too much wine" (Acts 2:13), because of the similarity of influence.

Of course, there are many important differences between alcohol and the Holy Spirit. Alcohol's influence leads to greater enslavement, while the Spirit gives great freedom. Alcohol eclipses our personality, while the Spirit reanimates it. And Satan uses alcohol to control us as God controls us through the Spirit. Still, alcohol provides an example of a foreign influence (albeit a bad one) that can affect our will and behavior.

As demonstrated by alcohol, control is always a question of degrees. There are things we can do that hinder the Spirit's influence and things we can do to increase sensitivity to the Spirit's leading. This is at the heart of walking in step—or being filled—with the Spirit. (The word "filled" means filled like a sail, not filled like a cup. When we think about the sail metaphor, we rightly think about adjusting ourselves to catch the existing wind of the Spirit. When we think about filling a cup, we wrongly think about increasing the amount of the Spirit like pouring in more of a drink.)

So, what constitutes the Spirit-filled life? What leads to the Spirit having maximum influence over our lives? This is not comprehensive, but what follow are the primary vehicles affecting the Spirit's influence upon our thoughts, heart, will, and emotions.

### *Lordship*

How does one become more drunk? (Or should I say drunkerer?) One consumes more alcohol. In the case of the Holy Spirit, we have all of Him that we will ever have. So the major determinant of the Spirit's influence is how much of us we let Him consume, meaning how much of our lives we allow Him to control.

The question we must ask ourselves is this: Do we desire to live for Christ in every area of our life (dating, vocation, relationships, and so on)? We sometimes call this a "lordship" decision.

It is often when we relinquish these areas, like a drain coming unclogged, that we experience a special empowerment, or increased influence of the Lord. This frequently happens during revival. While the new degree of influence can create a powerful experience, equilibrium soon follows, and the Spirit's influence becomes normative as we continue to stay yielded to the Lord's direction. Again, following Paul's alcohol analogy, for a consistent drinker or smoker, alcohol and nicotine in the bloodstream at some point normalizes, sans elation.

Lordship is a declaration to follow Christ wherever He leads, to whatever end. This commitment, like any commitment, initiates an ongoing process. Over time we'll discover deeper roots of sin and uncover areas disconnected from His control. In submitting these areas to Christ, we continue in, and affirm, His lordship and our commitment to live under it.

### *Confession*

Throughout the day, week, and year there are times when we make choices to sin. Sin is seizure of control. We take control of the direction of our life and steer it toward our sinful wants and desires. Confession cleanses and removes the barrier of sin, and it places the control of our life back under the Spirit's subtle but determining influence.

*Reliance (Unceasing Prayer)*

Throughout each day we experience neediness, weakness, and lack in the form of anxiety, loneliness, insecurity, trials, unholy desires, negative feelings, and so on. All of us have a natural inclination to meet these needs through reliance on something. Watch cigarette smokers. Every time they sense a need in their life, they light up. If they feel lonely, they light up. If they feel scared or nervous, they light up. If they need confidence, they light up. And while we might not smoke, we can find ourselves doing the same thing with food, lust, shopping, music, coffee, or any number of other things.

Choosing throughout the day to turn to the Lord for wisdom, patience, empowerment, companionship, security, confidence, and every other need is called humble reliance. As the smoker is aided by nicotine's influence, so the believer can experience the Spirit's influence. Instead of turning to whatever it is we turn to, we connect with God: "Oh Lord, I'm nervous. Will You please strengthen me?" "Oh Lord, will You please give me wisdom?" All day long, like smoking a pack of cigarettes, we turn to the Lord. This is the idea of reliance and it is vital to experiencing the Spirit's influence.

(I apologize for all the drinking and smoking analogies, but the Scripture is the foundation for them, and they are helpful in understanding influence.)

*Renewing of Our Minds*

The Spirit's influence is always refreshed, directed, and supported by prayer and time in the Scriptures. Through both of these He leads and renews our thinking.

### *Praise and Thanksgiving*

If you've ever been to a college party or bar, you'll get this concept rather easily. It's the idea of atmosphere: the room is dark; the music is pulsing; clothes and conversation are sexually suggestive; and alcohol sands down inhibitions. An atmosphere has been created that's conducive to sin. Though no one forces you to drink, lust, or gossip, they don't have to. Just bask in the music and the glow of the lava lamp long enough, and you want to.

Going back to our Spirit-filled passage (Ephesians 5:19-20) again, notice what it says: "Speak to one another with psalms, hymns and spiritual songs. Sing and make music in your heart to the Lord, always giving thanks to God the Father for everything, in the name of our Lord Jesus Christ."

The description Paul gave is of an environment conducive to the empowering influence of the Holy Spirit. As we worship, give thanks, praise God, and sing, our hearts become like that party, only in a very good way. An environment is created where the Lord can freely reign, a channel for Him to affect our thoughts, actions, and emotions.

### *Community*

Last, it is in community with other Christians that we experience a dynamic of the Spirit-filled life that we can never experience alone, because we encounter the indwelling Spirit through the lives of others, and through them we are energized, empowered, and directed.

## In Summary

Participating in these activities daily constitutes walking in step with the Spirit, or walking in the Spirit. The degree to which we participate is the degree to which the Spirit has influence upon us. Whether the Spirit's influence is a slow IV drip or a flowing river depends on our participation in the spiritual life.

Revival, an excessive overpowering sense of the Spirit's presence, is not within our hands to control. We seek God in prayer to do such mighty works, especially for those who most desperately need it, such as nominal Christians and unbelievers. But whether we are empowered by the Spirit and renewed daily ... well, that *is* in our control.

We can forget these foundational truths about walking in the Spirit, and in some cases maybe we never learned them. What follows is called the Satisfied Prayer Experience, which provides a prayerful reflection and review of these ideas in the context of group prayer. There is an opportunity to confess barriers to the Spirit's control. And there are opportunities to praise, worship, and present all of ourselves to Christ's lordship, making sure that we are being maximally influenced and are under the Spirit's control. I strongly suggest that you go through it with the others you have called to join you in praying for revival and awakening.

### The Satisfied Prayer Experience

> NOTE: This prayer experience is intended to be adaptable to your prayer group.[2] It can be as short as forty minutes or as long as two hours, depending on how you use the optional sections. Don't feel constrained to follow this format. Adapt it to your group and environment. May God give you and your group a rich time of celebrating and experiencing the powerful presence of His Spirit!

*[Divide into groups of three or four. You don't want groups to be too large. You want everyone to actively participate and experience all God has for you during this time of prayer.]*

## The Promise of Satisfaction

*Satisfaction:* (n.) fulfillment of one's needs, longing, or desires

Begin by thinking back over the last thirty days. What three words would you use to describe your Christian life during the past month? Share these with one another, along with a brief explanation of why you chose those words.

Are you satisfied with your experience? Do you desire more? Usually answers will reflect a broad range from deeply dissatisfied, to somewhat dissatisfied, to feeling generally okay, to very satisfied. But I suspect that almost all of us would admit that we desire more in our relationship with God.

Jesus said, "If anyone is thirsty, let him come to me and drink. Whoever believes in me, as the Scripture has said, streams of living water will flow from within him." John goes on to tell us, "By this he meant the Spirit" (John 7:37-39). The Spirit is the source of the truly satisfying life, quenching our deepest thirsts and longings. It is the gift of the Spirit that will be the focus of our prayer together.

## The Divine Gift

*Divine:* (adj) given by God

God has given us His Spirit so that we can experience intimacy with Him and enjoy all He has for us. The Holy Spirit is the source of our deepest satisfaction.

> Optional. If time is short, skip to 1 Corinthians 2:12 below.
>
> Five times in the "Farewell Discourse" Jesus spoke of the gift of the Spirit. Work in groups of three or four, and use the promises of these verses as a basis of short conversational sentences of praise and worship. (It can be

helpful to have these passages projected on a screen or printed on a handout.)

I will ask the Father, and he will give you another Counselor to be with you forever—the Spirit of truth. The world cannot accept him, because it neither sees him nor knows him. But you know him, for he lives with you and will be in you. (John 14:16-17)

The Counselor, the Holy Spirit, whom the Father will send in my name, will teach you all things and will remind you of everything I have said to you. (John 14:26)

When the Counselor comes, whom I will send to you from the Father, the Spirit of truth who goes out from the Father, he will testify about me. And you also must testify, for you have been with me from the beginning. (John 15:26-27)

I tell you the truth: It is for your good that I am going away. Unless I go away, the Counselor will not come to you; but if I go, I will send him to you. When he comes, he will convict the world of guilt in regard to sin and righteousness and judgment: in regard to sin, because men do not believe in me; in regard to righteousness, because I am going to the Father, where you can see me no longer; and in regard to judgment, because the prince of this world now stands condemned. (John 16:7-11)

When he, the Spirit of truth, comes, he will guide you into all truth. He will not speak on his own; he will speak only what he hears, and he

> will tell you what is yet to come. He will bring glory to me by taking from what is mine and making it known to you. All that belongs to the Father is mine. That is why I said the Spirit will take from what is mine and make it known to you. (John 16:13-15)

Paul applied the Spirit's ministry of revealing truth and wisdom in his first letter to the Corinthian believers (1 Corinthians 2:9–3:4). He stated, "We have not received the spirit of the world but the Spirit who is from God, that we may understand what God has freely given us" (1 Corinthians 2:12).

*[In your groups of three or four, use short sentence prayers to thank God for many things that God has given us in Christ and that the Spirit has helped you understand and experience. Be specific. For example, "Thank You, Lord, for enabling me to know and experience Your love. I know and understand Your love through Your Spirit." Or "Thank You, Lord, that by Your Spirit I have come to know Your wisdom and knowledge."]*

**The Present Danger**

*Danger:* (n.) a thing that may cause injury, loss, or pain

We cannot experience intimacy with God and enjoy all He has for us if we fail to depend on His Spirit. Our failures are often rooted in one of two problems. The Christian life is like a road and we can slip into the ditch on either side.

In the one ditch we begin to trust our own efforts and strength to live the Christian life. This is, of course, a source of great frustration. "Are you so foolish? After beginning with the Spirit, are you now trying to attain your goal by human effort?" (Galatians 3:3).

When we discover the futility of that, we can cross over to the other ditch. We may give up and succumb to our own selfish desires, seeking to please ourselves rather than God. "The sinful nature desires what is contrary to the Spirit, and the Spirit what is contrary to the sinful nature. They are in conflict with each other, so that you do not do what you want" (Galatians 5:17). Then, as with the Corinthians, our lives begin to manifest symptoms of the flesh and worldliness. "Brothers, I could not address you as spiritual but as worldly—mere infants in Christ. I gave you milk, not solid food, for you were not yet ready for it. Indeed, you are still not ready. You are still worldly. For since there is jealousy and quarreling among you, are you not worldly? Are you not acting like mere men?" (1 Corinthians 3:1-3).

*[Spend the next segment of time in silent confession. Examine your life for symptoms of self-dependence or self-centered living. Confess them to God and claim His forgiveness according to 1 John 1:9.]*

**The Intimate Journey**

As we learn to walk in the Spirit, we increasingly experience intimacy with God and enjoy all He has for us. Walking in the Spirit is a moment-by-moment lifestyle, learning to depend upon the Holy Spirit for His abundant resources as a way of life. "Live by the Spirit, and you will not gratify the desires of the sinful nature. ... Since we live by the Spirit, let us keep in step with the Spirit" (Galatians 5:16, 25).

*[In your groups, share testimonies of how you first learned to walk in the Spirit.]*

As we walk in the Spirit, we experience intimacy with God and all He has for us. The fruit of the Spirit is one description of what we experience through the Spirit. "The fruit of the Spirit is love, joy, peace, patience, kindness, goodness, faithfulness, gentleness and self-control" (Galatians 5:22-23).

*[Think about the challenges you are currently facing. What do you need to experience most at this time? Remember, it is the role of the Spirit to produce it in your life. Pray in your groups, claiming the fruit you seek (such as love for specific relationships or joy for specific trials). As you become aware of more areas where your attitudes or responses have fallen short (Romans 3:23) and have been displeasing to God, breathe spiritually. That is, exhale by confessing your sins, thanking God for His forgiveness, and then inhale by expressing your dependence upon the Spirit.]*

**The Empowering Presence**

*Empower:* (v.) to give ability to

We are filled with the Spirit by faith, enabling us to experience intimacy with God and enjoy all He has for us. The essence of the Christian life is what God does in and through us, not what we do for God. Christ's life is reproduced in the believer by the power of the Holy Spirit. By faith we experience God's power through the Spirit.

Paul prayed that his beloved Ephesian believers would experience these realities. "I pray that out of his glorious riches he may strengthen you with power through his Spirit in your inner being, so that Christ may dwell in your hearts through faith" (Ephesians 3:16-17).

*[In your groups, pray Paul's request for yourself and each other. Pray that you would fully experience the Spirit's strengthening with power in your inner being, so that Christ would be living His life in and through you.]*

> Optional: In your groups, pray for others you care for or minister to by name. Pray that they would experience the empowering of the Spirit and know the love of God. "I pray that you, being rooted and established in love, may have

> power, together with all the saints, to grasp how wide and long and high and deep is the love of Christ, and to know this love that surpasses knowledge—that you may be filled to the measure of all the fullness of God" (Ephesians 3:17-19).

### The Turning Point

*Turning point:* time when a decisive change occurs

It is our desire that all of us would know with confidence that we are experiencing the fullness of the Spirit today and throughout the days ahead.

*[As we conclude this segment of prayer, examine your hearts one more time. Ask yourself these three questions.]*

◇ Am I genuinely surrendering control of my life to the Lord Jesus Christ (Romans 12:1-2)?

◇ Have I confessed my sins, according to 1 John 1:9, and genuinely turned from them and back to God?

◇ Am I sincerely desiring to be filled—that is, directed and empowered—by the Holy Spirit (John 7:37-39)?

If you confidently answer yes to each question, silently reaffirm your faith in the Spirit's filling in your life according to His command (Ephesians 5:18) and promise (1 John 5:14-15). Ask God to fill you with His Spirit, enabling you to understand and experience in greater ways your intimacy with Him and your enjoyment of all He has for you.

If, in the integrity of your heart, you are unable to answer yes to the above questions, let us encourage you to take some additional time alone to be honest with God about the issues that are blocking your experience of His love and provision. Then go to a trusted leader or friend and share with that person what you are struggling with, asking him or her to pray with you and for you.

We need each other! As the letter to the Hebrews says, "Encourage one another daily, as long as it is called Today, so that none of you may be hardened by sin's deceitfulness. We have come to share in Christ if we hold firmly till the end the confidence we had at first" (Hebrews 3:13-14).

NOTE: Provide each participant with a copy of the *Satisfied?* booklet. Encourage them to review it, to pray through it as you have today, and to share with others.

# NOTES

**Introduction**

1. Charles Malik, *The Two Tasks* (Westchester, IL: Cornerstone, 1980), p. 26.

**Chapter 1: Let's Turn the College Campus Right Side Up**

1. Quoted in David Bryant, *In the Gap* (Ventura, CA: Regal, 1984), p. 97.
2. Douglas A. Sweeney, *The American Evangelical Story* (Grand Rapids, MI: Baker, 2005), p. 27–48.
3. Found at joinus.campuscrusadeforchrist.com.
4. Quoted in John Telford, *The Life of John Wesley* (New York: Hunt & Eaton, n.d.), p. 117.
5. Wesley Duewel, *Revival Fire* (Grand Rapids, MI: Zondervan, 1995), p. 57.
6. Albert D. Belden, *George Whitefield—The Awakener* (London: Low, Marston, & Co., n.d.), p. 65.
7. Robert Coleman, *The Coming World Revival* (Wheaton, IL: Crossway, 1995), p. 25.
8. J. I. Packer, *A Quest for Godliness* (Wheaton, IL: Crossway, 1990), p. 36.

9. David Bryant, *The Hope at Hand* (Grand Rapids, MI: Baker, 1996), p. 74.
10. Quoted in *How to Make Your Mark* (San Bernardino, CA: Campus Crusade for Christ, 1983), p. 19.
11. Earle E. Cairns, *An Endless Line of Splendor* (Wheaton, IL: Tyndale, 1986), pp. 20–21.
12. Bill Bright, *The Coming Revival* (Orlando, FL: New Life), pp. 81–82.
13. Quoted in J. Edwin Orr, *Campus Aflame* (Chicago, IL: Moody Press, 1972), p.119.
14. Richard M. Riss, *20th Century Revival Movements* (Peabody, MA: Hendrickson, 1988), p. 125–30.
15. Charles Finney, *Revival Lectures* (Westwood, NJ: Revell, n.d.), p. 33.

**Chapter 2: Awakened at Sixteen; Awakener at Twenty-Six**

1. Ernest Baker, *The Revivals of the Bible* (Cape Town: T. Mashew Miller, 1986), p. 83.
2. Timothy C. Wallstrom, *The Creation of a Student Movement to Evangelize the World* (Pasadena, CA: William Carey International University Press, 1980), pp. 24–25.
3. J. Edwin Orr, *Campus Aflame* (Glendale, CA: Regal, 1972, p. 27.
4. Ibid., p. 54.
5. Quoted in Robert Coleman, *The Coming World Revival* (Wheaton, IL: Crossway, 1995), pp. 89–90.
6. Quoted in Richard M. Riss, *20th Century Revival Movements* (Peabody, MA: Hendrickson, 1988), p. 32.
7. Ibid.
8. Ibid., p. 35.
9. Ibid., p. 36.
10. Ibid., p. 40.
11. Ibid., p. 39.
12. Ibid., p. 46.
13. Peter Lundell and Elaine Pettit, *When God Bursts In*

(Kansas City, MO: Beacon Hill, 2005), pp. 39–40.
14. Quoted in Riss, pp. 31–32.

**Chapter 3: Five Prerequisites to Revival**

1. James Burns, *The Laws of Revival* (Grand Rapids, MI: Baker, 1960).
2. Quoted in Stephen F. Olford, *Lord, Open the Heavens* (Wheaton, IL: Harold Shaw, 1980), p. 92.
3. Quoted in Richard M. Riss, *20th Century Revival Movements* (Peabody, MA: Hendrickson 1988), p. 32.
4. Quoted in Dale Schalfer, *Revival 101* (Colorado Springs, CO: NavPress, 2003), pp. 13-14
5. Andrew Woolsey, *Channel of Revival* (Sandbach, Cheshire, UK: Faith Mission, 1982), p. 114.
6. Ibid., p. 120.
7. Kathie Walters, *Bright and Shining Revival* (Macon, GA: Good News Fellowship, 2000).

**Chapter 4: Humility and Its Role in Revival**

1. Jonathan Edwards, *The Works of Jonathan Edwards* (Carlisle, PA: Banner of Truth, 1979).
2. Philip E. Howard Jr., *The Life and Diary of David Brainerd* (Grand Rapids, MI: Baker, 1992).
3. Ibid.
4. Earle E. Cairns, *An Endless Line of Splendor* (Wheaton, IL: Tyndale, 1986), p. 166.
5. Wesley Duewel, *Revival Fire* (Grand Rapids, MI: Zondervan, 1995), p. 173.
6. J. Edwin Orr, *Evangelical Awakenings in Africa* (Minneapolis: Bethany, 1975), p. 58.
7. Richard M. Riss, *20th Century Revival Movements* (Peabody, MA: Hendrickson, 1988), p. 31–32.
8. Vinson Synan, *In the Later Days* (Fairfax, VA: Xulon Press), p. 58.
9. Bill Bright, *The Coming Revival* (Orlando, FL: New Life), p. 92.

10. J. Edwin Orr, *Campus Aflame* (Glendale, CA: Regal, 1971), p. 105.
11. John Pollack, *Billy Graham: The Authorized Biography* (Grand Rapids, MI: Zondervan, 1966), p. 52.
12. "The Church Search," *Time*, April 5, 1993, p. 49.

**Chapter 5: Confession and Repentance**

1. Charles Finney, *Revival Lectures* (Westwood, NJ: Fleming H. Revell, n.d.).
2. IVCF archives, June 1995, www.wheaton.edu.
3. J. Edwin Orr, *The Role of Prayer in Spiritual Awakening* (video), Campus Crusade for Christ;
4. J. Oswald Sanders, *Prayer Power Unlimited* (Chicago: Moody Press, 1977), pp. 147–8.
5. "Eight Days That Shook Asbury," *Worldwide Challenge*, March 1983, p. 19.
6. J. Edwin Orr, *Campus Aflame* (Glendale, CA: Regal, 1971), p. 231.
7. Wesley Duewel, *Revival Fire* (Grand Rapids, MI: Zondervan, 1995), p. 152.
8. Ibid., pp. 152–3.
9. Ibid., p. 154.
10. Orr, *Campus Aflame*, p. 114.
11. Stephen F. Olford, *Lord, Open the Heavens* (Wheaton, IL: Harold Shaw, 1980), p. 86.

**Chapter 6: The Supreme Example of Prayer**

1. S. D. Gordon, *Quiet Talks on Prayer* (Westwood, NJ: Revell, 1967), p. 11.
2. J. Edwin Orr, *Campus Aflame* (Chicago, IL: Moody Press, 1972).
3. Quoted in Stephen F. Olford, *Lord, Open the Heavens* (Wheaton, IL: Harold Shaw, 1980), pp. 62–63.
4. Arthur Wallis, *Revival: The Rain from Heaven* (Tappan, NJ: Revell, 1979), p. 51.
5. Wesley Duewel, *Revival Fire* (Grand Rapids, MI:

Zondervan, 1995), p. 134.
6. Quoted in Douglas A. Sweeney, *The American Evangelical Story* (Grand Rapids, MI: Baker, 2005), p. 43.
7. Quoted in J. Oswald Sanders, *Prayer Power Unlimited* (Chicago: Moody Press, 1977), p. 33.

**Chapter 7: The Power of Fervent Prayer**

1. Bill Bright, "The Great Adventure," *Worldwide Challenge*, May–June 1994, p. 45.
2. J. Edwin Orr, quoted from lectures given at Fuller Theological Seminary.
3. Charles Finney, *Revival Lectures* (Westwood, NJ: Revell, n.d.), pp. 72–73.
4. *America's Great Revivals* (Minneapolis: Bethany, 2004), pp. 52–58.
5. Jonathan Edwards, *A Call to United Extraordinary Prayer...* (Fearn, UK: Christian Focus, 2004).
6. Finney, p. 137.
7. Quoted by Manny Hooper, *Worldwide Awakening and Revivals, 1700 Onwards* (Pasadena, CA: Research Center for Revival and Missions, 1989), pp. 6–7.
8. David Bryant, *The Hope at Hand* (Grand Rapids, MI: Baker, 1996), p. 116.
9. J. Oswald Sanders, *Prayer Power Unlimited* (Chicago: Moody Press, 1977), p. 154.
10. Ibid.
11. Joon Gon Kim, "It Only Takes a Fireseed," U.S. campus ministry director's letter, Campus Crusade for Christ, April 27, 1982.
12. Bill Bright, "The Holy Spirit and Revival," letter to Campus Crusade for Christ headquarters staff, spring 1993.
13. Peter Gregg and Dave Roberts, *Red Moon Rising* (Orlando, FL: Relevant, 2005), pp. 119–22.
14. Quoted in Wesley Duewel, *Revival Fire* (Grand Rapids, MI: Zondervan, 1995), p. 217.
15. Ibid., p. 217.

16. Ibid., pp. 216–52.
17. Leonard Ravenhill, "No Wonder God Wonders," Great Commission Prayer League.

**Chapter 8: Results of Spiritual Awakening on Campus**

1. Quoted in J. Edwin Orr, *Campus Aflame* (Glendale, CA: Regal, 1971), p. 226.
2. Ibid., p. 77.
3. Robert Coleman, *One Divine Moment* (Tappan, NJ: Revell, 1970), pp. 27–43.
4. "Interview with James Montgomery Boice," *Discipleship Journal*, Issue 11, 1982, p. 43.
5. Quoted in Timothy C. Wallstrom, *The Creation of a Student Movement to Evangelize the World* (Pasadena, CA: William Carey International University Press, 1980), p. 35.
6. Joseph Tson, Revival Forum, www.sermonindex.net.
7. Quoted in C. L. Culpepper, *The Shantung Revival* (Atlanta: Crescendo, 1971), p. 30.
8. Coleman, *One Divine Moment*.
9. W. S. Tyler, *Prayer for Colleges* (New York: M. W. Dodd, 1855), pp. 142–3.
10. Robert Coleman, *The Coming World Revival* (Wheaton, IL: Crossway, 1995), p. 48.
11. Quoted in Culpepper, p. 63.
12. Erwin Lutzer, *Flames of Freedom* (Chicago, IL: Moody, 1976), p. 68.
13. Wesley Duewel, *Revival Fire* (Grand Rapids, MI: Zondervan, 1995), p. 134.

**Chapter 9: Conclusions**

1. Stephen F. Olford, *Lord, Open the Heavens* (Wheaton, IL: Harold Shaw, 1980), p. 11.
2. Jonathan Edwards, *A Call to United Extraordinary Prayer...* (Fearn, UK: Christian Focus, 2004), pp. 22–23.
3. Winston Churchill, *Churchill, The Life Triumphant* (New York: American Heritage, 1965), p. 91.

**Afterword: Satisfied?**

1. Rick James, *InTransition* (Orlando, FL: Cru Press, 2007), pp. 95–96.
2. Keith Davy, "Satisfied Prayer Experience" (Campus Crusade for Christ, 2005), found at www.godsquad.com

In memory of Innes Lloyd
1925–1991

# Contents

The **Complete** Talking Heads

Also by Alan Bennett

**FICTION**

*The Clothes They Stood Up In*

*The Laying On of Hands*

**PLAYS**

*Plays One* (Forty Years On, Getting On, Habeas Corpus, Enjoy)

*Plays Two* (Kafka's Dick, The Insurance Man, The Old Country, An Englishman Abroad, A Question of Attribution)

*Office Suite*

*The Wind in the Willows*

*The Madness of George III*

*The Lady in the Van*

**TELEVISION PLAYS**

*The Writer in Dialogue*

*Objects of Affection* (BBC)

**SCREENPLAYS**

*A Private Function*

*Prick Up Your Ears*

*The Madness of King George*

**AUTOBIOGRAPHIES**

*The Lady in the Van*

*Writing Home*

# The **Complete** *Talking* Heads

**Alan Bennett**

**PICADOR**
**NEW YORK**

For information, address Picador, 175 Fifth Avenue, New York, N.Y. 10010.

www.picadorusa.com

Picador® is a U.S. registered trademark and is used by St. Martin's Press under license from Pan Books Limited.

For information on Picador Reading Group Guides, as well as ordering, please contact the Trade Marketing department at St. Martin's Press.
Phone: 1-800-221-7945 extension 763
Fax: 212-677-7456
E-mail: trademarketing@stmartins.com

*A Woman of No Importance* was first published by BBC Books in *Objects of Affection* in 1982. © Forelake Ltd 1982
*A Chip in the Sugar, Bed Among the Lentils, A Lady of Letters, Her Big Chance, Soldiering On,* and *A Cream Cracker Under the Settee* were first published by BBC Books in *Talking Heads* in 1988. Forelake Ltd 1988
*The Hand of God, Miss Fozzard Finds Her Feet, Playing Sandwiches, The Outside Dog, Nights in the Gardens of Spain,* and *Waiting for the Telegram* were first published by BBC Worldwide in *Talking Heads 2* in 1998. © Forelake 1998

Photographs: pp. 38, 57, 63, 104 Jeremy Grayson; pp. 153, 156, 163, 166, 175, 178, 187, 192 Simon Mein © Slow Motion; all other photos © BBC Worldwide 1998



ISBN 0-312-42308-X

First published in Great Britain by BBC Worldwide Ltd.

10 9 8 7 6

# Introduction

This collection includes the first and second series of *Talking Heads*, twelve monologues in all, together with the introductions I wrote for each series. However, it seems appropriate to include with them an earlier monologue, *A Woman of No Importance*, which was first televised in 1982 and for which I did this introduction.

I wrote *A Woman of No Importance* thinking I might direct it myself. I have never directed either for the stage or television and the possibility of having to do so accounts for the simplicity (not to say crudity) of the form: the piece is for one actress, who speaks directly to camera.

Thinking I would be able to manage at the most two cameras, I planned the play as a series of midshots with the camera tracking in very slowly to a close-up, holding the close-up for a while then, just as slowly, coming out again. I didn't figure on there being any cuts within scenes, though this would place a heavy burden on the performer, some sections being pretty lengthy: the first speech, for instance lasts twelve minutes. To shoot in such a way makes cutting virtually impossible: one fluff, and it's back to the top of the scene again. Autocue is one answer, but Patricia Routledge, for whom the piece was written, was anxious to avoid this, and quite rightly. Even when a performer is in full command of the text, the sight of it slowly reeling down over the camera lens exercises an hypnotic effect, and an element of the rabbit fascinated by the snake enters in. I therefore planned on using a second camera, shooting Miss Schofield in profile. This would provide a shot to which one could cut if it proved necessary to do so.

In the event, because I was working on one of the other plays, I didn't direct the piece, which was done by Giles Foster. He adhered faithfully to the form I'd given the play, though to begin with finding the restrictions it imposed irksome and unnerving. He began by moving the play around, with Miss Schofield traversing the studio to match the movements described in the text. Rehearsal was a process of simplification whereby these movements were taken back inside the character, who ended up static in front of the camera as I had originally imagined. There are in fact some cuts within sections, when a gesture or slight turn of the head make it possible to switch to a slightly different shot without being false to the fairly relentless nature of the piece. Of course such directness and simplicity may not be thought to work. 'Talking heads' is a synonym in television for boredom, and here is just one head, not two. And Miss Schofield is a bore. But to have her in full close-up, retailing in unremitting detail how she borrowed the salt in the canteen takes one, I hope, beyond tedium.

The first few lines of the play are poached. In the Festival of Britain, which I visited as a boy, there was a pavilion (I suspect I might be irritated by it now) called The Lion and the Unicorn, devoted to Englishness. It included a console where, by pressing a button, one heard snatches of typical English conversation. These had been written by (I think) Stephen Potter and were performed by Joyce Grenfell. One in particular concerned a disaster that befell a middle-class lady, and began: 'I was perfectly all right on the Monday. I was perfectly all right on the Tuesday. I was perfectly all right on the Wednesday. I was perfectly all right on the Thursday until lunchtime, when I just ate a little poached salmon: five minutes later I was *rolling about the floor*.'



With the experience accumulated from the later monologues there are other observations I can add about the technique appropriate for their presentation. The more still (and even static) the speaker is the better the monologue works. However much the text might seem to demand it too much movement dissipates interest and raises awkward questions, chief among them, 'Whom does this person think they're talking to?' Whereas if the speaker is relatively still and the camera has them in a medium to close shot such questions do not arise. I don't know why this should be but it is so.



There are also certain patterns in the form which, to begin with, I was unaware of but which I now see are essential to the action – and for all that there is just one person talking there is quite a bit of action. A section will often end with a seemingly throwaway remark that carries the plot forward: Violet's remarks about Francis at the end of several of the sections of *Waiting for the Telegram* chart his separate decline; in *The Outside Dog* Marjory's, 'He seems to have lost another anorak, this one fur-lined,' strikes the first note of unease about her murderous husband; and in *Playing Sandwiches* Wilfred's 'On my way home I called in at the sweet shop,' alerts the audience to the fact that something dreadful is about to happen. And, of course, by the beginning of the next section it has happened as the action of these stories generally takes place in the intervals between sections, what has happened recalled by the speaker rather than narrated as it occurs.

It would be quite possible to tell these stories in a different (and a more conventional) way, a question that will be found in the introduction to the first *Talking Heads* series.

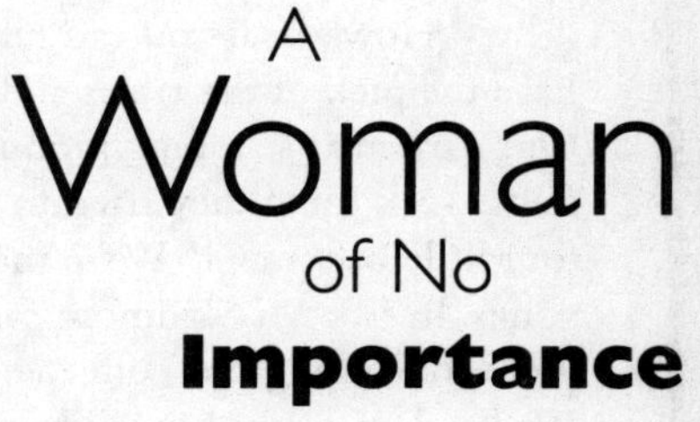


**Peggy:** Patricia Routledge

PRODUCED BY **INNES LLOYD** DIRECTED BY **GILES FOSTER**
DESIGNED BY **VIC MEREDITH** MUSIC BY **GEORGE FENTON**

PEGGY IS A MIDDLE-AGED WOMAN. SHE TALKS DIRECTLY TO CAMERA AGAINST A NEUTRAL BACKGROUND.

I was all right on the Monday. I was all right on the Tuesday. And I was all right on the Wednesday until lunchtime, at which point all my nice little routine went out of the window.

Normally, i.e. provided Miss Hayman isn't paying us one of her state visits, come half past twelve and I'm ready to down tools and call it a morning. I put on a lick of paint, slip over and spend a penny in Costing...I should technically use the one in Records but I've told them, that lavatory seat is a death trap. And I'm not ringing up again. 'Try a bit of sellotape.' What are they paid for? I'll then rout out Miss Brunskill from 402 and we'll meander gently over for our midday meal. But you just have to hit it right because, give it another five minutes, and believe me that canteen is dog eat dog.





However if you can manage to nip in before the avalanche you have the pick of the tables and there's still some semblance of hygiene. Our particular stamping ground is just the other side of the bamboo framework thing they tried to grow ivy up. It's what Miss Brunskill calls 'our little backwater'. We're more or less fixtures there and have been for yonks. In fact Mr Skidmore came by with his tray last week just as we were concluding our coffee and he said, 'Well, girls. Fancy seeing you!' We laughed. Girls! Mr Skidmore generally gravitates to the table in the far corner under that silly productivity thermometer-type thing. 'Export or Die'. It's actually broken – stuck anyway – but it's where management tend to foregather since we've had this absurd 'All Barriers Down' policy. Once upon a time management had tables roped off. That's gone, only they still congregate there. 'Huddling together for warmth,' Mr Rudyard calls it. I said to Mr Cresswell, 'You can tell who's an activist.' We laughed, because anybody more conformist than Mr Rudyard you couldn't want, and he has beautiful fingernails. Of course once the management started frequenting that particular table sure enough Miss Hayman and the Personnel brigade pitch camp next door. And she'll turn around and chat to Mr Skidmore over the back of her chair. She never used to have all that hair.

Our table though we're very much the happy family. There's me, Miss Brunskill, Mr Cresswell and Mr Rudyard, Pauline Lucas, who's ex-Projects...to tell the truth she's still Projects, only she's in Presentation wearing her Projects hat. Then there's Trish Trotter (when she's not in one of her 'bit of cheese and an apple' phases); Joy Pedley pays us the occasional visit, but by and large that's the hard core. Trish Trotter is the only one with a right weight problem but we're all salad fanatics and keep one another in line. I have to watch my stomach anyway and salad suits Miss Brunskill because she's a big Christian Scientist. But to add that bit of excitement I bring along some of my home-made French dressing. Mr Cresswell keeps pestering me to give Mr Rudyard what he calls 'the secret formula'. He's a keen cook, Mr Rudyard. Little moustache, back like a ramrod, you'd never guess it. I pretend there's a mystery ingredient and won't let on. We laugh.

People are a bit envious of us, I know. I ran into Mr McCorquodale the other day when we were both queueing in (guess!) Accounts and he said, 'You do seem to have a good time at your table, Peggy. What do you talk about?' And I didn't know. I mean, what do we talk about? Pauline's mother keeps getting a nasty rash that affects her elbows. We'd been discussing that. Mr Cresswell and Mr Rudyard were going in for some new curtains for their lounge and were debating about whether to have Thames Green. And I was saying if Thames Green was the green I thought it was I liked it in a front door but wasn't keen on it in curtains. So that made for some quite lively discussion. And Trish Trotter had got hold of some new gen on runner beans as part of a calorie-controlled diet, and we kicked that around for a bit. But honestly, that was all it was. I don't know what we do talk about half the time! My secret is, I don't talk about myself. When Joy Pedley went to Thirsk on a 'Know Your Client' course that was apparently the whole gist of it: concentrate on the other person. I said, 'Well, I've no need to go to Thirsk to learn that. It's something I've been born with.' We laughed.

Once we've lined up our eats and got the table organised Miss B. gets her nose into her crossword while I scan the horizon for the rest of the gang. I have to be on my toes because there's always some bright spark wanting to commandeer them and drag them off elsewhere. I don't think people like to see other people enjoying themselves, basically. Take Pauline Lucas. The other day, she came in with young Stuart Selby. He's ginger, and when Mr Oyston went up into Accounts and Mrs Ramaroop moved to Keighley, Stuart did a bit of a dog's hind leg and got into Costing. Him and Pauline were making a bee-line for the window, which is in the Smoking area. Now Pauline doesn't smoke, in fact rather the reverse. So I sang out, 'You're not deserting us, are you Pauline? Fetch Stuart over here. See how the other half lives!' So she did. Only halfway he ran into Wendy Walsh and it ended up just being me and Pauline. I said to her, 'That was a narrow escape.' She said, 'Yes.' We laughed. Her acne's heaps better.

And then look at Mr Cresswell and Mr Rudyard. It's the biggest wonder last week they didn't get sat with the truck drivers. They were dawdling past with their trays and there was room but luckily I just happened to be going by en route for some coffee and saw which way the wind was blowing and rescued them in the nick of time. They were so grateful. I said 'You two! You don't know you're born!' They laughed.

However, as I say, on this particular Wednesday I'm in the office, it's half past twelve and I'm just thinking, 'Time you were getting your skates on, Peggy,' when suddenly the door opens and nobody comes in. I didn't even look up. I just said, 'Yes, Mr Slattery?' He was on his hands and knees with a pro forma in his mouth. Anybody else would have got up. Not him. He crawls up to me, pretending to be a dog and starts begging, this bit of paper in his mouth! I thought, 'You're a grown man. You've got a son at catering college; your wife's in and out of mental hospital and you're begging like a dog.' I enjoy a joke, but I didn't laugh.





Surprise, surprise he's after a favour. The bit of paper is the Squash Ladder. Would I run him off two dozen copies? I said, 'Yes. By all means. At two o'clock.' He said, 'No. Now.' Wants to put them round in the lunch hour. I said, 'Sorry. No can do.' I haven't forgotten the works outing. Running round with that thing on his head. He was like a crazed animal. I said, 'Anybody with an atom of consideration would have come down earlier. Squash Ladder! It's half past twelve.' He said, 'It's not for me.' I said 'Who's it for?' He said, 'Mr Skidmore.'

*Pause.*

Well, as luck would have it I hadn't actually switched the machine off. And, knowing Trevor Slattery, Mr Skidmore had probably asked him to do it first thing and he'd only just got round to it. I know Mr Skidmore: courtesy is his middle name. But it did mean I didn't get out of the office until twenty to, by which time of course there's no Miss Brunskill. Any delay and La Brunskill's off like a shot from a gun, plastic hip or no plastic hip.

By this time of course the canteen is chock-a-block. I was five minutes just getting inside the door, and if I'd waited for a please or thank you I'd be stood there yet. They looked to be about to introduce martial law round the salad bowl so I thought, 'Little adventure, I'll opt for the hot dish of the day, steak bits or chicken pieces.' I knew the woman doling it out because she gets on the 56. She's black but I take people as they come, and seeing it was me she scrapes me up the last of the steak bits. I topped it off with some mushrooms, and trust me if I didn't get the last of the yogurts as well. I heard somebody behind me say 'Damn'. I laughed.

I beetled over to our table but no Pauline, no Mr Cresswell and no Mr Rudyard. It's a cast of unknowns and only Miss Brunskill that I recognise. I said, 'Didn't you save me a place?' She said, 'I thought you'd been and gone.' Been and gone? How could I have been and gone, she knows I'm meticulous. But I just said, 'Oh' rather pointedly, and started touring round.

Eventually I pinpoint Pauline sat with little Stuart Selby, only there's no room there either. 'Scattered to the four winds today, Pauline,' I said. 'Yes,' she said, and he laughed. I see she's starting another spot.

I trek over to the far side and blow me if Mr Cresswell and Mr Rudyard aren't sat with all the maintenance men, some of them still in their overalls. Mr Cresswell is smoking between courses, something he never does with us, a treacle sponge just stuck there, waiting. Mr Rudyard is having a salad and I wave my jar of French dressing in case he wants some but he doesn't see me because for some reason he's not wearing his glasses.





Just then I spot somebody vacating a place up at the top end. I say, 'Room for a little one?' only nobody takes on. They're young, mostly from Design, moustaches and those little T-shirty things, having some silly conversation about a topless Tandoori restaurant. I start on my steak bits, only to find that what she's given me is mainly gristle. I don't suppose they distinguish in Jamaica. I thought, 'Well, I'll have a little salt, perk it up a bit,' but as luck would have it there's none on the table, so I get up again and go in quest of some. The first salt I spot is on the table opposite, which happens to be the table patronised by the management; and who should be sat there but Mr Skidmore. So I asked him if I could borrow their salt. 'Excuse me, Mr Skidmore,' was what I said, 'but could I relieve you temporarily of your salt?' I saw Miss Hayman's head come round. She'd naturally think I was crawling. I wasn't. I just wanted some salt. Anyway, Mr Skidmore was very obliging. 'By all means,' he said. 'Would you like the pepper too?' I said, 'That's most civil of you, but I'm not a big pepper fan.' So I just took the salt, put a bit on the side of my plate and took it back. 'Much obliged,' I said. 'Don't mention it,' Mr Skidmore said. 'Any time.' He has impeccable manners, they have a big detached house at Alwoodley, his wife has had a nervous breakdown, wears one of those sheepskin coats.

I suddenly bethought me of the Squash Ladder, so just after I'd replaced the salt I said, 'Oh, by the way, I ran you off those copies of the Squash Ladder,' not in a loud voice, just person to person. He said, 'What?'

I said, 'I ran you off those copies of the Squash Ladder.' He said, 'Squash Ladder?' I said, 'Yes.' He said, 'Not my pigeon.' I said, 'Why?' He said, 'Didn't you know? There's been a flare-up with my hernia.' Well I didn't know. I can't see how I would be expected to know. Somebody laughed. I said, 'Oh, I am sorry.' He said, 'I'm not. Blessing in disguise. Squash is Slattery's pigeon now.'

I went back to my table and sat down. I felt really sickened. He'd done it on me had Mr Slattery.

After a bit Trish Trotter rolls up and parks herself next to me. She says, 'Are you not eating your steak bits?' I said, 'No.' She said, 'Don't mind if I do,' and helps herself. She shouldn't wear trousers.

Anyway it was that afternoon that I first began to feel really off it. I went home at half past four.



FADE QUICKLY TO BLACK. *Still shot of her desk: very neat. A single flower in a glass. Typewriter with its cover on.*

*I want the tableaux between scenes to look like still life paintings.*

*Peggy is now sat against another neutral background, wallpaper possibly – something to indicate she is at home.*



I don't run to the doctor every five minutes. On the last occasion Dr Copeland sat me down and said, 'Miss Schofield. If I saw my other patients as seldom as I see you I should be out of business.' We laughed.

He's always pleased to see me: gets up when I come into the room, sits me down, then we converse about general topics for a minute or two before getting down to the nub of the matter. He has a picture of his children on the desk, taken years ago because the son's gone to Canada now and his daughter's an expert in man-made fibres. He never mentions his wife, I think she left him, he has a sensitive face. Cactuses seem to be his sideline. There's always one on his desk and he has a Cactus Calendar hung up. This month's was somewhere in Arizona, huge, a man stood beside it, tiny. I looked at it while he was diddling his hands after the previous patient.

There was a young man in the room and Dr Copeland introduced me. He said, 'This is Miss…' (he was looking at my notes) 'Miss Schofield. Mr Metcalf is a medical student; he's mistaken enough to want to become a doctor.' We laughed, but the boy kept a straight face. He had on one of those zip-up cardigans I think are a bit common so that didn't inspire confidence. Dr Copeland said would I object to Mr Metcalf conducting the examination provided he was standing by to see I came to no actual physical harm? We both laughed but Mr Metcalf was scratching a mark he'd found on the knee of his trousers.

Dr Copeland put him in the picture about me first: 'Miss Schofield has been coming to me over a period of twelve years. Her health is generally good, wouldn't you say, Miss Schofield?' – and he was going on, but I interjected. I said, 'Well, it is good,' I said, 'but it's quite likely to seem better than it is because I don't come running down to the surgery with every slightest thing.' 'Yes,' he said. 'If I saw my other patients as seldom as I see Miss Schofield I should be out of business.' He laughed. The student then asked me what the trouble was and I went through the saga of the steak bits and my subsequent tummy upset.

He said, 'Is there anything else beside that?' I said, 'No.' He said, 'Any problems at work?' I said, 'No.' He said, 'Any problems at home?' I said, 'No.' He said, 'You're single.' I said, 'Yes.' He said, 'Where are your parents?' I said, 'Mother's in her grave and father is in a Sunshine Home at Moortown.' He said, 'Do you feel bad about that?' (He didn't look more than seventeen.) I said, 'No. Not after the life he's lived.'

I saw him look at Dr Copeland, only he was toying with the calendar, sneaking a look at what next month's cactus was going to be. So this youth said, 'What life did he lead?' I said, 'A life that involved spending every other weekend at Carnforth with a blondified piece from the cosmetics counter at Timothy Whites and Taylors.' He said, 'Is that a shoe shop?' I said, 'You're thinking of Freeman, Hardy and Willis. It's a chemist. Or was. It's been taken over by Boots. And anyway she now has a little gown shop at Bispham. His previous was a Meltonian shoe cream demonstrator at Manfields, and what has this to do with my stomach?'

Dr Copeland said, 'Quite. I think it's about time you took an actual look at the patient, Metcalf.' So the young man examined me, the way they do pressing his hands into me and whatnot, and then calls over Dr Copeland to have a look. 'That's right,' I said. 'Make way for the expert.' Only neither of them laughed.

Dr Copeland kneaded me about a bit, but more professionally and while he was washing his hands he said, 'Miss Schofield. I'm not in the least bit worried by your stomach. But, you being you, it wants looking at. There aren't many of us left!' We laughed. 'So just to be on the safe side I want to make an appointment for you to see a specialist, Mr Penry-Jones.' I said, 'Isn't his wife to do with the Music Festival?' He said, 'I don't know, is she?' I said, 'She is. I've seen a picture of her talking to Lord Harewood.' He took me to the door of the consulting room, which he doesn't do with everybody, and he took my hand (and I'm not a private patient). 'Thank you,' he said. 'Thank you for being a guinea pig.' We laughed. Only it's funny, just as I was coming out I saw the student's face and he was looking really pleased with himself.

*She very slightly presses her hand into her stomach.*

FADE TO BLACK AND UP AGAIN *to still shot of bedside table. Clock. Bedside lamp. A bottle of white medicine.*

FADE TO BLACK AND UP AGAIN: *Peggy is in a hospital bed.*



I've just had a shampoo and set. She's not done it too badly, bearing in mind she doesn't know my hair. Lois, her name is. She has a little salon. You go past Gyney, and it's smack opposite Maternity. It's a bit rudimentary, they just have it to perk up the morale of the pregnant mums basically, but, as Lois says, it's an open door policy just so long as you can find your way because this place is a rabbit warren. Lois said my hair was among the best she'd come across. It's the sort Italians make into wigs apparently, they have people scouring Europe for hair of this type. I should have had a perm last Tuesday only when Mr Penry-Jones whipped me in here it just went by the board.

Caused chaos at work. Miss Brunskill said after I'd rung up Mr McCorquodale and Mr Skidmore went into a huddle for fully half an hour and at the end of it they still couldn't figure out a way to work round me. In the finish Miss Hayman had to come down from the fifth floor – though not wearing her Personnel hat, thank God – and Pauline did her usual sideways jump from Records, but it's all a bit pass the parcel. Miss Brunskill says everybody is on their knees praying I come back soon.

I'd actually been feeling a lot better when I went along to see Mr Penry-Jones. He's got one of those big double-fronted houses in Park Square: vast rooms, wicked to heat. There was just one other woman in the waiting room, smartish, looked to have arthritis. I said, 'I wouldn't like this electricity bill,' but she just smiled. Then the housekeeper came and conducted me upstairs. I made some remark about it being spring but she didn't comment, a lot of them are Spanish these days. Mr Penry-Jones though was a very courtly oldish man, blue pin-striped suit, spotted bow-tie. I said, 'What a lovely fireplace.' He said, 'Yes. These are old houses.'

I said, 'Georgian, I imagine.' 'Oh,' he said. 'I can see I'm in the presence of a connoisseur.' We laughed.

He examined me and I went through the story again, though I didn't actually mention the steak bits, and it was a beautiful carpet. Then he looked out of the window and asked me one or two questions about my bowels. I said, 'I believe your wife has a lot to do with the Music Festival.' He said, 'Yes.' I said, 'That must be very satisfying.' He says, 'Yes. It is. Last week she shook hands with the Queen.' I said, 'Well that's funny, because I stood as near to her as I am to you, at York in 1956. What an immaculate complexion!'

When I'd got dressed he said, 'Miss Schofield, you are a puzzle. I'm very intrigued.' I said, 'Oh?' He said, 'Have you got anything special on in the next couple of weeks?' he said. 'Because ideally what I would like to do is take you in, run a few tests and then go on from there. I'm absolutely certain there's nothing to get worked up about but we ought to have a little look. Is that all right?' I said, 'You're the doctor.' We laughed.



He made a point of coming downstairs with me. It was just as some other doctor was helping the better-class-looking woman with arthritis into a car – it looked to be chauffeur driven. I went and sat on a seat in the square for a bit before I got the bus. The trees did look nice.



GO TO BLACK AND UP AGAIN. *Miss Schofield is now sat by her hospital bed in a candlewick dressing gown.*

I've appointed myself newspaper lady. I go round first thing taking the orders for the papers, then I nip down and intercept the trolley on its way over. I said to Sister Tudor, 'Well, with a candlewick dressing gown I might as well.' Most of the others have these silly shorty things. Mine's more of a housecoat. The shade was called Careless Pink, only that's fifteen years ago. It's mostly the *Sun* or the *Mirror*, there's only two of us get the *Mail* and she's another Miss. I could tell straight away she was a bit more refined. Hysterectomy.

Of course I shan't be able to do the papers tomorrow because of my op.

When Princess Alexandra came round, this was the bed she stopped at, apparently.

I get on like a house on fire with the nurses. We do laugh. Nurse Trickett says I'm their star patient. She's little and a bit funny-looking but so goodhearted. 'How's our star patient?' she says. 'I hope you've been behaving yourself.' We laugh. She hasn't got a boy friend. I've promised to teach her shorthand typing. Her mother has gallstones, apparently. Nurse Gillis is the pretty one. I think she's just marking time till she finds the right man. And then there's Nurse Conkie, always smiling. I said to her, 'You're always smiling, you're a lesson to any shop steward, you.' She laughed and laughed the way they do when they're black.

Sister came in while she was laughing and said wasn't it time Mrs Boothman was turned over. She's all right is Sister, but she's like me: she has a lot on her plate. I said to her, 'I'm a professional woman myself.' She smiled.

*Pause. Miss Schofield turns the name tag she has on her wrist.*

Name on my wrist now: 'Schofield, Margaret, Miss.'



*Pause.*



Mr Penry-Jones comes round on a morning, and he fetches his students and they have to guess what's wrong. I said to Miss Brunskill, 'It's a bit of a game. If he doesn't know what the matter is, they won't.' He said, 'Gentlemen, a big question mark hangs over Miss Schofield's stomach.' They all laughed.

So tomorrow's the big day. He was telling the students what he's going to do. 'I'm just going to go in,' he said, 'and have a look round. We're not going to do anything, just a tour of inspection.' I chipped in, 'More of a guided tour, if all these are there.' They did laugh. Not Sister though. She can't afford to, I suppose. He's like a God to them, Mr Penry-Jones.

I do my bit here in different ways. I'm always going round the beds, having a word, particularly when someone isn't mobile. I run them little errands and tell the nurse if there's anything anybody's wanting. Mrs Maudsley opposite's on a drip and she was going on about getting her toenails cut, they catch on the sheet. I located Nurse Gillis and told her, only it must have slipped her mind because when I went across later on Mrs Maudsley was still on about it. I mentioned it again to Nurse Gillis just in case she'd forgotten and she said, 'I don't know how we managed before you came, Miss Schofield, I honestly don't.' Actually I found out later her toenails had been cut. Apparently Nurse Conkie must have cut them the same day as she cut mine, the day before yesterday, only Mrs Maudsley wouldn't know because she's no feeling in her feet.

Mrs Boothman's another of my regulars. Can't move. Can't speak. Doesn't bother me. I sit and chat away to her as if it was the most normal thing in the world. She'll sometimes manage a little movement of her hand, but the look in her eyes is enough.

Miss Brunskill's been down to see me. Nobody else much. Plenty of cards. I've got more cards than anybody else on this side.

*She reads them.*

'Feel kinda sick without you. Trish.' Trish Trotter. Picture of an elephant. 'Wishing you a speedy recovery. All in 406.' 'It's not the same without you. You're missed more than words can tell. So I'm sending this card to say, Please hurry and get well.' It says 'from all on the fifth floor' but I bet it's Mr Skidmore, it's such a classy card. A thatched cottage. I should imagine it can be damp, though, thatch. Silly one from Mr Cresswell and Mr Rudyard. 'Sorry you're sick. Hope you'll soon be back to normal. Whatever that is!'

I thought they might have been popping down, but Mr Cresswell hates hospitals, apparently, and they're going in for a new dog. A Dandy Dinmont. They think it'll be company for Tina, their Jack Russell. Well, they're out all day.

*Pause.*

Miss Brunskill's knitting me a bedjacket. I said, 'You'll have to be sharp, I shall be home next week.'

*Pause.*

I've got one nice neighbour, one not so nice. She's been quite ill. Just lies on her side all day. Karen, her name is. I offered her one of my women's books but she just closed her eyes. She's young. But however poorly I was I think I'd still try to be pleasant. The woman this side is as different again. Very outgoing. Talks the whole time. She's in with her chest. She's a lifelong smoker, so I don't wonder. Her daughter's marrying a computer programmer whose father was a prisoner of the Japanese, and she's inundated with visitors. She's a big TV fan so she's often down the other end. I reckon to be asleep sometimes when she's going on. You can't always be on your toes.

*Pause.*

Could just drink a cup of tea. Can't when you're having an op. They get you up at six, apparently. Give you a jab. Nurse Trickett says I won't even know I've gone and I'll be back up here by twelve. I've warned sister I shan't be able to get the papers, she thinks they'll manage.

*Pause.*

Solve the mystery anyway.

GO TO BLACK.

*Still of the bedhead. Bed empty, as if she has gone for her operation.*



GO TO BLACK AND UP AGAIN.

*Miss Schofield is sitting by a radiator near a window in her dressing gown.*



Hair in my dinner again today. Second time this week. Someone must be moulting. I mentioned it to Sister and she said she'd take it up with the kitchen staff and get back to me. She hasn't though. It isn't that she's nasty. Just crisp. I don't complain. Nurse Gillis can be sharp as well, but I try and meet her halfway. I said, 'Don't apologise. I deal with people myself. They don't realise, do they?'

*Pause.*

I'd such a shock yesterday. Nurse Conkie and Nurse Trickett had just given me my bath, and the little trainee nurse with the bonny face and cold hands was combing my hair, when I bethought me of the bedjacket Miss Brunskill had knitted me. I'd put it away in my locker because she'd made it too tight round the sleeves, but I tried it on again and it was just right. She says she hates knitting. I'm the only person she'll knit for, apparently. Of course, I paid for the wool. She's never ailed a thing, Miss Brunskill. Still, I hadn't until this do. Anyway I'd just got the bedjacket on and she'd fetched Nurse Conkie to see how nice I looked and they got me out my lipstick and I put a bit of that on. I was just sitting there and Nurse Conkie said, 'All dressed up and nowhere to go,' and a voice said, 'Hello. Long time no see!' And it's Mr Skidmore!

And I said it, loud, like that 'Mr Skidmore!' I said to him, I said, 'Five minutes earlier and you'd have seen me being bathed.' He said 'That's the story of my life.' We laughed.

He chatted about work. Said they were still only limping along. Said my job is open whenever I feel up to it and what's more it'll stay that way. They've got a special dispensation from Mr Strudwick. He says it's open-ended. They've never done that before. When Wendy Walsh had her infected sinus they ended up giving her a deadline. Still she wasn't the lynch-pin I am.

He did say there were other factors quite unconnected pushing them towards some degree of revamping. 'But,' he said, and patted my hand, 'in that event we shall find you a niche.' I said, 'Well I'm honoured. Fancy making a special journey for me.' Only it transpires that Mrs Skidmore's mother is in the psychiatric wing with another of her depression do's, and he'd left Mrs Skidmore sitting with her while he popped along to see me. 'Killing two birds with one stone,' he said. Then realised. 'I didn't mean that,' he said. 'Don't be silly,' I said. We laughed. He does look young when he laughs.

He'd just gone when Nurse Conkie came down to turn Mrs Boothman over. Great big smile. 'Who was your gentleman friend?' she said. She's got a nice sense of humour. I said 'That was my boss. He says they can't wait till I'm back.' 'I'm not sure we can spare you,' she said. We laughed.

I've been here the longest now, apart from Mrs Boothman and she's been resuscitated once. I potter around doing this and that.

Mr Penry-Jones is very proud of my scar. He fetches his students round to see it nearly every week. He says he's never seen a scar heal as quickly as mine. It's to do with the right mental attitude apparently. They stop longer at my bed than with anybody. What he does is take the students a bit away, talks to them quietly, then they come up, one by one and ask me questions. I whisper to them 'He doesn't know what it is, so don't worry if you don't.' Mrs Durrant on this side, she won't have them. She goes on about 'patients' rights'. She's a schoolteacher, though you'd never guess it to look at her. Long hair, masses of it. And I've heard her swear when they've given her a jab.

*Pause.*

I have a laugh with the porters that take me down for treatment. There's one in particular, Gerald. He's always pleased when it turns out to be me. 'My sweetheart,' he calls me. 'It's my sweetheart.' He's black too. I get on with everybody.

*Pause.*

I've started coming and looking out of this window. I just find it's far enough. There's naught much to see. There's the place where they put the bins out and a cook comes out now and again and has a smoke. And there's just the corner of the nurses' annexe. A young lad comes there with a nurse. He kisses her then goes away. Always the same lad. Nice. Though I don't like a lot of kissing, generally.



*Pause.*



I keep wondering about my Dad.

GO TO BLACK.

*Up on a jug and tumbler on the bedside table.*

BLACK.

*Up again on Miss Schofield in bed. Her hair should be straight, as if it has been washed but not set. The speeches are more disjointed, and feebler.*

I'm lucky. I'm standard size. I've got stuff off the peg and people have thought I'd had it run up specially. I've got a little fawn coat hanging up at home that I got fifteen years ago at Richard Shops. I ring the changes with scarves and gloves and whatnot, but it's been a grand little coat.

*Pause.*

I fetched up ever such a lot of phlegm this morning. Nurse Gillis was on. She was pleased. She said I'd fetched up more phlegm than anyone else on the ward. I said 'Was there a prize?' She laughed. I've never had that trouble before, but that's the bugbear when you're lying in bed, congestion.

*Pause.*

She said it's a good job all the patients aren't as little trouble as me or else half the nurses would be out of work. Funny, I didn't use to like her, but she's got a lot nicer lately. Her boy friend's a trainee something-or-other. I forget what. She did tell me. They're planning on moving to Australia.



*Pause.*

I've never been to Australia. She said if I wanted I could come out and visit them. I said, 'Yes.' Only I couldn't go. I couldn't be doing with all that sun.



*Pause.*

When Princess Alexandra came round this was the bed she stopped at, apparently.

*Pause.*

Sister's been better lately, too. The one I can't stand is Nurse Conkie. Never stops smiling. Great big smile. When they took old Mrs Boothman away just the same. Great big smile.

*Pause.*

Vicar round today. Think it was today. Beard. Sports jacket. Student, I thought, at first.

*Pause.*

Chatted. Bit before he got round to God. Says God singles you out for suffering. If you suffer shows you're somebody special in the eyes of God. He said he knew this from personal experience. His wife suffers from migraine.

*Pause.*

Do without being somebody special, this lot.

*Pause.*

There's a vicar goes round at Farnley, where my Dad is. Sits.

*Pause.*

Miss Brunskill came. Revolution at work. 406 and 405 knocked into one. Do your own photocopying now. Do it yourself, cut out the middleman. I said, 'Where did I fit in?' and she was telling me, only I must have dropped off and when I woke up she'd gone. Niche somewhere.

*Pause.*

I've been lucky with buses when I think back. I don't know what it is but just as I get to the bus stop up comes the bus. It must be a knack. I don't think I've ever had to wait more than two minutes for a bus, even when it's been a really spasmodic service.

*Pause.*

I wish they wouldn't laugh.

*Pause.*

There shouldn't be laughing.

*Pause.*

If they just left me alone I should be all right. 'Schofield, Margaret, Miss.' I've got a fly: keeps coming down. Must like me. There's a woman comes over and talks to me sometimes. Telling some tale. I close my eyes.

*Pause.*

Somebody was telling me about Rhyl. Still very select, apparently. No crowds.

*Pause.*

Here's my friend. This fly.



*She smiles.*

I said to Nurse Gillis, 'It's singled me out.' She laughed.



GO TO BLACK THEN UP. *The final shot is of an empty bed with the mattress folded back. The light is hard and white.*

FADE OUT.

# Introduction to *Talking Heads*

These six monologues were written and recorded for BBC television in 1987. Forms, one is often led to think, dictate themselves, the material demanding to be written in a particular way and no other. I would be happy to think this were so with these pieces but I'm not sure it's true. *A Chip in the Sugar*, for instance, or *Bed Among the Lentils* could both have been written as plays proper. It would be fun to see Mr Turnbull, Mrs Whittaker's fancy man, in the flesh (and his three-quarter-length windcheater), or Mrs Shrubsole doing her ruthless flower arranging – see them for ourselves, that is, rather than through the eyes of Graham and Susan who narrate those respective stories. But then they would be different stories, more objective, rounded and altogether fairer to the people the narrator is talking about. None of these narrators after all is telling the whole story. Geoffrey, Susan's husband, may be a nicer, more forbearing man than her account of him might lead us to suppose; and Mr Turnbull may not be quite the common fellow ('could have been a bookie') the jealous Graham is so ready to disparage. And were these monologues plays there would be room for qualification and extenuation, allowances could be made, redemptions hinted at, a different point of view. Instead there is a single point of view, that of the speaker alone with the camera, and with the rest of the story pictured and peopled by the viewer more effort is demanded of the imagination. In this sense to watch a monologue on the screen is closer to reading a short story than watching a play.





Admittedly it is a stripped-down version of a short story, the style of its telling necessarily austere. 'Said' or 'says' is generally all that is required to introduce reported speech, because whereas the novelist or short story writer has a battery of expressions to choose from ('exclaimed', 'retorted', 'groaned', 'lisped'), in live narration such terms seem literary and self-conscious. Adverbs too ('she remarked, tersely') seem to over-egg the pudding or else acquire undue weight in the mouth of a supposedly artless narrator. And these narrators are artless. They don't quite know what they are saying and are telling a story to the meaning of which they are not entirely privy. In *A Chip in the Sugar* Graham would not accept that he is married to his mother, or Miss Ruddock in *A Lady of Letters* that she is not a public-spirited guardian of morals. In *Soldiering On* Muriel ends up knowing her husband ruined her daughter but is no closer to realising that she had a hand in it too. Lesley in *Her Big Chance* thinks she has a great deal to offer both as an actress and a person, and Susan, the vicar's wife in *Bed Among the Lentils*, doesn't realise it's not just the woman in the off-licence but the whole parish that knows she's on the drink. Only Doris, the old lady who has fallen and broken her hip in *A Cream Cracker Under the Settee*, knows the score and that she is done for, but though she can see it's her determination to dust that's brought about her downfall, what she doesn't see is that it's the same obsession that tidied her husband into the grave.

I am disturbed as I was with a previous collection of television plays to note so many repetitions and recurrences. There are droves of voluntary workers, umpteen officials from the social services, and should there be a knock on the door it's most likely to be a bearded vicar. Even Emily Brontë turns up twice. If I'm guilty of repeating myself, on another count I plead innocence. The suspicion of child abuse in *A Lady of Letters* and the hint of it in *Soldiering On* might suggest I am straining after topicality. My instinct is generally to take flight in the opposite direction and in fact both these pieces were written and recorded before the subject began regularly to hit the headlines, which it may well have ceased to do by the time the programmes are transmitted. Since several of the characters fare badly at the hands of social and community workers I might seem to be taking a currently fashionable line here also. In the popular press nowadays social workers are generally (and easily) abused. I have little experience of them and to seem to line up with the *Sun* or the *Daily Express* would dismay me. My quarrel with social work is not with its praiseworthy practicalities but with the jargon in which it's sometimes conducted. Graham's 'I am not being defensive about sexual intercourse; she is my mother' is a protest about language.

Some of the events in these stories stem from actual occurrences in my life, though they are often joined to it by a very narrow isthmus. The funeral with which *Soldiering On* begins (though none of the characters in it) was suggested by the funeral of the composer George Fenton's father, who had been in Colditz and like Ralph had touched life at many points. Though much of the church stuff in *Bed Among the Lentils* (including Mr Medlicott the verger) comes from my childhood, the disaffection of Susan, the vicar's wife, I can trace to opening a hymn book in the chapel of Giggleswick School and finding in tiny, timid letters on the fly leaf, 'Get lost, Jesus'. Of these six characters only Lesley, the small-part actress, is wholly modern (while being quite old-fashioned). She and dozens like her have auditioned for films and plays I've done in the last twenty years. One of the first Lesley-like characters was a boy who came up for a part in *Forty Years On*. The director asked him what he had done:

'I was in George Bernard Shaw.'

'What did you play?'

'The drums.'

Perky, undefeated, their hopes of stardom long since gone, these actors retail the films and plays one might have glimpsed them in, playing waiters or barmen or, like Lesley, travelling on the back of a farm cart next to the star, wearing a shawl, the shawl 'original nineteenth-century embroidery, all hand done'. I saw an actor for a part not long ago who had been in a few episodes of *Emmerdale Farm*. 'I played the postman,' he said, 'only I haven't done any since. They don't seem to be getting much mail.'

Another obsession goes back to childhood. The dog dirt outside Buckingham Palace that spoils Miss Ruddock's Awayday and the 'little hairs all up and down' that rule out a dog for Doris betray a prejudice inherited from my father, who was a butcher in Leeds. He was plagued by dogs: 'Get out, you nasty lamppost-smelling little article,' he shouted once as he raced some unfortunate mongrel from the shop, and now thirty years later Doris has the line. It was my father too who had a craze for fretwork, but whereas for Doris's husband Wilfred fretwork is just one of his dreams ('toys and forts and whatnot, no end of money he was going to make'), with Dad it was no dream. Sitting at his little treadle saw with plans from *Hobbies Magazine* beside him he made forts and farms for my brother and me, a toy butcher's shop once and wonderfully elaborate constructions of ramps and trapdoors into which we shot marbles. This was at the start of the Second War when toys were scarce, and for a few years he was able to make a little money selling some of his stuff to a toyshop down County Arcade off Briggate. It wasn't much though. 'You want to ask a bit more,' my mam used to say. 'They take advantage of you. That's your trouble, Walt, you won't push yourself.' Which sounds like Doris again. Toy penguins were Dad's speciality, made out of three-ply and set on a sturdy green four-wheeled cart. Did we ever come across a child pulling one of these creations it was a big event and we would trail behind, scanning the face of its small owner for any evidence of pleasure in this (to me very dull) toy, Dad presumably experiencing some of the same pleasure a writer gets when he catches someone reading his book.

It's with mixed feelings that I see tattoos are (twice) sniffed at, along with red paint, yellow gloves and two-tone cardigans. These disparagements too date back to home and childhood, where they were items in a catalogue of disapproval that ranged through (fake) leopardskin coats, dyed (blonde) hair to slacks, cocktail cabinets and statuettes of ladies with alsatian dogs on leash. In our house and in my mother's idiosyncratic scheme of things they were all common. Common is not an easy term to define without seeming to brand the user as snobbish or socially pretentious, which my mother wasn't. But it was always her distinction:

I never remember my father making it, and both in its use and application common tended to be a woman's term. 'She's a common woman' one heard more often (was more common) than 'He's a common feller', perhaps because in those days women had more time and inclination to make such distinctions. A common woman was likely to swear or drink (or drink 'shorts'), to get all dolled up and go out leaving the house upside down and make no bones about having affairs. Enjoy herself, possibly, and that was the trouble; a common woman sidestepped her share of the proper suffering of her sex. What was also being criticised was an element of pretension and display (the dyed blonde hair, the too-tight slip-over, the face plastered with make-up). Elsie Tanner was a common woman, as with her curlers and too ready opinions is Hilda Ogden. And so, I thought as a child, was Mary Magdalene.

Sudden money augmented the risk and pools winners would find it hard to avoid the epithet. Hence the unfortunate tale of Vivien Nicholson, the Yorkshire pools winner and heroine of Jack Rosenthal's *Spend, Spend, Spend*. Her persistent car crashes and the dramas and notorieties of her personal life were never out of the *Evening Post*. 'Well,' my mother used to say, as Mrs N wrote off yet another of her cars and her lovers in some frightful motorway pile-up, 'she's a common woman.' No other explanation was necessary.

Places could be common too, particularly at the seaside. Blackpool was common (people enjoying themselves), Morecambe less so (not enjoying themselves as much), and Grange or Lytham not common at all (enjoyment not really on the agenda). If we ever did get to Blackpool we stayed at Cleveleys or Bispham, the refined end. To my brother and me (and I suspect to the local estate agents) refined just meant furthest away from the funfair. Not that where we stayed made much difference to the type of boarding house or the mixed bag we found there. To some extent my mother's nice distinctions were subjective and self-fulfilling: we met a better class of person where we stayed because we kept out of the way of the rest, Palm Court rather than bathing beauties, not the knobbly knees contest but a Wallace Arnold to Windermere. Package holidays came too late for my parents but had they ever ventured abroad they would have taken their attitudes with them. My mam would soon have located the Bispham end of Benidorm, a select part to Sitges. 'Well, we don't like it all hectic, do we, Dad?'

Common persists. It's not a distinction I'd want to be detected making but to myself I make it still. There are some lace (or more likely nylon) curtains popular nowadays that are gathered up for some reason in the middle. They look to me like a woman who's been to the lav and got her underskirt caught up behind her. They're absurd but that's not my real objection. They're common. The mock Georgian doorways that disfigure otherwise decent houses, the so-called Kentucky fried Georgian, offend me because they're cheap, inappropriate, ill-proportioned...and common.

Finally vicars who, Anglican though not always specified as such, turn up in all but one of these pieces, earnest, visitant and resolutely contemporary. Several are bearded, one is in trainers and most are in mufti. I have no particular wish to lock the clergy out of the wardrobe or ban them the boutique, but along with postmen and porters I wish they had not abandoned black. Just as postmen nowadays look like members of the Rumanian airforce so cassocks come in beige and even lilac, and if a parson submits to the indignity of a dog collar the chances are it has gone slimline, peeping coyly above a modish number in some fetching pastel shade. Nuns too have lost their old billowing, wimpled innocence and now look like prison wardresses on the loose. Even hearses have gone grey, black altogether too uncompromising a colour, life something to be shaded out of when, after much suffering tastefully borne, we blend nicely into the grave.





The clergy not wanting to look the part has something to do with the dismantling of the Book of Common Prayer. Anxious not to sound like parsons they can hardly be blamed for not wanting to look like them either. The 'underneath this cassock I am but a man like any other' act that Geoff does in *Bed Among the Lentils* must be a familiar routine at many a church door. And it's not of course new. Priests have always hankered after the world, or at any rate the worldly, and consorting as He did with publicans and sinners it was Jesus who started the rot. Or so Susan would say.

I don't know why it should be only Catholics who are thought never to escape their religious upbringing; I have never managed to outgrow mine. When I was sixteen and not long confirmed I was devoutly religious, a regular communicant who knew the service off by heart. It might be thought this would rejoice a vicar's heart and maybe it did, but actually I think the parish clergy found my fervour faintly embarrassing. A fervent Anglican is a bit of a contradiction in terms anyway, but I was conscious that my constant presence at the Eucharist, often midweek as well as Sundays, was thought to be rather unhealthy. As the celebrant sallied forth from the vestry on a cold winter's morning and found me sitting or (like Miss Frobisher, never one to let an opportunity slip) getting in a spot of silent prayer, he must have felt like a doctor opening the surgery door and discovering the sole occupant of the waiting room some tiresome hypochondriac (I was that too actually). Shy, bespectacled and innocent of the world I knew I was a disappointment to the clergy. What they wanted were brands to pluck from the burning and that was not me by a long chalk; I'd never even been near the fire.

Those early morning services with just a handful of regulars in the side chapel, the others generally maiden ladies who had cycled there on tall bicycles through the autumn mists, were to me the stuff of religion, the real taste of God. But though I did not admit it myself I knew that what the clergy preferred were occasions like Christmas Eve when the church was packed to the doors, the side aisles full, people even standing at the back like they did in those days at the cinema. For many in the congregation this was their one visit to church in the year. Plumping to my knees with split-second timing I would scornfully note how few of these festive communicants knew the service. Most of them didn't even kneel but sat, head in hand as if they were on the lavatory, this their one spiritual evacuation of the year.





Fastidious worshipper that I was, when I got to the altar rail I was even more choosy. Christmas and Easter, those joyous festivals of the Christian year, figured in my calendar as fearful health hazards and a true test of faith. At the sparsely attended eucharists that were the norm the rest of the year one could bank on finding oneself at the communion rail alongside a person of proven piety and blameless life. As my turn came for the chalice I would think of the TB or the cancer I might catch but come the Watch Night services at Christmas and Easter these ailments were forgotten. Then it was VD that was the bugbear. With the church chock-a-block with publicans and sinners one never knew who was going to be one's drinking companion. It was all my mother's fault. She had brought us up never to share a lemonade bottle with other boys, and wiping it with your hand, she said, was no protection, so I knew the dainty dab with the napkin the priest gave the chalice made no difference at all. There was God of course, in whose omnipotence I was supposed to believe: He might run to some mystical antisepsis. But then He might not. That I should catch syphilis from the chalice might be all part of His plan. The other place I was frightened of contracting it was the seat of a public lavatory, and that the rim of the toilet should be thus linked with the rim of the chalice was also part of the wonderful mystery of God. It was on such questions of hygiene rather than any of theology that my faith cut its teeth. I see myself walking back from the altar and plunging to my knees, then at the first opportunity surreptitiously spitting into my handkerchief.

But I knew that if God had marked me down for VD and a test of faith no amount of spitting was going to help. It was all chickenfeed to the Ancient of Days.

Switching on the Test Match at Headingley by mistake nowadays, I see the scene of these early spiritual struggles. 'Why, Headingley!' I might say, parodying Larkin, 'I was re-born here.' The camera pans along the Cardigan Road boundary and there above the trees is the spire of St Michael's, designed by J.L. Pearson who built Truro Cathedral, St Michael's with St Bartholomew's at Armley, the best of the nineteenth-century churches in Leeds, and in those days I knew them all. Around the time I was spitting into my handkerchief David Storey, the novelist and playwright, was playing rugby for Wakefield and so was often on the Headingley ground. For him too St Michael's was a symbol of hope. Cold, wet and frightened in the middle of a game he would look longingly at the spire and tell himself that within the hour he would be stood opposite the church waiting for a tram; the match would be over and he would be going home. That is by the way, but then so is much of this reminiscence, my childhood itself fairly by the way, or so it seemed at the time. Brought up in the provinces in the forties and fifties one learned early the valuable lesson that life is generally something that happens elsewhere.

# A **Chip** in the Sugar

**Graham:** Alan Bennett

PRODUCED BY **INNES LLOYD** DIRECTED BY **STUART BURGE**
DESIGNED BY **TONY BURROUGH** MUSIC BY **GEORGE FENTON**

GRAHAM IS A MILD MIDDLE-AGED MAN. THE PLAY IS SET IN HIS BEDROOM, A SMALL ROOM WITH ONE WINDOW AND ONE DOOR.
IT IS FURNISHED WITH A SINGLE BED, A WARDROBE, TWO CHAIRS AND NOTHING MUCH ELSE.

I'd just taken her tea up this morning when she said, 'Graham, I think the world of you.' I said, 'I think the world of you.' And she said, 'That's all right then.' I said, 'What's brought this on?' She said, 'Nothing. This tea looks strong, pull the curtains.' Of course I knew what had brought it on. She said, 'I wouldn't like you to think you're not Number One.' So I said, 'Well, you're Number One with me too. Give me your teeth. I'll swill them.'

What it was we'd had a spot of excitement yesterday: we ran into a bit of Mother's past. I said to her, 'I didn't know you had a past. I thought I was your past.' She said, 'You?' I said, 'Well, we go back a long way. How does he fit in vis-à-vis Dad?' She laughed. 'Oh, he was pre-Dad.' I said, 'Pre-Dad? I'm surprised you remember him, you don't remember to switch your blanket off.' She said, 'That's different. His name's Turnbull.' I said, 'I know. He said.'

I'd parked her by the war memorial on her usual seat while I went and got some reading matter. Then I waited while she went and spent a penny in the disabled toilet. She's not actually disabled, her memory's bad, but she says she prefers their toilets because you get more elbow room. She always takes for ever, diddling her hands and whatnot, and when she eventually comes back it turns out she's been chatting to the attendant. I said, 'What about?' She said, 'Hanging. She was in favour of stiffer penalties for minor offences and I thought, "Well, we know better, our Graham and me." I wish you'd been there, love; you could have given her the statistics, where are we going for our tea?'

The thing about Mam is that though she's never had a proper education, she's picked up enough from me to be able to hold her own in discussions about up-to-the-minute issues like the environment and the colour problem, and for a woman of her age and background she has a very liberal slant. She'll look at my *Guardian* and she actually thinks for herself. Doctor Chaudhury said to me, 'Full marks, Graham. The best way to avoid a broken hip is to have a flexible mind. Keep up the good work.'

They go mad round the war memorial so when we cross over I'll generally slip my arm through hers until we're safely across, only once we're on the pavement she'll postpone letting it go, because once upon a time we got stopped by one of these questionnaire women who reckons to take us for husband and wife. I mean, Mam's got white hair. She was doing this dodge and I said, 'Mam, let go of my arm.' I didn't really wrench it, only next thing I knew she's flat on the pavement. I said, 'Oh my God, Mother.'

People gather round and I pick up her bag, and she sits up and says, 'I've laddered both my stockings.' I said, 'Never mind your stockings, what about your pelvis?' She says, 'It's these bifocals. They tell you not to look down. I was avoiding some sick.' Somebody says, 'That's a familiar voice,' and there's a little fellow bending over her, green trilby hat, shorty raincoat. 'Hello,' he says, 'remember me?'

Well, she doesn't remember people, I know for a fact because she swore me down she'd never met Joy Buckle, who teaches Flowers in Felt and Fabric at my day centre. I said, 'You have met Joy, you knitted her a tea cosy.' That's all she can knit, tea cosies. And bed socks. Both outmoded articles. I said to her, 'Branch out. If you can knit tea cosies you can knit skiing hats.' She says, 'Well, I will.' Only I have to stand over her or else she'll still leave a hole for the spout. 'Anyway,' I said, 'you do remember Joy because you said she had some shocking eyebrows.' She said, 'I hope you didn't tell her that.' I said, 'Of course I didn't.' She said, 'Well, I don't remember.' And that's the way she is, she doesn't remember and here's this little fellow saying, 'Do you remember me?' So I said, 'No she won't. Come on, Mother. Let's get you up.' Only she says, 'Remember you? Of course. It's Frank Turnbull. It must be fifty years.' He said, 'Fifty-two. Filey. 1934.' She said, 'Sea-Crest.' He said, 'No sand in the bedrooms.' And they both cracked out laughing.

Meanwhile she's still stuck on the cold pavement. I said, 'Come along, Mother. We don't want piles.' Only he butts in again. He says, 'With respect, it's advisable not to move a person until it's been ascertained no bones are broken. I was in the St John's Ambulance Brigade.' 'Yes,' said Mother, 'and who did you learn your bandaging on?' And they both burst out laughing again. He had on these bright yellow gloves, could have been a bookie.

Eventually, I get my arms round her waist and hoist her up, only his lordship's no help as he claims to have a bad back. When I've finally got her restored to the perpendicular she introduces him. 'This is Frank Turnbull, a friend of mine from the old days.' What old days? First time I knew there were any old days. Turns out he's a gents' outfitter, semi-retired, shop in Bradford and some sort of outlet in Morecambe. I thought, 'Well, that accounts for the yellow gloves.'

Straight off he takes charge. He says, 'What you need now, Vera, is a cup of coffee.' I said, 'Well, we were just going for some tea, weren't we, Mother?' Vera! Her name's not Vera. She's never been called Vera. My Dad never called her Vera, except just once, when they were wheeling him into the theatre. Vera. 'Right,' he says, 'follow me.' And puts his arm through hers. 'Careful,' she says. 'You'll make my boy friend jealous.' I didn't say anything.

*Pause.*

Now the café we generally patronise is just that bit different. It's plain but it's classy, no cloths on the tables, the menu comes on a little slate and the waitresses wear their own clothes and look as if they're doing it just for the fun of it. The stuff's all home-made and we're both big fans of the date and walnut bread. I said, 'This is the place.' Mr Turnbull goes straight past. 'No,' he says, 'I know somewhere, just opened. Press on.'

Now, if there's one thing Mother and me are agreed on it's that red is a common colour. And the whole place is done out in red. Lampshades red. Waitresses in red. Plates red, and on the tables those plastic sauce things got up to look like tomatoes. Also red. And when I look there's a chip in the sugar. I thought, 'Mother won't like this.' 'Oh,' she says, 'this looks cheerful, doesn't it, Graham?' I said, 'There's a chip in the sugar.' 'A detail,' he says, 'they're still having their teething troubles. Is it three coffees?' I said, 'We like tea,' only Mother says, 'No. I feel like an adventure. I'll have coffee.' He gets hold of the menu and puts his hand on hers. 'Might I suggest,' he says, 'a cheeseburger?' She said, 'Oh, what's that?' He said, 'It's fresh country beef, mingled with golden-fried onions, topped off with toasted cheese served with french fries and lemon wedge.' 'Oh, lemon wedge,' said Mother. 'That sounds nice.' I thought, 'Well, I hope you can keep it down.' Because it'll be the pizza story all over again. One mouthful and at four o'clock in the morning I was still stuck at her bedside with the bucket. She said, 'I like new experiences in eating. I had a pizza once, didn't I, Graham?' I didn't say anything.

They fetch the food and she's wiring in. He said, 'Are you enjoying your cheeseburger?' She said, 'I am. Would I be mistaken in thinking that's tomato sauce?' He said, 'It is.' She says, 'Give us a squirt.' They both burst out laughing. He said, 'Glass cups, Graham. Be careful or we'll see up your nose.' More laughter. She said, 'Graham's quite refined. He often has a dry sherry.'

'Well, he could do with smartening up a bit,' Mr Turnbull said. 'Plastic mac. He wants one of these quilted jobs, I've shifted a lot of those.'

'I don't like those quilted jobs,' I said. 'He sweats,' Mother said. 'There's no excuse for that in this day and age,' Mr Turnbull said, 'the range of preparations there are on the market. You want to invest in some roll-on deodorant.' Everybody could hear. 'And flares are anathema even in Bradford.'

'Graham doesn't care, do you, Graham?' Mother said. 'He reads a lot.' 'So what?' Mr Turnbull said. 'I know several big readers who still manage to be men about town. Lovat green's a nice shade. I tell you this, Graham,' he said, 'if I were squiring a young lady like this around town I wouldn't do it in grey socks and sandals. These shoes are Italian. Feel.' 'I always think Graham would have made a good parson,' Mother said, feeling his foot, 'only he doesn't believe in God.' 'That's no handicap these days,' Mr Turnbull said. 'What do you do?'

'He's between jobs at present,' Mother said. 'He used to do soft toys for handicapped children. Then he was making paper flowers at one stage.' I went to the toilet.

*Pause.*

When I came back he said, 'I don't believe in mental illness. Nine times out of ten it's a case of pulling your socks up.' I didn't say anything. Mother said, 'Yes, well, I think the pendulum's gone too far.' She didn't look at me. 'It's like these girls, not eating,' he said, 'they'd eat if they'd been brought up like us, Vera, nothing to eat.' 'That's right,' Mother said, 'they have it too easy. Did you marry?' 'Twice,' he said. 'I buried Amy last May. I was heartbroken but life has to go on. I've a son lives in Stevenage. I've got two grandsons, one at the motorbike stage. Do you drive?' 'No,' I said. 'You do,' Mother said. 'You had that scooter.' 'It was only a moped,' I said. 'Well, a moped, Graham. They're all the same. I can't get him to blow his own trumpet.'

'I've got a Rover 2000,' Mr Turnbull said, 'handles like a dream. I think the solution to mental illness is hard physical work. Making raffia mats, I'd go mad.' 'Yes,' says Mother, 'only they do pottery as well. I've seen some nice ashtrays.' 'Featherbedding,' Mr Turnbull said. 'Do you like these Pakistanis?' 'Well in moderation,' Mother said. 'We have a nice newsagent. Graham thinks we're all the same.' I said, 'I thought you did.' She said, 'Well, I do when you explain it all to me, Graham, but then I forget the explanation and I'm back to square one.' 'There is no explanation,' Mr Turnbull said. 'They sell mangoes in our post office, what explanation is there for that?' 'I know,' Mother said, 'I smelled curry on my *Woman's*

*Own*. You have to be educated to understand.' I didn't say anything.

He ran us home, promised to give her a tinkle next time he was in the neighbourhood. Said he was often round here tracking down two-tone cardigans. 'Your Mother's a grand woman,' he said. 'You want to cherish her.' 'He does, he does,' Mother said. 'You're my boy friend, aren't you, Graham?' She put her arm through mine.

GO TO BLACK.

*Come up on Graham standing looking out of the window. It is late afternoon. He sits on the arm of the chair.*





There must be a famine on somewhere because we were just letting our midday meal go down when the vicar calls with some envelopes. Breezes in, anorak and running shoes, and he says, 'I always look forward to coming to this house, Mrs Whittaker.' (He's got the idea she's deaf, which she's not; it's one of the few things she isn't.) He says, 'Do you know why? It's because you two remind me of Jesus and his mother.' Well, I've always thought Jesus was a bit off-hand with his mother, and on one occasion I remember he was quite snotty with her, but I didn't say anything. And of course Madam is over the moon. In her book if you can't get compared with the Queen Mother the Virgin Mary's the next best thing. She says, 'Are you married?' (She asks him every time, never remembers.) He said, 'No, Mrs Whittaker. I am married to God.' She says, 'Where does that leave you with the housework?' He said, 'Well, I don't do as well as your Graham. He's got this place like a palace.' She says, 'Well, I do my whack. I washed four pairs of stockings this morning.' She hadn't. She put them in the bowl then they slipped her mind, so the rest of the operation devolved on me.

He said, 'How are you today, Mrs Whittaker?' She says, 'Stiff down one side.' I said, 'She had a fall yesterday.' She says, 'I never did.' I said, 'You did, Mother. You had a fall, then you ran into Mr Turnbull.'

*Pause.*

She says, 'That's right. I did.' And she starts rooting in her bag for her lipstick. She says, 'That's one of them anoraky things, isn't it? They've gone out now, those. If you want to look like a man about town you want to get one of those continental quilts.' He said, 'Oh?' I said, 'She means those quilted jackets.' She said, 'He knows what I mean. Where did you get those

shoes?' He said, 'They're training shoes.' She said, 'Training for what? Are you not fully qualified?' He said, 'If Jesus were alive today, Mrs Whittaker, I think you'd find these were the type of shoes he would be wearing.' 'Not if his mother had anything to do with it,' she said. 'She'd have him down Stead and Simpson's and get him into some good brogues. Somebody was telling me the Italians make good shoes.'

The vicar takes this as his cue to start on about people who have no shoes at all and via this to the famine in Ethiopia. I fork out 50p which he says will feed six families for a week and she says, 'Well, it would have bought me some Quality Street.' When he's at the door he says, 'I take my hat off to you, Graham, I've got a mother myself.' When I get back in she said, 'Vicar! He looked more like the paper boy. How can you look up to somebody in pumps?' Just then there's a knock at the door. 'Get down,' she says, 'he's back.' Only it isn't. It's Mr Turnbull.

*Graham stands up.*

New outfit this time: little suede coat, corduroy collar, maroon trousers.

She says, 'You're colourful.' 'We just happen to have these slacks on offer,' he says. 'I was wondering whether you fancied a run out to Bolton Abbey?' 'Bolton Abbey?' she says. 'Oh, that's right up our street, isn't it, Graham? Graham's good with buildings, aren't you, Graham? He knows all the periods of houses. There's one period that's just come in. Other people don't like it yet but we do, don't we, Graham?' 'I don't know,' I said. 'You do. What is it?' 'Victorian,' I said. 'That's it, Victorian. Only there's a lot been pulled down.' Mr Turnbull yawns. 'I've got a little bungalow.' 'That's nice,' Mother says. 'I like a nice bungalow, don't you, Graham?' 'Yes,' I said, 'provided it's not a blot on the landscape.' 'Mine's architect designed,' says Mr Turnbull. 'It has a patio and a breakfast bar, it overlooks a beauty spot.' 'Oh,' said Mother, 'sounds tip-top. We'd better be getting our skates on, Graham.' He said, 'I've got to pick up a load of green three-quarter-length windcheaters in Ilkley; there won't really be room for a third party. Isn't there anything on at the pictures?' 'Oh he'll be happy reading,' Mother said. 'Won't you, Graham?' 'Anyway,' Mr Turnbull said, 'you don't always want to be with your Mother at your age, do you, Graham?' I didn't say anything.





*He sits on the chair arm again.*

I've been laid on my bed reading one of my magazines. I've a feeling that somebody's looking at the house, only I can't see anybody. Once or twice I think I've heard a knock on the door, but I haven't gone in case there's nobody there.

GO TO BLACK.

*Come up on Graham sitting on his unmade bed in his pyjamas. Night.*

Today they went over to York. It was after seven when he dropped her off. He generally comes in but not this time. Just gives her a little kiss. She has to bend down. I said, 'Have you had a good time?' She said, 'Yes. We had egg and chips, tea, bread and butter, we've got a lot in common and there's a grand new car park.' I said, 'Did you go in the Minster?' She said, 'No. Frank's not keen on old buildings. We need to look more to the future. He says they've built a spanking new precinct in Bradford, so that's going to be next on the agenda. You're quiet.' I said, 'Well, do you wonder? Doctor Chaudhury says I should have a stable environment. This isn't a stable environment with your fancy men popping in every five minutes.'

She said, 'He isn't my fancy man.' I said, 'Well, he's your fancy man in embryo.' She said, 'You know I don't know what that means.' I said, 'How old are you?' She said, 'I don't know.' I said, 'You do know.' She said, 'I don't. Tell me.' I said, 'You're seventy-two.' 'That's not so old. How old was Winston Churchill?' I said, 'When?' She said, 'You think you've got it over me, Graham Whittaker. Well, I'll tell you something, my memory's better with Frank. He was telling me about the economy. You've got it all wrong.' I said, 'How?' 'I can't remember but you have. Blaming it on the government. Frank says it's the blacks.' I didn't say anything, just came upstairs.

When I went down again she's still sat there with her hat and coat on. I said: 'Do you want to knit him a tea cosy?' She said, 'I don't think he's the tea-cosy type. When I first knew him he had a motorbike and sidecar. Besides, I think it's got beyond the tea-cosy stage.' I said, 'What do you mean?' She said, 'Graham. My one aim in life is for you to be happy. If I thought that by dying I would make you happy I would.' I said, 'Mother, your dying wouldn't make me happy. In fact the reverse. It would make me unhappy. Anyway, Mother, you're not going to die.' She said, 'No. I'm not going to die. I'm going to get married. And the honeymoon is in Tenerife. Have one of your tablets.'

She made a cup of tea. I said, 'How can you go to Tenerife, you're smothered at Scarborough?' She said, 'It's a four-star hotel with tip-top air-conditioning, you get your breakfast from a long table.' I said, 'What about your bowels?' She said, 'What about my bowels?' 'Well, you said they were unpredictable at Morecambe. Get them to the Canary Islands and they're going to be all over the place.' She said, 'Who's talking about the Canary Islands? I'm going to Tenerife.' 'And what about post-Tenerife? Where are you going to live?' She said, 'Here. Frank says he'll be away on and off on business but he wants to call this home.' I said, 'What about me?' She went into the kitchen. 'Well, we wondered whether you'd prefer to go back to the hostel. You were happy at the hostel. You rubbed shoulders with all sorts.' I said, 'Mam. This is my home.' She said, 'A man shouldn't be living with his mother at your age, Frank says. Did you take a tablet?'

Now it's four o'clock in the morning and I can't sleep. There's a car parked outside. I can't see but I think there's somebody in it, watching like they used to do before. I thought all that chapter was closed.

GO TO BLACK.

*Come up on Graham sitting on an upright chair. Evening.*

This morning I went to Community Caring down at the Health Centre. It caters for all sorts. Steve, who runs it, is dead against what he calls 'the ghetto approach'. What he's after is a nice mix of personality difficulties as being the most fruitful exercise in problem-solving and a more realistic model of society generally. There's a constant flow of coffee, 'oiling the wheels' Steve calls it, and we're all encouraged to ventilate our problems and generally let our hair down. I sometimes feel a bit out of it as I've never had any particular problems, so this time when Steve says 'Now chaps and chappesses who's going to set the ball rolling?' I get in quick and tell them about Mother and Mr Turnbull. When I'd finished Steve said, 'Thank you, Graham, for sharing your problem with us. Does anybody want to kick it around?'

First off the mark is Leonard, who wonders whether Graham has sufficiently appreciated that old people can fall in love and have meaningful relationships generally, the same as young people. I suppose this is understandable coming from Leonard because he's sixty-five, only he doesn't have meaningful relationships. He's been had up for exposing himself in Sainsbury's doorway. As Mother said, 'Tesco, you could understand it.'

Then Janice chips in. 'Had they been having sexual intercourse?' I said I didn't want to think about it. Steve said, 'Why?' I said I didn't know. So he said, 'Maybe what we should be talking about is why Graham is being so defensive about sexual intercourse.' I said, 'Steve. I am not being defensive about sexual intercourse. She is my mother.' Jackie, who's nine parts Lesbian, said, 'Graham. She is also A Woman.' I couldn't believe this. I said, 'Jackie. You're an ex-battered wife. I thought you didn't approve of marriage.' She said, 'Graham. I approve of caring marriage.' I said, 'Jackie. This is not caring marriage.' She said, 'Graham, what's Tenerife? That's caring. All I got was a black eye and a day trip to Fleetwood.' Then they all have a go. Get Graham. Steve summed up. 'The general feeling of the group is that Graham could be more open.' I said, 'How can I be more open? There's somebody sat outside the house watching.' I wanted to discuss that only Leonard leaped in and said he felt the need to talk through an episode behind British Home Stores. I stuck it a bit longer and then came home.

Mother's sat there, all dolled up. Earrings on, chiffon scarf, lathered in make-up. She said, 'Oh, I thought you were Mr Turnbull.' I said, 'No.' She said, 'I'll just go to the lav.' She goes three times in the next ten minutes. I said, 'You're not getting married today, are you?' She said, 'No. There's a new Asda superstore opened at Bingley and we thought we'd give it the once over. Frank says they have a very good selection of sun tan lotions.' I said, 'Mother, there's somebody watching the house.' She said, 'I want to pick out some tissues and Frank's looking for a little chammy for his windscreen. He's promised me something called a cheeseburger, there's a café that's part of the complex.'

Just then there's a little toot on the horn and she runs to the lav again. I said, 'Don't go. Don't leave me, Mam.' She said, 'I'm not giving in to you, you're a grown man. Is my underskirt showing?' He toots again. She says, 'Look at your magazines, make yourself a poached egg.' I said, 'Mam.' She said, 'There's that bit of chicken in the fridge. You could iron those two vests. Take a tablet. Give us a kiss. Toodle pip.'

I thought I'd go sit in the back room where they couldn't see me. I pulled the curtains and I'm sitting there in the dark and I think I hear a knock at the front door. I don't move and there's another knock. Louder. I do like Doctor Chaudhury says and tell myself it's not happening, only it is. Somebody shouts through the letter-box. 'I know you're in there. Open this door.' So I do. And there is someone. It's a woman.



She said, 'Are you the son?' I said, 'What?' She said, 'Are you the son? I'm the daughter.' I said, 'Have you been watching the house?' She said, 'On and off. Why?' I said, 'Nothing.' She said, 'I don't know what there is to look so suited about.' I said, 'You'd better come in.'



GO TO BLACK.

*Come up on Graham as he puts a magazine on top of the wardrobe. He sits down in the easy chair. Night.*

It's nine o'clock when I hear the car outside. I'm sitting watching TV. I say, 'Oh hello. Did you have a nice time?' She said, 'Yes. Yes we did, thank you.' 'Did you get your sun tan lotion?' She said, 'What sun tan lotion?' 'You were going to get some sun tan lotion. Never mind. You've forgotten. How's Mr Turnbull?' 'Frank? He's all right.' She took her things off. 'I'm sure you could get to like him, Graham, if only you got to know him.' I said, 'Well, you should have brought him in.' 'Well, I will next time. It'd be nice if now and again we could go off as a threesome. What have you done?' 'Nothing,' I said. 'Just sat here.' 'You've been all right?' 'Mmm.'

'You see,' she said, 'there wasn't anybody outside.' 'Oh yes there was.' She said, 'Oh Graham. Have you had a tablet? Have a tablet.' 'I don't want a tablet. I'll tell you who was sat outside. Mrs Pamela Musgrave.' She said, 'Who's she?' 'Née Turnbull. The daughter of your hubby to be.' She

said, 'He hasn't got a daughter. He's got a son down south. He hasn't got a daughter,' she said, 'you're making stuff up now, have a tablet.' I said, 'I'm not making it up. And there's something else I'm not making up. Mrs Turnbull.' She said, 'There isn't a Mrs Turnbull. She's dead. I'm going to the lav.' I said, 'She's not dead. She's in a wheelchair with a broken heart. He's been having you on.'

After a bit she comes out. 'You're just saying all this.' 'The number's on the pad. Ring up. She's disabled is his wife. Has been for ten years. Their daughter looks after them. You're not the first. He's always doing it. One woman, it was going to be Barbados. Somebody spotted you together at Bolton Abbey. A well-wisher. Tenerife!'

Later on I took her a cup of tea. She'd been crying. She said, 'I bought this little bedjacket.' I said, 'I'm sorry, Mam.' She said, 'He was right enough. What can you expect at my age? How old am I?' 'Seventy-two.' 'That's another thing. I remembered with him. I don't remember with you.' I said, 'I'm sorry.' She said, 'You're not sorry. How are you sorry? You didn't like him.' I said, 'He wasn't good enough for you.' She said, 'I'm the best judge of that. He was natty, more than can be said for you.' And starts crying again. I said, 'I understand, Mam.' She said, 'You don't understand. How can you understand, you, you're not normal?' I said, 'I'm going to bed.'

In a bit she comes shouting outside the door. 'You think you've got it over me, Graham Whittaker. Well, you haven't. I've got it over you.' I said, 'Go back to bed.' She said, 'I know the kind of magazines you read.' I said, 'Chess. You'll catch cold.' She said, 'They never are chess. Chess with no clothes on. Chess in their birthday suits. That kind of chess. Chess men.' I said, 'Go to bed. And turn your blanket off.'

*Pause.*

Next day she's right as rain. Forgotten it. Never mentions it anyway, except just as we're coming out of the house she said, 'I do love you, Graham.' I said, 'I love you too.' She said, 'Anyway he had a hearing aid.' She said, 'What's on the agenda for today, then?' I said, 'I thought we might have a little ride to Ripon.' She said, 'Oh yes, Ripon. That's nice. We could go to the cathedral. We like old buildings, don't we, you and me?'

She put her arm through mine.

FADE OUT.

# Bed **Among** the Lentils

**Susan:** Maggie Smith

PRODUCED BY **INNES LLOYD** DIRECTED BY **ALAN BENNETT**
DESIGNED BY **TONY BURROUGH** MUSIC BY **GEORGE FENTON**

SUSAN IS A VICAR'S WIFE. SHE IS THIN AND NERVOUS AND PROBABLY SMOKES. SHE SITS ON AN UPRIGHT CHAIR IN THE KITCHEN. IT IS EVENING.

Geoffrey's bad enough but I'm glad I wasn't married to Jesus. The lesson this morning was the business in the Garden of Gethsemane when Jesus prays and the disciples keep falling asleep. He wakes them up and says, 'Could you not watch with me one hour?' It's my mother.

I overslept this morning, flung on a cardigan and got there just as everybody was standing up. It was Holy Communion so the militants were out in force, the sub-zero temperature in the side-chapel doubtless adding to the attraction.

Geoffrey kicks off by apologising for his failure to de-frost the church. (Subdued merriment.) Mr Medlicott has shingles, Geoffrey explains, and, as is well known, has consistently refused to initiate us lesser mortals into the mysteries of the boiler. (Helpless laughter.)





Mrs Belcher read the lesson. Mr Belcher took the plate round. 'Big day for you,' I said to them afterwards.

The sermon was about sex. I didn't actually nod off, though I have heard it before. Marriage gives the OK to sex is the gist of it, but while it is far from being the be all and end all (you can say that again) sex is nevertheless the supreme joy of the married state and a symbol of the relationship between us and God. So, Geoffrey concludes, when we put our money in the plate it is a symbol of everything in our lives we are offering to God and that includes our sex. I could only find 10p.

Thinking about the sermon during the hymn I felt a pang of sympathy for the Deity, gifted with all this sex. No fun being made a present of the rare and desiccated conjunctions that take place between Geoffrey and me. Or the frightful collisions that presumably still occur between the Belchers. Not to mention whatever shamefaced fumblings go on between Miss Budd and Miss Bantock. 'It's all right if we offer it to God, Alice.' 'Well, if you say so, Pauline.'

Amazing scenes at the church door. Geoffrey had announced that after Easter the bishop would be paying us a visit so the fan club were running round in small circles, Miss Frobisher even going as far as to squeeze my elbow. Meanwhile, Geoffrey stands there the wind billowing out his surplice and ruffling his hair, what 'Who's Who in the Diocese of Ripon' calls 'his schoolboy good looks'. I helped put away the books while he did his 'underneath this cassock I am but a man like anybody else' act. 'Such a live wire,' said Mrs Belcher, 'really putting the parish on the map.'

'That's right,' burbles Mrs Shrubsole, looking at me. 'We must cherish him.'

We came back and I cherished him with some chicken wings in a tuna fish sauce. He said, 'That went down well.' I said, 'The chicken wings?' He said, 'My sermon. I felt it hit the nail on the head.' He put his hand over mine, hoping, I suppose, that having hit one nail he might hit another, but I said I had to go round with the parish magazine. 'Good girl,' he said. 'I can attack my paperwork instead.'

Roads busy. Sunday afternoon. Families having a run out. Wheeling the pram, walking the dog. Living. Almighty God unto whom all hearts be open, and from whom no secrets are hid, cleanse the thoughts of our hearts by the inspiration of thy holy spirit that we may perfectly love thee and worthily magnify thy glorious name and not spend our Sunday afternoons parked in a lay-by on the Ring Road wondering what happened to our life.

When I got back Geoffrey was just off to Evensong, was I going to come? When I said 'No' he said, 'Really? Then I'd better pretend you have a headache.'

Why? One of the unsolved mysteries of life, or the unsolved

mysteries of my life, is why the vicar's wife is expected to go to church at all. A barrister's wife doesn't have to go to court, an actor's wife isn't at every performance, so why have I always got to be on parade? Not to mention the larger question of whether one believes in God in the first place. It's assumed that being the vicar's wife one does but the question has never actually come up, not with Geoffrey anyway. I can understand why, of course. To look at me, the hair, the flat chest, the wan smile, you'd think I was just cut out for God. And maybe I am. I'd just like to have been asked that's all. Not that it matters of course. So long as you can run a tight jumble sale you can believe in what you like.

It could be that Geoffrey doesn't believe in God either. I've always longed to ask him only God never seems to crop up. 'Geoffrey,' I'd say. 'Yes, Susan?' 'Do you really believe in God? I mean, cards on tables, you don't honestly, do you? God's just a job like any other. You've got to bring home the bacon somehow.' But no. Not a word. The subject's never discussed.

After he'd gone I discovered we were out of sherry so I've just been round to the off-licence. The woman served me. Didn't smile. I can't think why. I spend enough.





GO TO BLACK.

*Come up on Susan on the steps of the side-chapel, polishing a candlestick. Afternoon.*

We were discussing the ordination of women. The bishop asked me what I thought. Should women take the services? So long as it doesn't have to be me, I wanted to say, they can be taken by a trained gorilla. 'Oh yes,' Geoffrey chips in, 'Susan's all in favour. She's keener than I am, aren't you, darling?' 'More sprouts anybody?' I said.

On the young side for a bishop, but he's been a prominent sportsman at university so that would explain it. Boxing or rugby. Broken nose at some stage anyway. One of the 'Christianity is common sense' brigade. Hobby's bricklaying apparently and refers to me throughout as 'Mrs Vicar'. Wants beer with his lunch and Geoffrey says he'll join him so this leaves me with the wine. Geoffrey's all over him because the rumour is he's shopping round for a new Archdeacon. Asks Geoff how outgoing I am. Actually says that. 'How outgoing is Mrs Vicar?' Mr Vicar jumps in with a quick rundown of my accomplishments and an outline of my punishing schedule. On a typical day, apparently, I kick off by changing the wheel on the Fiesta, then hasten to the bedside of a dying pensioner, after which, having done the altar flowers and dispensed warmth and appreciation to sundry parishioners en route, I top off a thrill-packed morning by taking round Meals on Wheels…somehow – 'and this to me is the miracle,' says Geoffrey – 'somehow managing to rustle up a delicious lunch in the interim', the miracle somewhat belied by the flabby lasagna we are currently embarked on. 'The ladies,' says the bishop. 'Where would we be without them?'

Disaster strikes as I'm doling out the tinned peaches: the jug into which I've decanted the Carnation milk gets knocked over, possibly by me. Geoffrey, for whom turning the other cheek is part of the job, claims it caught his elbow and his lordship takes the same line, insisting he gets doused in Carnation milk practically every day of his life. Still, when I get a dishcloth and sponge off his gaiters I catch him giving me a funny look. It's Mary Magdalene and the Nivea cream all over again. After lunch Geoffrey's supposed to be taking him on a tour of the parish but while we're having a cup of instant he claps his hand to his temple because he's suddenly remembered he's supposed to be in Keighley blessing a steam engine.

We're stacking the dishwasher and I ask Geoffrey how he thinks it's gone. Doesn't know. 'Fingers crossed,' I say. 'I think there are more constructive things we could do than that,' he says crisply, and goes off to mend his inner tube. I sit by the Aga for a bit and as I doze off it comes to me that by 'constructive things' he perhaps means prayer.

When I wake up there's a note from Geoffrey. 'Gone to talk to the Ladies Bright Hour. Go to bed.' I'm not sleepy and anyway we're running low on sherry so I drive into Leeds. I've stopped going round the corner now as I owe them a bit on the side and she's always so surly. There's a little Indian shop behind the Infirmary I've found. It's a newsagents basically but it sells drink and anything really, the way they do. Open last thing at night, Sundays included, my ideal. Ramesh he's called. Mr Ramesh I call him, though Ramesh may be his Christian name. Only not Christian of course. I've been once or twice now, only this time he sits me in the back place on a sack of something and talks. Little statuette of a god on the wall. A god. Not The God. Not the definite article. One of several thousand apparently. 'Safety in numbers,' I said but he didn't understand. Looks a bit more fun than Jesus anyway. Shows me pictures of other gods, getting up to all sorts. I said, 'She looks a very busy lady. Is that yoga?' He said, 'Well, it helps.' He's quite athletic himself apparently, married, but his wife's only about fourteen so they won't let her in. He calls me Mrs Vicar too, only it's different. He has lovely teeth.

Go to black.

*Come up on Susan in the kitchen near the Aga. Morning.*

Once upon a time I had my life planned out…or half of it at any rate. I wasn't clear about the first part, but at the stroke of fifty I was all set to turn into a wonderful woman…the wife to a doctor, or a vicar's wife, Chairman of the Parish Council, a pillar of the WI. A wise, witty and ultimately white-haired old lady, who's always stood on her own feet until one day at the age of eighty she comes out of the County Library, falls under the weight of her improving book, breaks her hip and dies peacefully, continently and without fuss under a snowy coverlet in the cottage hospital. And coming away from her funeral in a country churchyard on a bright winter's afternoon people would say, 'Well, she was a wonderful woman.'





Had this been a serious ambition I should have seen to it I was equipped with the skills necessary to its achievement. How to produce jam which, after reaching a good, rolling boil, successfully coats the spoon; how to whip up a Victoria sponge that just gives to the fingertips; how to plan, execute and carry through a successful garden fête. All weapons in the armoury of any upstanding Anglican lady. But I can do none of these things. I'm even a fool at the flower arrangement. I ought to have a PhD in the subject the number of classes I've been to but still my efforts show as much evidence of art as walking sticks in an umbrella stand. Actually it's temperament. I don't have it. If you think squash is a competitive activity try flower arrangement.

On this particular morning the rota has Miss Frobisher and Mrs Belcher down for the side aisles and I'm paired with Mrs Shrubsole to do the altar and the lectern. My honest opinion, never voiced needless to say, is that if they were really sincere about religion they'd forget flower arrangement altogether, invest in some permanent plastic jobs and put the money towards the current most popular famine. However, around mid-morning I wander over to the church with a few dog-eared chrysanthemums. They look as if they could do with an immediate drink so I call in at the vestry and root out a vase or two from the cupboard where Geoffrey keeps the communion wine.

It not looming very large on my horizon, I assume I am doing the altar and Mrs Shrubsole the lectern, but when I come out of the vestry Mrs S is at the altar well embarked on her arrangement. I said, 'I thought I was doing the altar.' She said, 'No. I think Mrs Belcher will bear me out. I'm down to do the altar. You are doing the lectern. Why?' She smiled sweetly. 'Do you have a preference?' The only preference I have is to shove my chrysanthemums up her nose but instead I practise a bit of Christian forbearance and go stick them in a vase by the lectern. In the best tradition of my floral arrangements they look like the poles of a wigwam, so I go and see if I can cadge a bit of backing from Mrs Belcher. 'Are you using this?' I say, picking up a bit of mouldy old fern. 'I certainly am. I need every bit of my spiraea. It gives it body.' I go over and see if Miss Frobisher has any greenery going begging only she's doing some Japanese number, a vase like a test-tube half filled with gravel, in which she's throttling a lone carnation. So I retire to the vestry for a bit to calm my shattered nerves, and when I come out ready to tackle my chrysanths again Mrs Shrubsole has apparently finished and fetched the other two up to the altar to admire her handiwork. So I wander up and take a look.

Well, it's a brown job, beech leaves, teazles, grass, that school of thought. Mrs Shrubsole is saying, 'It's called Forest Murmurs. It's what I did for my Highly Commended at Harrogate last year. What do you think?' Gert and Daisy are of course speechless with admiration, but when I tentatively suggest it might look a bit better if she cleared up all the bits and pieces lying around she said, 'What bits and pieces?' I said, 'All these acorns and fir-cones and whatnot. What's this conker in aid of?' She said, 'Leave that. The whole arrangement pivots on that.' I said, 'Pivots?' 'When the adjudicator was commenting on my arrangement he particularly singled out the hint I gave of the forest floor.' I said, 'Mrs Shrubsole. This is the altar of St Michael and All Angels. It is not The Wind in the Willows.' Mrs Belcher said, 'I think you ought to sit down.' I said, 'I do not want to sit down.' I said, 'It's all very well to transform the altar into something out of Bambi but do not forget that for the vicar the altar is his working surface. Furthermore,' I added, 'should the vicar sink to his knees in prayer, which since this is the altar he is wont to do, he is quite likely to get one of these teazle things in his eye. This is not a flower arrangement. It is a booby trap. A health hazard. In fact,' I say in a moment of supreme inspiration, 'it should be labelled HAZFLOR. Permit me to demonstrate.' And I begin getting down on my knees just to prove how lethal her bloody Forest Murmurs is. Only I must have slipped because next thing I know I'm rolling down the altar steps and end up banging my head on the communion rail.

Mrs Shrubsole, who along with every other organisation known to man has been in the St John's Ambulance Brigade, wants me left lying down, whereas Mrs Belcher is all for getting me on to a chair. 'Leave them lying down,' says Mrs Belcher, 'and they inhale their own vomit. It happens all the time, Veronica.' 'Only, Muriel,' says Mrs Shrubsole, 'when they have vomited. She hasn't vomited.' 'No,' I say, 'but I will if I have to listen to any more of this drivel,' and begin to get up. 'Is that blood, Veronica?' says Mrs Belcher pointing to my head. 'Well,' says Mrs Shrubsole, reluctant to concede to Mrs B on any matter remotely touching medicine, 'it could be, I suppose. What we need is some hot sweet tea.' 'I thought that theory had been discredited,' says Mrs Belcher. Discredited or not it sends Miss Frobisher streaking off to find a teabag, and also, it subsequently transpires, to telephone all and sundry in an effort to locate Geoffrey. He is in York taking part in the usual interdenominational conference on the role of the church in a hitherto uncolonised department of life, underfloor central heating possibly. He comes haring back thinking I'm at death's door, and finding I'm not has nothing more constructive to offer than I take a nap.



This gives the fan club the green light to invade the vicarage, making endless tea and the vicar his lunch and, as he puts it, 'spoiling him rotten'. Since this also licenses them to conduct a fact-finding survey of all the housekeeping arrangements or absence of same ('Where does she keep the Duroglit, Vicar?'), a good time is had by all. Meanwhile Emily Brontë is laid out on the sofa in a light doze.



I come round to hear Geoffrey saying, 'Mrs Shrubsole's going now, darling.' I don't get up. I never even open my eyes. I just wave and say, 'Goodbye, Mrs Shrubsole.' Only thinking about it as I drift off again I think I may have said, 'Goodbye, Mrs Subsoil.' Anyway I meant the other. Shrubsoil.

When I woke up it was dark and Geoffrey'd gone out. I couldn't find a thing in the cupboard so I got the car out and drove into Leeds. I sat in the shop for a bit, not saying much. Then I felt a bit wanny and Mr Ramesh let me go into the back place to lie down. I must have dozed off because when I woke up Mr Ramesh has come in and started taking off his clothes. I said, 'What are you doing? What about the shop?' He said, 'Do not worry about the shop. I have closed the shop.' I said, 'It's only nine. You don't close till eleven.' 'I do tonight,' he said. I said, 'What's tonight?' He said, 'A chance in a million. A turn-up for the books. Will you take your clothes off please.' And I did.

GO TO BLACK.

*Come up on Susan sitting in the vestry having a cigarette. Afternoon.*

You never see pictures of Jesus smiling, do you? I mentioned this to Geoffrey

once. 'Good point, Susan,' is what he said, which made me wish I'd not brought it up in the first place. Said I should think of Our Lord as having an inward smile, the doctrine according to Geoffrey being that Jesus was made man so he smiled, laughed and did everything else just like the rest of us. 'Do you think he ever smirked?' I asked, whereupon Geoffrey suddenly remembered he was burying somebody in five minutes and took himself off.

If Jesus is all man I just wish they'd put a bit more of it into the illustrations. I was sitting in church yesterday, wrestling with this point of theology, when it occurred to me that something seemed to have happened to Geoffrey. The service should have kicked off ages ago but he's still in the vestry. Mr Bland is filling in with something uplifting on the organ and Miss Frobisher, never one to let an opportunity slip, has slumped to her knees for a spot of unscheduled silent prayer. Mrs Shrubsole is lost in contemplation of the altar, still adorned with Forest Murmurs, a trail of ivy round the cross the final inspired touch. Mr Bland now ups the volume but still no sign of Geoff. 'Arnold,' says Mrs Belcher, 'there seems to be some hiatus in the proceedings,' and suddenly the fan club is on red alert. She's just levering him to his feet when I get in first and nip in there to investigate.





His reverence is there, white-faced, every cupboard open and practically in tears. He said, 'Have you seen it?' I said, 'What?' He said, 'The wine. The communion wine. It's gone.' I said, 'That's no tragedy,' and offer to pop out and get some ordinary. Geoffrey said, 'They're not open. Besides, what does it look like?' I said, 'Well, it looks like we've run out of communion wine.' He said, 'We haven't run out. There was a full bottle here on Friday. Somebody has drunk it.'

It's on the tip of my tongue to say that if Jesus is all he's cracked up to be why doesn't he use tap-water and put it to the test when I suddenly remember that Mr Bland keeps a bottle of cough mixture in his cupboard in case any of the choirboys gets chesty. At the thought of celebrating the Lord's Supper in Benylin Geoffrey now has a complete nervous breakdown but, as I point out, it's red and sweet and nobody is going to notice. Nor do they. I see Mr Belcher licking his lips a bit thoughtfully as he walks back down the aisle but that's all. 'What was the delay?' asks Mrs Shrubsole. 'Nothing,' I said, 'just a little hiccup.'

Having got it right for once I'm feeling quite pleased with myself, but Geoffrey obviously isn't and never speaks all afternoon so I bunk off Evensong and go into Leeds.

Mr Ramesh has evidently been expecting me because there's a bed made up in the storeroom upstairs. I go up first and get in. When I'm in bed I can put my hand out and feel the lentils running through my fingers. When he comes up he's put on his proper clothes. Long white shirt, sash and whatnot. Loincloth underneath. All spotless. Like Jesus. Only not. I watch him undress and think about them all at Evensong and Geoffrey praying in that pausy way he does, giving you time to mean each phrase. And the fan club lapping it up, thinking they love God when they just love Geoffrey. Lighten our darkness we beseech thee O Lord and by thy great mercy defend us from all perils and dangers of this night. Like Mr Ramesh who is twenty-six with lovely legs, who goes swimming every morning at Merrion Street Baths and plays hockey for Horsforth. I ask him if they offer their sex to God. He isn't very interested in the point but with them, so far as I can gather, sex is all part of God anyway. I can see why too. It's the first time I really understand what all the fuss is about. There among the lentils on the second Sunday after Trinity.



I've just popped into the vestry. He's put a lock on the cupboard door.

GO TO BLACK.

*Come up on Susan sitting in the drawing-room of the vicarage. Much smarter than in previous scenes, she has had her hair done and seems a different woman. Evening.*



I stand up and say, 'My name is Susan. I am a vicar's wife and I am an alcoholic.' Then I tell my story. Or some of it anyway. 'Don't pull any punches,' says Clem, my counsellor. 'Nobody's going to be shocked, believe me love, we've all been there.' But I don't tell them about Mr Ramesh because they've not been there. 'Listen, people. I was so drunk I used to go and sleep with an Asian grocer. Yes, and you won't believe this. I loved it. Loved every minute.' Dear oh dear. This was a real drunken lady.

So I draw a veil over Mr Ramesh who once, on the feast of St Simon and St Jude (Choral Evensong at six, daily services at the customary hour), put make-up on his eyes and bells on his ankles, and naked except for his little belt danced in the back room of the shop with a tambourine.

'So how did you come to AA?' they ask. 'My husband,' I say. 'The vicar. He persuaded me.' But I lie. It was not my husband, it was Mr Ramesh, the exquisitely delicate and polite Mr Ramesh who one Sunday night turned his troubled face towards me with its struggling moustache and asked if he might take the bull by the horns and enquire if intoxication was a prerequisite for sexual intercourse, or whether it was only when I was going to bed with him, the beautiful Mr Ramesh, twenty-six, with wonderful legs, whether it was only with him I had to be inebriated. And was it, asked this slim, flawless and troubled creature, was it perhaps his colour? Because if not he would like to float the suggestion that sober might be even nicer. So the credit for the road to Damascus goes to Mr Ramesh, whose first name turns out also to be Ramesh. Ramesh Ramesh, a member of the community council and the Leeds Federation of Trade.

But none of this I say. In fact I never say anything at all. Only when it becomes plain to Geoffrey (and it takes all of three weeks) that Mrs Vicar is finally on the wagon, who is it gets the credit? Not one of Mr Ramesh's jolly little gods, busy doing everything under the sun to one another, much like Mr Ramesh. Oh no. It's full marks to Geoffrey's chum, the Deity, moving in his well-known mysterious way.





So now everything has changed. For the moment I am a new woman and Geoffrey is a new man. And he brings it up on the slightest pretext. 'My wife's an alcoholic, you know. Yes. It's a great challenge to me and to the parish as extended family.' From being a fly in the ointment I find myself transformed into a feather in his cap. Included it in his sermon on Prayers Answered when he reveals that he and the fan club have been having these jolly get togethers in which they'd all prayed over what he calls 'my problem'. It practically sent me racing back to the Tio Pepe even to think of it. The fans, of course, never dreaming that their prayers would be answered, are furious. They think it's brought us closer together. Geoffrey thinks that too. We were at some doleful diocesan jamboree last week and I'm stuck there clutching my grapefruit juice as Geoffrey's telling the tale to some bearded cleric. Suddenly he seizes my hand. 'We met it with love,' he cries, as if love were some all-purpose antibiotic, which to Geoffrey it probably is.

And it goes on, the mileage in it endless. I said to Geoffrey that when I stood up at AA I sometimes told the story about the flower arranging. Result: he starts telling it all over the diocese. The first time was at a conference on The Supportive Parish. Gales of deep, liberated, caring laughter. He's now given it a new twist and tells the story as if he's talking about a parishioner, then at the end he says, 'Friends I want to tell you something. (Deep hush.) That drunken flower-arranger was my wife.' Silence...then the applause, *terrific*.

I've caught the other young, upwardly mobile parsons sneaking looks at me now and again and you can see them thinking why weren't they smart enough to marry an alcoholic or better still a drug addict, problem wives whom they could do a nice redemption job on, right there on their own doorstep. Because there's no stopping Geoffrey now. He grips my hand in public, nay *brandishes* it. 'We're a team,' he cries. Looks certain to be rural dean and that's only the beginning. As the bishop says, 'Just the kind of man we're looking for on the bench…someone with a seasoned compassion, someone who's looked life in the face. Someone who's been there.'

Mr Ramesh sold his shop. He's gone back to India to fetch his wife. She's old enough now apparently. I went down there on Sunday. There was a boy writing Under New Management on the window. Spelled wrong. And something underneath in Hindi, spelled right probably. He said he thought Mr Ramesh would be getting another shop, only in Preston.

They do that, of course, Asians, build something up, get it going nicely, then take the profit and move on. It's a good thing. We ought to be more like that, more enterprising.

My group meets twice a week and I go. Religiously. And that's what it is, of course. The names are different, Frankie and Steve, Susie and Clem. But it's actually Miss Frobisher and Mrs Shrubsole all over again. I never liked going to one church so I end up going to two. Geoffrey would call that the wonderful mystery of God. I call it bad taste. And I wouldn't do it to a dog. But that's the thing nobody ever says about God…he has no taste at all.

FADE OUT.

# A Lady of Letters

**Irene Ruddock:** Patricia Routledge

PRODUCED BY **INNES LLOYD** DIRECTED BY **GILES FOSTER**
DESIGNED BY **TONY BURROUGH** MUSIC BY **GEORGE FENTON**

MISS RUDDOCK IS AN ORDINARY MIDDLE-AGED WOMAN. THE ROOM IN WHICH WE SEE HER IS SIMPLY FURNISHED AND THERE IS A BAY WINDOW. IT IS AFTERNOON.

I can't say the service was up to scratch. It smacked of the conveyor-belt. In fact I wrote to the crematorium. I said I thought the hallmark of a ceremony of that nature was reverence, whereas the word that kept coming into my mind was brisk. Moreover, I added, grief-stricken people do not expect to emerge from the Chapel of Rest to find grown men skulking in the rhododendrons with tab-ends in their mouths. If the hearse drivers must smoke then facilities should be provided. I'd heard good reports of this crematorium, but I hoped that they would agree with me that on this occasion it had let itself down.





Of course if I'd happened to be heartbroken I'd have felt much worse. I didn't let on to the crematorium because I thought it might get them off the hook but I actually didn't know her all that well. I used to see her getting on the 37 and we'd pass the time of day. She lost her mother round about the time I lost mine, she had a niece in Australia and I have the one cousin in Canada, then she went in for gas-fired central heating just a few weeks before I did, so one way and another we covered a lot of the same ground. I'd spent years thinking she was called Hammersley, which was way off the mark because her name turns out to be Pringle. There was a picture of her in the *Evening Post* (she'd been a big voluntary worker) with details of the funeral on the Wednesday afternoon, which is the one time I'm dangling my feet a bit, so I thought I'd get out my little maroon coat and put in an appearance. At least it's an outing. And I was glad I'd gone but, as I say, the ceremony was a bit lack-lustre and topped off by these young fellers smoking, so I thought the least I could do was write.

Anyway I had a charming letter back from the director of operations, a Mr Widdop. He said he was most grateful I'd drawn this matter to his attention and, while he was aware the practice sometimes went on, if he personally caught anybody smoking he would jump on the culprits with both feet. He knew I would appreciate that discipline within the chapel precincts presented special problems as it wasn't always convenient to tear a strip off somebody when there were grief-stricken people knocking about. What he personally preferred to do was to keep a low profile, then come down on the offenders like a ton of bricks once the coast was clear. With regard to my remarks about facilities, they had no plans to provide a smoking area in the Chapel of Rest in the foreseeable future as I must understand that space was at a premium and top of their list of priorities at the present moment was the provision of a temporary temple for the use of racial minorities. However, he would bear my remarks in mind, and if I were to come across any similar infringements in the future I was not to hesitate to get in touch.

I wrote him a little letter back thanking him for his prompt and courteous reply and saying that though I hoped not to be making any further visits to the crematorium in the near future (joke) I took his point. I also dropped a line to the relatives, care of the undertakers, saying that I was an acquaintance of Miss Pringle, had been present at the ceremony and had taken the liberty of entering into correspondence with the crematorium over the unfortunate lapse. I enclosed a copy of Mr Widdop's reply but they didn't write back, which I can understand because the one thing death always entails is a mass of correspondence. When Mother died I had fifty-three letters. Besides, they may not have even seen them smoking, they were probably blinded with grief. I see we've got a new couple moved in opposite. Don't look very promising. The kiddy looks filthy.



GO TO BLACK.



*Come up on Miss Ruddock in the same setting. Morning.*

A card from the opticians this morning saying that their records indicate that it's two years since they supplied me with spectacles and that by now they would almost certainly be in need of verification and suggesting I call at my earliest convenience. I thought that was nice so I took my trusty Platignum and dashed off an answer forthwith. I said I thought it was very considerate of them to have kept me in mind and while I was quite satisfied with my spectacles at the present moment I was grateful to them for drawing the matter to my attention and in the event of my noticing any deterioration I would in due course get in touch with them. (*She picks up her pen.*) It's stood me in good stead has this pen. Mother bought it me the last time she was able to get over to Harrogate. It's been a real friend. (*She glances in the direction of the window.*)

Angie her name is. I heard him shout of her as I went by en route for the Post Office. He was laid out underneath his car wanting a spanner and she came out, transistor in one hand, kiddy in the other. Thin little thing, bruise on its arm. I thought, 'Well, you've got a car, you've got a transistor, it's about time you invested in some curtains.' She can't be more than twenty and by the look of her she's expecting another.

I passed the place where there was the broken step I wrote to the council was a danger to the public. Little ramp there now, access for the disabled. Whenever I pass I think, 'Well, that's thanks to you, Irene.' My monument that ramp. Only some dog had gone and done its business right in the middle of it. I'm sure there's more of that than there used to be. I had a little Awayday to London last year and it was dog dirt everywhere. I spotted some on the pavement right outside Buckingham Palace. I wrote to the Queen about it. Had a charming letter back from a lady in waiting saying that Her Majesty appreciated my interest and that my letter had been passed on to the appropriate authority. The upshot eventually is I get a long letter from the chief cleansing officer to Westminster City Council apologising profusely and enclosing a rundown of their Highways and Maintenance Budget. That's been my experience generally...people are only too grateful to have these things pointed out. The keynote is participation. Of course I wrote back to thank him and then blow me if I didn't get another letter thanking me for mine. So I wrote back saying I hadn't been expecting another letter and there was no need to have written again and was this an appropriate use of public resources? They didn't even bother to reply. Typical.





*Pause.*

I'm just waiting for the paper coming. Not that there's much in it. The correspondence I initiated on the length of the Archbishop of Canterbury's hair seems to have gone off the boil. Till I wrote up to Live Letters nobody'd actually spotted it. Various people took up the cudgels until there was an impassioned letter from the Rural Dean of Halifax who has a beard and that seems to have put the tin hat on it.

Getting dark.

The couple opposite just having their tea. No cloth on. They must have put the kiddy to bed. When I put the milk bottle out I heard it crying.

GO TO BLACK.

*Come up on Miss Ruddock sitting in an easy chair reading the newspaper. Afternoon.*

Prison, they have it easy. Television, table tennis, art. It's just a holiday camp, do you wonder there's crime? And people say, 'Well, what can you do?' Well, you can get on to your MP for a start. I do, regularly. Got a reply to one letter this morning. I'd written drawing his attention to a hitherto unnoticed factor in the rise in crime, namely the number of policemen these days who wear glasses. What chance would they have against a determined assailant? He noted my comments and promised to make them known in the proper quarter. He's Labour but it's always very good notepaper and beautifully typed.

When I'd dusted round and done my jobs I had a walk on to the end and bought a little packet of pork sausage and some Basildon Bond. Big black hair in the sausage. So I wrote off to the makers enclosing the hair. Stuck it under a bit of Sellotape. Little arrow: 'This is the hair.' I emphasised that I didn't want a substitute packet, as it was plainly manufactured under unhygienic conditions, so would they send me a refund of the purchase price plus the cost of postage. I don't want inundating with sausage.



I keep wondering about the kiddy opposite. Haven't seen it for a week or two. And they're out all the time. Every single night they go off, and the kiddy doesn't go. And nobody comes in to sit. It can't be more than five. Where do they get the money to go out, that's what I'd like to know? Because he's not working. Spends all day tinkering with that car. There wants to be a bit less of the car and a bit more of the kiddy. It never plays out and they want fresh air do kiddies, it's a well-known fact. You don't hear it crying now, nothing. And I've never seen a cloth on. Teapot stuck there. Milk bottle. It'll surprise me if they're married. He has a tattoo anyway.



GO TO BLACK.

*Come up on Miss Ruddock sitting on a dining chair in the window. Dusk.*

My mother knew everybody in this street. She could reel off the occupants of every single house. Everybody could, once upon a time. Now, they come and they go. That's why these tragedies happen. Nobody watching. If they knew they were being watched they might behave. I'd talk to next door's about it only there hasn't been any contact since the business over the dustbins. And this other side's Asians so they won't know what's normal and what isn't. Though I've a feeling he's been educated and their kiddies are always beautifully turned out. I just wish they'd do something about their privet.

I thought I'd go and have a word with the doctor, drop a hint there somehow. There used to be just one doctor. Now they've all amalgamated so it's a bit of a lucky dip. Young fellow. I said I was getting upset, like I did before. 'Before what?' he said. I said, 'It's in my notes.' So he read them and then said, 'You've been getting a bit upset, like you did before. I'll give you something to take.' So I told him about the kiddy, and he said, 'Well, these tablets will help you to take a more balanced view.' I gave them three or four days and they didn't seem to me to make much difference so I went along again. Different doctor this time. Same rigmarole. I said I didn't want any more tablets, I just wanted the name of the firm manufacturing the ones I'd already had, because I think they ought to be told if their product isn't doing the trick. The doctor said it would be easier if he gave me some new tablets and anyway I couldn't write, the firm was Swiss. I said, 'What difference does that make, everybody speaks English now.' He said, 'We don't want to get into that, do we?' and writes me another prescription. I shan't bother with it. In fact I put it down the toilet. I don't know who you write to about doctors.





After I'd had my tea I sat in the front room in the dark watching the house. He's messing about with the car, one of those little vests on they have now without sleeves. Radio going hammer and tongs. No kiddy still. I don't even know their name.

GO TO BLACK.

*Come up on Miss Ruddock in her hat and coat against a bare background.*

Thinking about it afterwards, I realised it must have been the doctor that alerted the vicar. Came round anyway. Not the old vicar. I'd have known him. This was a young fellow in a collar and tie, could have been anybody. I didn't take the chain off. I said, 'How do I know you're the vicar, have you any identification?' He shoves a little cross round the door. I said, 'What's this?' He said, 'A cross.' I said, 'A cross doesn't mean anything. Youths wear crosses nowadays. Hooligans. They wear crosses in their ears.' He said, 'Not like this. This is a real cross. A working cross. It's the tool of my trade.' I was still a bit dubious, then I saw he had cycle clips on so I let him in.

He chats for a bit, this and that, no mention of God for long enough. They keep him up their sleeve for as long as they can, vicars, they know it puts people off. Went through a long rigmarole about love. How love comes in different forms...loving friends, loving the countryside, loving music. People would be surprised to learn, he said (and I thought, 'Here we go'), people would be surprised to learn that they loved God all the time and just didn't know it. I cut him short. I said, 'If you've come round here to talk about God you're barking up the wrong tree. I'm an atheist.' He was a bit stumped, I could see. They don't expect you to be an atheist when you're a miss. Vicars, they think if you're a single person they're on a good wicket. He said, 'Well, Miss Ruddock, I shall call again. I shall look on you as a challenge.'

He hadn't been gone long when there's another knock, only this time it's a policeman, with a woman policeman in tow. Ask if they can come in and have a word. I said, 'What for?' He said, 'You know what for.' I said, 'I don't,' but I let them in. Takes his helmet off, only young and says he'll come straight to the point: was it me who'd been writing these letters? I said, 'What letters? I don't write letters.' He said, 'Letters.' I said, 'Everyone writes letters. I bet you write letters.' He said, 'Not like you, love.' I said, 'Don't love me. You'd better give me your name and number. I intend to write to your superintendent.'



It turns out it's to do with the couple opposite. I said, 'Well, why are you asking me?' He said, 'We're asking you because who was it wrote to the chemist saying his wife was a prostitute? We're asking you because who was it gave the lollipop man a nervous breakdown?' I said, 'Well, he was interfering with those children.' He said, 'The court bound you over to keep the peace. This is a serious matter.' I said, 'It is a serious matter. I can't keep the peace when there's cruelty and neglect going on under my nose. I shouldn't keep the peace when there's a child suffering. It's not my duty to keep the peace then, is it?' So then madam takes over, the understanding approach. She said didn't I appreciate this was a caring young couple? I said if they were a caring young couple why did you never see the kiddy? If they were a caring young couple why did they go gadding off every night, leaving the kiddy alone in the house? She said because the kiddy wasn't alone in the house. The kiddy wasn't in the house. The kiddy was in hospital in Bradford, that's where they were going every night. And that's where the kiddy died, last Friday. I said, 'What of? Neglect?' She said, 'No. Leukaemia.'



*Pause.*

He said, 'You'd better get your hat and coat on.'

GO TO BLACK.

*Come up on. Miss Ruddock back at home. Day.*

I've got two social workers come, one white, one black. Maureen I'm supposed to call the white one, shocking finger nails, ginger hair, and last week a hole in her tights as big as a 50p piece. She looks more in need of social work than I do. Puts it all down to men. 'We all know about men, don't we, Irene.' I never said she could call me Irene. I don't want to be called Irene. I want to be called Miss Ruddock. I'm not Irene. I haven't been Irene since Mother died. But they all call me Irene, her, the police, everybody. They think they're being nice, only it's just a nice way of being nasty. The other one's Asian, Mrs Rabindi, little red spot on her forehead, all that. Sits, talks. She's right enough. Said I'd be useful in India. You can earn a living writing letters there apparently as they're all illiterate. Something daubed on her door last week. She says it's what you get to expect if you're Asian. I said, 'Well, there's all sorts gets chucked over my wall.' We sit and talk, only she's a bit of a boring woman. I tell her I loved my mother and she says how she loved her mother. I tell her I'm frightened to walk the streets and she tells me how she's been attacked herself. Well, it doesn't get you any further. It's all 'me too'. Social work, I think it's just chiming in.





I'm on what's called a suspended sentence. It means you have to toe the line. If I write any more letters I get sent to prison. The magistrate said I was more to be pitied than anything else. I said, 'Excuse me, could I interject?' He said, 'No. Your best plan would be to keep mum.' Big fellow, navy blue suit, poppy in his buttonhole. Looked a bit of a drinker.

Maureen says I should listen to local radio. Join these phone-in things. Chat to the disc jockey and choose a record. She says they're very effective in alleviating loneliness and a sense of being isolated in the community. I said, 'Yes and they're even more effective in bumping up the phone bill.' Maureen's trying to get me on reading. I suppose to get me off writing. She says books would widen my horizon. Fetches me novels, but they don't ring true. I mean, when somebody in a novel says something like 'I've never been in an air crash', you know this means that five minutes later they will be. Say trains never crash and one does. In stories saying it brings it on. So if you get the heroine saying, 'I don't suppose I shall ever be happy', then you can bank on it there's happiness just around the corner. That's the rule in novels. Whereas in life you can say you're never going to be happy and you never are happy, and saying it doesn't make a ha'porth of difference. That's the real rule. Sometimes I catch myself thinking it'll be better the second time round. (*Pause.*) But this is it. This has been my go.

*Pause.*

New policeman now. Walks the streets, the way they used to. Part of the new policy. Community policing. Smiles. Passes the time of day. Keeping an eye on things.

Certainly keeps an eye on No. 56. In there an hour at a stretch. Timed it the other day and when eventually he comes out she's at the door in just a little shorty housecoat thing.

He's in there now.

*Pause.*

He wants reporting.

GO TO BLACK.

*Come up on Miss Ruddock against a plain institutional background. She is in a tracksuit, speaks very quickly and is radiant.*

I ought to be writing up my diary. Mrs Proctor's got us all on keeping diaries as part of Literary Appreciation. The other girls can't think what to put in theirs, me I can't think what to leave out. Trouble is I never have time to write it up, I'm three days behind as it is.

I'm that busy. In a morning it's Occupation and I've opted for bookbinding and dressmaking. In dressmaking Mrs Dunlop's chucked me in at the deep end and I'm running up a little cocktail dress. I said, 'I never have cocktails.' She said, 'Well, now you've got the dress, you can.' That's what it's geared to, this place, new horizons. It's in shantung with a little shawl collar. Lucille's making me a chunky necklace for it in Handicrafts.

I share a room with Bridget, who's from Glasgow. She's been a prostitute on and off and did away with her kiddy, accidentally, when she was drunk and upset. Bonny little face, you'd never think it. Her mother was blind, but made beautiful pastry and brought up a family of nine in three rooms. You don't know you're born I think. I'm friends with practically everyone though besides Bridget. I'm up and down this corridor; more often than not I'm still on my rounds when the bell goes.

They laugh at me, I know, but it's all in good part. Lucille says, 'You're funny you, Irene. You don't mind being in prison.' I said, 'Prison!' I said, 'Lucille. This is the first taste of freedom I've had in years.'

Of course I'm lucky. The others miss the sex. Men, men, men. They talk about nothing else.

Mind you, that's not quite the closed book it used to be. Bridget's taken me through the procedure step by step and whereas previous to this if I'd ever found myself in bed with a man I should have been like a fish out of water, now, as Bridget says, at least I know the rudiments. Of course I can't ever see it coming to that at my age, but still it's nice to have another string to your bow. They've got me smoking now and again as well. I mean, I shan't ever be a full-time smoker, I'm not that type, and I don't want to be, but it means that if I'm ever in a social situation when I'm called on to smoke, like when they're toasting the Queen, I shan't be put off my stroke. But you see, that's the whole philosophy of this place: acquiring skills.

I sailed through the secretarial course, Miss Macaulay says I'm their first Grade I. I can type like the wind. Miss Macaulay says we mustn't let the grass grow under our feet and if she goes down on her knees in Admin they might (repeat might) let me have a go on their word processor. Then the plan is: Stage One, I go on day release for a bit, followed by Stage Two a spell in a resettlement hostel where I'll be reintegrated into the community. Then finally Stage Three a little job in an office somewhere. I said to Miss Macaulay, 'Will it matter my having been in prison?' She said, 'Irene, with your qualifications it wouldn't matter if you'd been in the SS.'

But the stuff some of them come out with! You have to smile. They have words for things I didn't know there were words for, and in fact I swear myself on occasion now, though only when the need arises. The other evening I'm sat with Shirley during Association. Shirley's very obese, I think it's glandular, and we're trying to put together a letter to her boy friend. Well, she says it's her boy friend only I had to start the letter three times because first go off she says his name's Kenneth, then she says it's Mark, and finally she settles on Stephen. She stammers does Shirley and I think she just wanted a name she could say. I don't believe she has a boy friend at all, just wants to be in the swim. She shouldn't actually be in here in fact, she's not all there but there's nowhere else to put her apparently, she sets fire to places. Anyway, we're sitting in her room concocting this letter to her pretend boy friend when Black Geraldine waltzes in and drapes herself across the bed and starts chipping in, saying was this boy friend blond, did he have curly hair, and then nasty personal-type questions she should know better than to ask Shirley. And Shirley's getting confused and stammering and Geraldine's laughing, so finally I threw caution to the winds and told Geraldine to fuck up.

She screams with laughing and goes running down the corridor saying, 'Do you know what Irene said, do you know what Irene said?'

When she'd gone Shirley said, 'You shouldn't have said that.' I said, 'I know, but sometimes it's necessary.' She said, 'No, Irene. I don't mean you shouldn't have said it. Only you got it wrong. It's not fuck up.' I said, 'What is it?' She said, 'It's fuck off.' She's good-hearted.

*Pause.*

Sometimes Bridget will wake up in the middle of the night shouting, dreaming about the kiddy she killed, and I go over and sit by the bed and hold her hand till she's gone off again. There's my little clock ticking and I can hear the wind in the poplar trees by the playing field and maybe it's raining and I'm sitting there. And I'm so *happy*.

FADE OUT.

# Her Big Chance

**Lesley:** Julie Walters

PRODUCED BY **INNES LLOYD** DIRECTED BY **GILES FOSTER**
DESIGNED BY **TONY BURROUGH** MUSIC BY **GEORGE FENTON**

LESLEY IS IN HER EARLY THIRTIES. SHE IS IN HER FLAT. MORNING.

I shot a man last week. In the back. I miss it now, it was really interesting. Still, I'm not going to get depressed about it. You have to look to the future. To have something like that under your belt can be quite useful, you never know when you might be called on to repeat the experience.

It wasn't in the line of duty. I wasn't a policewoman or someone who takes violence in their stride. It was with a harpoon gun actually, but it definitely wasn't an accident. My decision to kill was arrived at only after a visible tussle with my conscience. I had to make it plain that once I'd pulled the trigger things were never going to be the same again: this was a woman at the crossroads.



It wasn't *Crossroads*, of course. They don't shoot people in *Crossroads*, at any rate not with harpoon guns. If anybody did get shot it would be with a weapon more suited to the motel ambience. I have been in *Crossroads* though, actually. I was in an episode involving a fork lunch. At least I was told it was a fork lunch, the script said it was a finger buffet. I said to the floor manager, I said, 'Rex. Are you on cans because I'd like some direction on this point. Are we toying or are we tucking in?' He said, 'Forget it. We're losing the food anyway.' I was playing Woman in a Musquash Coat, a guest at a wedding reception, and I was scheduled just to be in that one episode. However in my performance I tried to suggest I'd taken a fancy to the hotel in the hope I might catch the director's eye and he'd have me stay on after the fork lunch for the following episode which involved a full-blown weekend. So I acted an interest in the soft furnishings, running my fingers over the Formica and admiring the carpet on the walls. Only Rex came over to say that they'd put me in a musquash coat to suggest I was a sophisticated woman, could I try and look as if I was more at home in a three star motel. I wasn't at home in that sort of motel I can tell you. I said to the man I'd been put next to, who I took to be my husband, I said, 'Curtains in orange nylon and no place mats, there's not even the veneer of civilisation.' He said, 'Don't talk to me about orange nylon. I was on a jury once that sentenced Richard Attenborough to death.' We'd been told to indulge in simulated cocktail chit-chat so we weren't being unprofessional, talking. That is something I pride myself on, actually: I am professional to my fingertips.



Whatever it is I'm doing, even if it's just a walk-on, I must must must get involved, right up to the hilt. I can't help it. People who know me tell me I'm a very serious person, only it's funny, I never get to do serious parts. The parts I get offered tend to be fun-loving girls who take life as it comes and aren't afraid of a good time should the opportunity arise-type-thing. I'd call them vivacious if that didn't carry overtones of the outdoor life. In a nutshell I play the kind of girl who's very much at home on a bar stool and who seldom has to light her own cigarette. That couldn't be more different from me because for a start I'm not a smoker. I mean, I can smoke if a part requires it. I'm a professional and you need as many strings to your bow as you can in this game. But, having said that, I'm not a natural smoker and what's more I surprise my friends by not being much of a party-goer either. (Rather curl up with a book quite frankly.) *However*, this particular party I'd made an exception. Thing was I'd met this ex-graphic designer who was quitting the rat race and going off to Zimbabwe and he was having a little farewell do in the flat of an air hostess friend of his in Mitcham, would I go? I thought, well it's not every day you get somebody going off to Zimbabwe, so I said 'Yes' and I'm glad I did because that's how I got the audition.



Now my hobby is people. I collect people. So when I saw this interesting-looking man in the corner, next thing is I find myself talking to him. I said, 'You look an interesting person. I'm interested in interesting people. Hello.' He said, 'Hello.' I said, 'What do you do?' He said, 'I'm in films.' I said, 'Oh, that's interesting, anything in the pipeline?' He said, 'As a matter of fact, yes,' and starts telling me about this project he's involved in making videos for the overseas market, targeted chiefly on West Germany. I said, 'Are you the producer?' He said, 'No, but I'm on the production side, the name's Spud.' I said, 'Spud! That's an interesting name, mine's Lesley.' He said, 'As it happens, Lesley, we've got a problem at the moment. Our main girl has had to drop out because her back's packed in. Are you an actress?' I said, 'Well, Spud, interesting that you should ask because as a matter of fact I am.' He said, 'Will you excuse me one moment, Lesley?' I said, 'Why, Spud, where are you going?' He said, 'I'm going to go away, Lesley, and make one phone call.'



It transpires the director is seeing possible replacements the very next day, at an address in West London. Spud said, 'It's interesting because I'm based in Ealing.' I said, 'Isn't that West London?' He said, 'It is. Where's your stamping ground?' I said, 'Bromley, for my sins.' He said, 'That's a far-ish cry. Why not bed down at my place?' I said, 'Thank you, kind sir, but I didn't fall off the Christmas tree yesterday.' He said, 'Lesley, I have a son studying hotel management and a daughter with one kidney. Besides, I've got my sister-in-law staying. She's come up for the Ideal Home Exhibition.'

The penny began to drop when I saw the tattoo. My experience of tattoos is that they're generally confined to the lower echelons, and when I saw his vest it had electrician written all over it. I never even saw the sister-in-law. Still traipsing round Olympia probably.

GO TO BLACK.

*Come up on Lesley in the same setting. Afternoon.*

I know something about personality. There's a chapter about it in this book I'm reading. It's by an American. They're the experts where personality is concerned, the Americans; they've got it down to a fine art. It makes a big thing of interviews so I was able to test it out.



The director's not very old, blue suit, tie loose, sleeves turned back. I put him down as a university type. Said his name was Simon, which I instantly committed to memory. (That's one of the points in the book: purpose and use of name.) He said, 'Forgive this crazy time.' I said, 'I'm sorry, Simon?' He said, 'Like 9.30 in the morning.' I said, 'Simon. The day begins when the day begins. You're the director.' He said, 'Yes, well. Can you tell me what you've done?'



I said, 'Where you may have seen me, Simon, is in *Tess*. Roman Polanski. I played Chloë.' 'I don't remember her,' he said. 'Is she in the book?' I said, 'Book? This is *Tess*, Simon. Roman Polanski. Chloë was the one on the back of the farm cart wearing a shawl. The shawl was original nineteenth-century embroidery. All hand done. Do you know Roman, Simon?' He said, 'Not personally, no.' I said, 'Physically he's quite small but we had a very good working relationship. Very open.' He said that was good, because Travis in the film was very open. I said, 'Travis? That's an interesting name, Simon.' He said, 'Yes. She's an interesting character, she spends most of the film on the deck of a yacht.' I said, 'Yacht? That's interesting, Simon. My brother-in-law has a small power boat berthed at Ipswich.' He said, 'Well! Snap!' I said, 'Yes, small world!' He said, 'In an ideal world, Lesley, I'd be happy to sit here chatting all day but I have a pretty tight schedule and, although I know it's only 9.30 in the morning, could I see you in your bra and panties?' I said, '9.30 in the morning, 10.30 at night, we're both professionals, Simon, but,' I said, 'could we just put another bar on because if we don't you won't be able to tell my tits from goose-pimples.' He had to smile. That was another of the sections in the personality book: humour, usefulness of in breaking the ice.

When I'd got my things off he said, 'Well, you've passed the physical. Now the oral. Do you play chess?' I said, 'Chess, Simon? Do you mean the musical?' He said, 'No, the game.' I said, 'As a matter of fact, Simon, I don't. Is that a problem?' He said, 'Not if you water-ski. Travis is fundamentally an outdoor girl, but we thought it might be fun to make her an intellectual on the side.' I said, 'Well, Simon, I'm very happy to learn both chess and water-skiing, but could I make a suggestion? Reading generally indicates a studious temperament and I'm a very convincing reader,' I said, 'because it's something I frequently do in real life.' I could tell he was impressed. And so I said, 'Another suggestion I could make would be to kit Travis out with some glasses. Spectacles, Simon. These days they're not unbecoming and if you put Travis in spectacles with something in paperback, that says it all.' He said, 'You've been most helpful.' I said, 'The paperback could be something about the environment or, if you want to maintain the water-skiing theme, something about water-skiing and the environment possibly. I mean, Lake Windermere.'

He was showing me out by this time but I said, 'One last thought, Simon, and that is a briefcase. Put Travis in a bikini and give her a briefcase and you get the best of every possible world.' He said, 'I'm most grateful. You've given me a lot of ideas.' I said, 'Goodbye, Simon. I hope we can work together.' The drill for saying goodbye is you take the person's hand and then put your other hand over theirs, clasp it warmly while at the same time looking into their eyes, smiling and reiterating their name. This lodges you in their mind apparently. So I did all that, only going downstairs I had another thought and I popped back. He was on the phone. 'You won't believe this,' he was saying. I said, 'Don't hang up, Simon, only I just wanted to make it crystal clear that when I said briefcase I didn't mean the old-fashioned type ones, there are new briefcases now that open up and turn into a mini writing-desk. Being an up-to-the-minute girl, that would probably be the kind of briefcase Travis would have. She could be sitting in a wet bikini with a briefcase open on her knee. I've never seen that on screen so it would be some kind of first. Ciao, Simon. Take care.'

*Pause.*

That was last Friday. The book's got charts where you check your interview score. Mine was 75. Very good to excellent. Actually, I'm surprised they haven't telephoned.

GO TO BLACK.

*Come up on Lesley, who is now made up and her hair done, sitting in a small bleak room in her dressing-gown. Morning.*

You'd never think this frock wasn't made for me. I said to Scott, who's Wardrobe, 'She must be my double.' He said, 'No. You're hers. The stupid cow.'

Talk about last-minute, though. Eleven o'clock on Tuesday night I'm just wondering about having a run round with the dustette, six o'clock next morning I'm sitting in Lee-on-Solent in make-up. When the phone went telling me I'd got the part I assumed it was Simon. So I said, 'Hello Simon.' He said, 'Try Nigel.' So I said, 'Well, Nigel, can you tell Simon that I haven't let the grass grow under my feet. I now play a rudimentary game of chess.' He said, 'I don't care if you play a championship game of ice hockey, just don't get pregnant.'





It transpires the girl they'd slated to do the part had been living with a racing driver and of course the inevitable happened, kiddy on the way. So my name was next out of the hat. I said to Scott, 'I know why. They knew I had ideas about the part.' He said, 'They knew you had a 38-inch bust.' His mother's confined to a wheelchair, he's got a lot on his plate.

Anyway, I'm ready. I've been ready since yesterday morning. It was long enough before anybody came near. I had a bacon sandwich which Scott went and fetched for me while I was under the dryer. I said, 'Wasn't there a croissant?' He said, 'In Lee-on-Solent?' On *Tess* there were croissants. On *Tess* there was filter coffee. There was also some liaison.

I wanted to talk to somebody about the part, only Scott said they were out in the speed boat doing mute shots of the coastline. On *Tess* you were never sitting around. Roman anticipated every eventuality. We filmed in the middle of a forest once and the toilet arrangements were immaculate. There was also provision for a calorie-controlled diet. I said to Scott, 'I'm not used to working like this.' He said, 'Let's face it, dear. You're not used to working. Why didn't you bring your knitting?' I said, 'I do not knit, Scott.' He said, 'Well, file your nails then, pluck an eyebrow, be like me, do something constructive.' He's as thin as a rail and apparently an accomplished pianist and he seems to be make-up as well as wardrobe. On *Tess* we had three caravans for make-up alone.

Eventually Simon puts his head round the door. I said, 'Hello, Simon.' I said, 'Long time no see. Did Nigel tell you I've learned chess?' He said, 'Chess? Aren't you the one who can water-ski?' I said 'No.' He said 'Bugger' and disappeared. I said to Scott, 'Simon's on the young side for a director.' He said, 'Director? He couldn't direct you to the end of the street. He just does all the running about.' I said, 'Who is the director?' He said, 'Gunther.' I said, 'Gunther? That sounds a continental name.' He said, 'Yes. German.' I said, 'That's interesting. I went to Germany once. Dusseldorf.' He said, 'Well, you'll have a lot to talk about.' I've a feeling Scott may be gay. I normally like them only I think he's one of the ones it's turned bitter.

I'm still sitting there hours later when this other young fellow comes in. I said, 'Gunther?' He said, 'Nigel.' I said, 'We spoke on the phone.' He said, 'Yes. I'm about to commit suicide. I've just been told. You don't water-ski.' I said, 'Nigel. I could learn. I picked up the skateboard in five minutes.' He said, 'Precious. Five minutes is what we do not have. You don't by any chance have fluent French?' I said, 'No, why?' He said, 'They'd wondered about making her French.' I said, 'Nigel. How can she be French when she's called Travis? Travis isn't a French name.' He said, 'The name isn't important.' I said, 'It is to me. It's all I've got to build on.' He said, 'I'll get back to you.' I said, 'Nigel. I don't have French but what I do have is a smattering of Spanish, the legacy of several non-package type holidays on the Costa del Sol. Could Travis be half Spanish?' He said to Scott, 'We wanted someone with fluent French who could water-ski. What have we got? Someone with pidgin Spanish who plays chess.' Scott said, 'Well, don't tell me. I started off a landscape gardener.'





I was still waiting to be used in the afternoon which is when they did the water-skiing. Some girl from the local sub-aqua did it. She works part-time in the quayside restaurant where they all ate last night apparently. I saw her when she came in for make-up. Pleasant enough but didn't look a bit like me. I'm quite petite, only she was on the large side and whereas my hair is auburn hers was definitely ginger. I didn't say anything at the time but I thought if she's supposed to be me they'll be into big continuity problems so I thought I'd go in quest of the director and tell him. Nobody about on the yacht except a man who's dusting the camera. He said not to worry, the shot was p.o.v. water-skis so we'd only be seeing her elbow. I said, 'Will that work?' He said, 'Oh yes. You know, Cinema, the magic of.' Mind you, he said, if it was up to him personally, he'd rather see my elbow than hers any day. His name was Terry, what was mine? I said, 'It's a relief to find someone civil.' He said, 'It's the usual story, Lesley, Art comes in at the door, manners go out of the window. Why is making a film like being a mushroom?'

I said, 'Why, Terry?' He said, 'They keep you in the dark and every now and again somebody comes and throws a bucket of shit over you.' He laughed. I said, 'That's interesting, only Terry, they don't grow mushrooms like that now. It's all industrialised.' He said, 'You sound like a cultured person, what say we spend the evening exploring the delights of Lee-on-Solent?'

His room's nicer than mine. His bathroom's got a hair-dryer.

GO TO BLACK.

*Come up on Lesley now in a bikini and wrap. An anonymous hotel room. Evening.*

Please don't misunderstand me. I've no objection to taking my top off. But Travis as I was playing her wasn't the kind of girl who would take her top off. I said, 'I'm a professional, Nigel. Credit me with a little experience. It isn't Travis.'





I'd been sitting on the deck of the yacht all day as background while these two older men had what I presumed was a business discussion. One of them, who was covered in hair and had a real weight problem, was my boy friend apparently. You knew he was my boy friend because at an earlier juncture you'd seen him hit me across the face. Travis is supposed to be a good-time girl, though you never actually see me having a good time, just sat on this freezing cold deck plastering on the sun tan lotion. I said to Nigel, 'I don't know whether the cameraman's spotted it, Nigel, but would I be sunbathing? There's no sun.' Nigel said, 'No sun is favourite.' Nigel's first assistant, here there and everywhere. Gunther never speaks, not to me anyway. Just stands behind the camera with a little cap on. Not a patch on Roman. Roman had a smile for everybody.

Anyway, I'm sitting there as background and I say to Nigel, 'Nigel, am I right in thinking I'm a denizen of the cocktail belt?' He said, 'Why?' a bit guardedly. I said, 'Because to me, Nigel, that implies a cigarette-holder,' and I produced quite a modest one I happened to have brought with me. He went and spoke to Gunther, only Gunther ruled there was to be no smoking. I said, 'On grounds of health?' Nigel said, 'No. On grounds of it making continuity a bugger.' I'd also brought a paperback with me just to make it easier for props (which seemed to be Scott again). Only I'd hardly got it open when Nigel relieved me of it and said they were going for the sun tan lotion. I said, 'Nigel, I don't think the two are incompatible. I can apply sun tan lotion and read at the same time. That is what professionalism means.' He checked with Gunther again and he came back and said, 'Forget the book. Sun tan lotion is favourite.' I said, 'Can I

ask you something else?' He said, 'Go on.' I said, 'What is my boy friend discussing?' He said, 'Business.' I said, 'Nigel. Would I be right in thinking it's a drugs deal?' He said, 'Does it matter?' I said, 'It matters to me. It matters to Travis. It helps my character.' He said, 'What would help your character is if you took your bikini top off.' I said, 'Nigel. Would Travis do that?' I said, 'We know Travis plays chess. She also reads. Is Travis the type to go topless?' He said, 'Listen. Who do you think you're playing, Emily Brontë? Gunther wants to see your knockers.'

I didn't even look at him. I just took my top off without a word and applied sun tan lotion with all the contempt I could muster. They did the shot, then Nigel came over and said Gunther liked that and if I could give him a whisker more sensuality it might be worth a close-up. So we did it again and then Nigel came over and said Gunther was liking what I was giving them and in this next shot would I slip off my bikini bottom. I said, 'Nigel. Trust me. Travis would not do that.' Talks to Gunther. Comes back. Says Gunther agrees with me. The real Travis wouldn't. But by displaying herself naked before her boy friend's business associate she is showing her contempt for his whole way of life. I said, 'Nigel. At last

Gunther is giving me something I can relate to.' He says, 'Right! Let's shoot it! Elbow the bikini bottom!'

*Pause.*

We wrapped about six (that's film parlance for packed up). I said to Nigel, 'Did I give Gunther what he wanted? Is he happy?' He said, 'Gunther is an artist, Lesley. He's never happy. But as he said this afternoon, "At last we're cooking with gas."' I said, 'Does that mean it's good?' He said, 'Yes.' I said, 'Oh. Because I prefer electricity.'

When I got back to the hotel, it took me some time to unwind. I'd become so identified with Travis it was only when I'd had a bath and freshened up I felt her loosening her hold on me. I was looking forward to relaxing with the crew, swapping anecdotes of the day's shooting in the knowledge of a day's work well done only when I got downstairs there was nobody about, just Scott and one of the drivers. Turns out all the rest of them had gone off to supper at the restaurant run by the fat girl who did the water-skiing.





I sat in the bar for a bit. Just one fellow in there. I said, 'My hobby is people, what do you do?' Lo and behold he's on the film too, the animal handler, Kenny. In charge of the cat. I said, 'That's interesting, Kenny. I didn't know there was going to be a cat. I love cats. I love dogs too, but I love cats.' He said, 'Would you care to see her? She's asleep on my bed.' I said, 'That's convenient.' He said, 'Lesley. Don't run away with that idea. I am wedded to my small charges.' So I go up and pal on with the cat a bit and Kenny tells me about all the animals he's handled, a zebra once, a seal, an alligator and umpteen ferrets. He has a trout there too in a tank. It was going to be caught later on in the film. Quite small, only they were going to shoot it in close-up so it would look bigger.

I sat on the bed and listened to him talk about animal behaviour. I said, 'Kenny, this is the kind of evening I like, two people just talking about something interesting.'

I woke up in the night and couldn't remember where I was. Then I saw the cat sitting there, watching the trout.

GO TO BLACK.

*Come up on Lesley back in her own flat and in her ordinary clothes. Dusk.*

When you've finished a shot on a film you have to wait and see whether there's what they call a hair in the gate. It's film parlance for the all clear. Thank God there wasn't because I couldn't have done it again. I'd created Travis and though it was her lover that got shot I felt it was the something in me that was Travis that had died.

My lover's name turned out to be Alfredo. That was my big line. 'Alfredo!' He was the head of some sort of crime syndicate only everybody in the yachting fraternity thought he was very respectable and to do with the building trade. One night while Alfredo and me were ashore at a building federation dinner and dance this young undercover policeman swims out to the yacht to search it in his underpants. However, as luck would have it Travis has a headache, so she and Alfredo return early from this ultra-respectable function with Alfredo in a towering rage. Originally I was down to say, 'I can't help it, Alfredo, I have a headache,' and we tried it once or twice only Gunther then thought it would be more convincing if my headache was so bad I couldn't actually speak and Alfredo just said, 'You and your headaches.' I said, 'If it's a migraine rather than a headache Travis probably wouldn't be able to speak,' and Gunther said, 'Whatever you say.' It's wonderful, that moment, when you feel a director first begin to trust you and you can really start to build.

Anyway Travis and Alfredo come into the cabin where they find this young man behind the sofa in his underpants and Alfredo takes out his gun and says, 'How lucky lovely Travis had a headache and we had to leave our glittering reception. I was cross with her then but now my mood has changed. Offer the gentleman a drink, Travis. Then go and take your clothes off. There's nothing I like better than making love after killing a policeman. Ha ha.' I then retire to the next cabin while Alfredo taunts this bare young policeman and says he is going to kill him, but before he does so, he tells him about his drug-smuggling operation in every detail, the way criminals tend to do the minute they get somebody at gunpoint. When Travis comes back with no clothes on the young policeman is talking about the evil drugs do, all the young lives ruined and so on. Only I forgot to say that there'd been some dialogue earlier, when I was supposed to be snorkelling, about how Travis had a little brother, Craig, and how he'd got hooked on drugs and how I was heartbroken and determined to revenge myself on the culprits should I ever come across them.

So when the policeman is saying all this about the horror of drugs you can see it comes as a revelation to Travis that her lover is involved in drugs: she thinks it's just been ordinary crime and stealing electrical goods. Anyway very quietly, 'almost pensively' Gunther said, Travis picks up an underwater spear gun that happens to be on the sideboard. Nigel came over and said that ideally at this point Gunther would like to see a variety of emotions chase themselves across Travis's face as her affection for her lover, Alfredo, fights with the demands of her conscience and the memories of her little brother, Craig. You see my lover's fat finger tighten on the trigger as he gets ready to shoot the policeman, only just then I say his name very quietly, 'Alfredo'. He spins round. Travis fires the harpoon and you see the spear come out of his back, killing him, and also ruining his dinner jacket. They then follow that with a big close-up with blood and everything, and me with a single tear rolling down my cheek.

We did this in one take, which Nigel said was almost unique in the annals of filming. Only Scott has to chip in and say good job, as just having one dinner jacket was fairly unique as well. I couldn't have done it again anyway. I'd got nothing left. Except I suddenly had a flash of inspiration, the way you do when you've been to the end of the world and back, and I said to Nigel, 'Don't you think that Travis, drained of all emotion by the death of her lover, would perhaps cling on to the policeman whose life she has saved, and that they would celebrate his deliverance by having sexual intercourse there and then?'

Big debate. Gunther really liked it, only the actor playing the policeman wasn't keen. I think he may have been gay too, he had a moustache. Eventually Nigel came over and said that favourite was for the policeman to look as if he was considering having sexual intercourse and for him to run his hand speculatively over Travis's private parts, only then pity drives out lust and instead he covers up her nakedness with an oriental-type dressing-gown, the property of her dead lover. Though even at this late stage you can tell he's not ruled out the possibility because as he's fastening the dressing-gown his fingers linger over Travis's nipples. Afterwards Gunther explained that if there had been any proper funny business at this point it would have detracted from the final scene when after all the excitement the undercover policeman goes home to his regular girl friend, who cooks him a hot snack and who's a librarian, and then the final scene is of them making love, the message being that sexual intercourse is better with someone you're in love with even though they are a bit homely and work in the county library than with someone like Travis who's just after a good time. As Gunther said to me that night, 'It's a very moral film only the tragedy is, people won't see it.' I said to him, I said, 'That's interesting because I saw it that way right from the start.'

When we were in bed I said, 'If only we could have done this before.' He said, 'Lesley. I make it a rule never to lay a finger on an actress until the whole thing's in the can.' I said, 'Gunther. There's no need to explain. We're both professionals. But Gunther,' I said, 'can I ask you one question? Was I Travis? Were you pleased with my performance?' He said, 'Listen. If someone is a bad actress I can't sleep with her. So don't ask me if I was pleased with your performance. This is the proof.' He's a real artist is Gunther.

When I woke up in the morning he'd gone. I wandered down for some coffee only there was nobody from the unit about. I'd planned to say goodbye to everybody but they were off doing some establishing shots of the marina. Anyway, I went and bought a card with a sinking ship on it and put 'Goodbye, gang! See you at the première!' and left it at the desk.

As I came out with my bags Scott was just loading the laundry. I said, 'Ciao, Scott. It's been a pleasure working with you.' He said, 'You win some, you lose some.' I said, 'Now it's back to real life.' He said, 'Some of us never left it.' It's funny the way their clothes are always too small.

The film's coming out in West Germany initially, then Turkey possibly. Gunther says it'll make me quite famous. Well, I suppose I shall have to live with that. Only I'm not just going to sit here and wait for the phone to ring. No fear. I'm going to acquire another skill. Spoken Italian. Selling valuable oil paintings. Canoeing. You see, the more you have to offer as a person the better you are as an actress. Acting is really just giving.

FADE OUT.

# Soldiering On

**Muriel:** Stephanie Cole

PRODUCED BY **INNES LLOYD** DIRECTED BY **TRISTRAM POWELL**
DESIGNED BY **TONY BURROUGH** MUSIC BY **GEORGE FENTON**

MURIEL IS A BRISK, SENSIBLE WOMAN IN HER LATE FIFTIES. SHE IS IN A TWEED SKIRT AND CARDIGAN WITH SOME PEARLS, AND WE COME ON HER SETTLED IN A CORNER OF HER COMFORTABLE HOME. IT IS AFTERNOON.

It's a funny time, three o'clock, too late for lunch but a bit early for tea. Besides, there were one or two brave souls who'd trekked all the way from Wolverhampton; I couldn't risk giving them tea or we'd have had a mutiny on our hands. And I think people like to be offered something even if they don't actually eat it. One's first instinct was to make a beeline for the freezer and rout out the inevitable quiche, but I thought, 'Muriel, old girl, that's the coward's way out,' so the upshot was I stopped up till two in the morning trundling out a selection of my old standards… chicken in a lemon sauce, beef en croute from the old Colchester days (I thought of Jessie Marchant), and bushels of assorted salads. As it happened it wasn't exactly a salady day, quite crisp for April actually, however Mabel warmed up the proceedings with one of her famous soups, conjured up out of thin air, so we lived to fight another day. Nobody could quite put their finger on the flavour, so I was able to go round saying, 'Have you guessed the soup yet?' and that broke the ice a bit. I don't know what had got into Mabel but she'd gone mad and added a pinch of curry and that foxed most people. It was cauliflower actually.

Still, it was a bit sticky at the start as these occasions generally are. There were people there one didn't know from Adam (all the Massey-Ferguson people for instance, completely unknown quantities to me), and then lots of people I knew I should know and didn't. But whenever I saw anyone looking lost I thought of Ralph and grabbed hold of someone I did know and breezed up saying, 'This is Jocelyn. She's at the Royal College of Art. I don't know your name but the odds are you're in agricultural machinery,' and then left them to it. It was a case of light the blue touch paper and retire.

Knowing Ralph, of course, it was a real mixed bag. Several there from the Sports Council and quite a contingent from Tonbridge, some Friends of Norwich Cathedral and the Discharged Prisoners Aid Society, Madge and Perce whom we met on the *Mauretania* on our honeymoon, Donald and Joyce Bannerman who were actually en route for Abu Dhabi, then Donald bought a paper at Heathrow, saw the announcement and came straight down. And one sweet old man who'd come all the way over from Margate. He said, 'You won't remember me, Mrs Carpenter, but I'm a member of the criminal fraternity.' I shrieked. As the vicar said: Ralph touched life at many points.

The children magnificent, of course, or Giles at any rate. Luckily Margaret didn't appear. But Giles took off all the Household Brigade people on a tour of the garden while Pippa coped with some of the bigwigs from the City. 'I don't think you know George,' I heard one of them say, 'George cracks the whip at Goodison, Brown.' Poor souls, they both of them deserved medals. And Crispin and Lucy angelic, Crispin popping in and out of people's legs reaching up to fill the glasses. I wanted them to have a rest. 'No,' said Giles, 'let them do it. They adored their grandpa.' 'Adored him,' said Pippa, 'like we all did.'

The church had been absolutely chocker and I'd managed not to blub until right at the finish when they struck up with 'I vow to thee my country'. And then I'd a hundred and one things to do so I was perfectly all right until I saw awful Angela Gillespie had made the mistake of talking to boring old Frank from the firm, and I heard the dreaded words 'fork-lift trucks' and thought how many times I used to have to shut Ralph up in similar circumstances, and the idea of shutting Ralph up at all set me off instantly and I had to nip into the pantry to staunch the flow, shortly to be followed by Mabel who'd just fallen over one of his old wellingtons and promptly gone into floods. So we had a good laugh and a good cry over that before powdering our noses and hurling ourselves back into the fray.





When everybody'd gone I'm just having five minutes in the chair before tackling the debris when Margaret comes plunging into the room. She said, 'What were all those people?' I said, 'It was a kind of party for Daddy.' She said, 'Why? Is he dead?' I said, 'You know he's dead.' She said, 'Who killed him?' I said, 'Don't be such a donkey. Come along and we'll find you a tablet.' Some of Ralph's medicine's still in the cupboard. Fat lot of good that did, I thought, and poured it down the lav. Then felt a bit choked.

Anyway the tablet did the trick. I heard her walking about at two in the morning but I didn't get up. Except then I had to get up anyway because it suddenly came to me, in all the excitement I'd completely forgotten to feed the dogs.

GO TO BLACK.

*Come up on Muriel sitting in an armchair. Evening.*

Everybody I run into says not to take any big decisions. I staggered into the Community Centre bearing Ralph's entire wardrobe which Angela Gillespie had nipped in smartish and earmarked for Muscular Dystrophy.

Five minutes later, Brenda Bousfield had come knocking at the door on behalf of Cystic Fibrosis. Knives out straightaway, I practically had to separate them. In fact I did separate them in the end, the City suits to Angela and Brenda the tweeds. All lovely stuff. Beautiful dinner jacket from Hawes and Curtis, done for Giles if he hadn't got so fat. Mind you, he didn't want the ties either. Angela did. 'Lovely jumble,' she said. 'How're you coping? Don't take any big decisions, one day at a time, I don't see any shoes.'

Actually I'd been silly and kept his shoes back. I loved his shoes. Always used to clean them. 'My shoeshine lady.' 'Whatever you do,' Angela said, 'don't give them to Brenda. They're top-heavy on staff, their group, it's well known. It all goes on the admin. We can use shoes.'

I thought I'd go into the library and see if Miss Dunsmore could find me something on bereavement. That's something I learned from Ralph: plug into other people's experience, pool your resources. 'A new experience is like travelling through unknown country. But remember, others have taken this road before you, old girl, and left notes. So Question no. 1: Is there a map? Question no. 2: Am I taking advantage of all the information available? It doesn't matter if you're going to get married, commit a burglary or keep a guinea pig; efficiency is the proper collation of information.' Oh Ralph.



Miss Dunsmore did a reconnoitre round, but the only information she could come up with was a book about burial customs in Papua New Guinea. I think even Ralph would draw the line at that. However, she thought the Health Centre did a pamphlet on bereavement. Miss Dunsmore said she wasn't offering this as consolation but apparently elephants go into mourning and so, very strangely, does the pike. So we chatted about that for a bit. Told me not to take any big decisions, and if I was throwing away any of his books could I steer them her way as she ran some sort of reading service for the disabled.

I dropped into the Health Centre and the receptionist said there was a pamphlet on death; they'd had some on the counter, only the tots kept taking them to scribble on, so they hadn't re-ordered. She said she'd skimmed through it and the gist of it was not to take any big decisions and to throw yourself into something. I said, 'You don't mean the canal?' She said, 'Come again?' Nobody expects you to make jokes. As I was going out she called me back and said did Ralph wear spectacles? Because if he did, not to throw away the old pairs as owing to cutbacks they'd started a spectacles recycling scheme.

Back at base Mabel said Margaret had been plonked on the chair in the passage all morning with her bag packed and her outside coat on, and for some reason wellington boots. Said the police were coming. We manhandled her upstairs, and after about seventeen goes I managed to smuggle in a tablet which did the trick and she'd just settled down for a little zizz when who should draw up at the door but Giles.

He'd cancelled all his appointments, eluded the guards at the office and just belted down the A12 because he suddenly thought I might need cheering up, bless him. He could always get round Mabel ever since he was little, so she agrees to hold the fort while he whisks me off to lunch at somewhere rather swish. I thought to myself, I hope you're watching, Ralph, you old rascal, and eating your words. Ralph and Giles never got on for more than five minutes whereas, it's funny, he was always dotty about Mags.



When eventually we get back, what with all the wine etc. (I mean pudding *and* cheese), I'm just longing to put my head down, but Giles cracks the whip and gets me to sign lots of papers. It turns out Ralph's left me very nicely off. What with the house and all his various holdings, one way and another I'm quite a rich lady. He's tied a bit up for Margaret, nothing specific for Giles, but he doesn't mind because of course he doesn't need any and when I go he'll get it all anyway. But what I do have is what Giles calls a liquidity problem, and the first item on the agenda is to give me some ready cash, hence the papers. Then something about buying a forest. Bit wary to start with, said, 'Can I not mull it?' and Giles said, 'Well you can, but the index is going down.' I said, 'What about Mr Sherlock?' Giles said, 'You know what lawyers are.' Wish old Ralph could have seen me, signing away. He never showed me any papers at all, whereas Giles took me through them and explained it all. I suppose it's a different generation. What he did do, which made me feel a tiny bit shifty, was to take away three or four of the best pictures, the two carriage clocks and a couple of other choice items. Said that when the sharks from the revenue came round to assess the stuff for estate duty these were just the items that would bump the figure up. I said, 'What about the inventory?' Giles said, 'I think we'll just drag our brogues on that one.' Apparently everybody does it. He's just going to keep the stuff under the bed at Sloane Street until the heat is off, then back they come.



Margaret still lying on the bed when I went upstairs. Asleep she looks quite presentable. Daddy's little girl. Not so little now, those great legs. But as Mabel says, 'It looks as if we're on the hospital trail again.' If she goes in, I could perhaps go to Siena. Except I've nobody to go with. One keeps forgetting that.

GO TO BLACK.

*Come up on Muriel sitting at a table writing letters. Afternoon.*

It's not an ideal place, no one is saying it is. Even Giles doesn't say that. In fact it's a perfect example of one of those places they're always famously about to scrap. Started life as a workhouse probably, during the Napoleonic Wars, and *qua* building not displeasing. As someone weaned on Nikolaus Pevsner and practically a founder member of the National Trust I wouldn't alter a single brick. And as an arts centre first rate. As a museum of industrial archaeology...couldn't be bettered. Or as a craft centre, weaving, pottery, a shop-window where craftsmen and craftswomen could make and display their wares...absolutely ideal, the very place. But as a mental hospital...oh no, no, no, no, no.



The food, for instance. The food has to cross a courtyard – the kitchen is so far away for all I know it may have to cross a frontier. One toilet per floor...I just put my head round the door and wished I hadn't; no telephone that I could see and the beds so crammed together if you got out of one you'd be into another. Dreadful.



And of course I keep thinking of Ridgeways, the cup of tea, the matron's parlour and that immaculate lawn. It would break old Ralph's heart. But Ridgeways costs money. It always did. First of the month, beg to inform, respectfully submit, all very nice but £600 on the dot. And more. And more. And as Giles says, 'Mummy no can do. That kind of money we do not have.' Well we do, but it's all tied up.

And whereas in normal circumstances one would have fought tooth and nail to keep her in the private sector, just out of respect for Daddy, nowadays we are in what Giles calls a different ball game. And the old thing minds. Goodness, he minds. I wanted him to come with me today but just the idea of the place upsets him so much he won't even set foot in it. And actually I feel the same, but where is that going to get us? I thought of Ralph (as if I ever think of anybody else) and I thought, 'Come on, Muriel. You're a widow lady, you've got time on your hands, if anybody's in a position to roll their sleeves up it's you.' So today when I paid Mags a visit I got the name of the hospital secretary, almoner it used to be called in my day, and bearded him in his den. He did have a beard actually and looked pretty sorry for himself besides. It turns out he has to precept for absolutely everything down to the last toilet roll, and if he does have any brainwaves about improvements and can sell them to his own management committee, he's still at the mercy of the regional spending programme.

I asked about a table-tennis table. He said, 'My point exactly.' A table-tennis table would mean going cap in hand to Ipswich, which he's not anxious to do since the vegetable steamer's on its last legs. And on the rare occasions he does have a bit of latitude he finds his hands are tied by NUPE. Well, the upshot is I'm writing sheaves of letters to everybody I've ever heard of in an effort to plug the hospital into the coffee-morning circuit and get a support group started. What I'm saying is that mental illness is a scourge. It's also a mystery, can occur in the best-regulated families and nobody knows why. I mean, take us. Why have we been singled out? Loving parents. Perfectly normal childhood, then this.

When I went in this afternoon, Margaret was weaving a basket, and not making a bad stab at it really, all things considered. It's lucky I arrived when I did because she'd just got to the part where she had to integrate the handle with the main body and she was making a real pig's breakfast of it. So I got cracking and showed her the whys and wherefores and actually ended up making both handles. Which seemed to make her a lot happier. She's never been much good with her hands. Giles was a real wizard.



A propos Giles there's a bit of a crisis with the funds apparently. Nothing serious. A chum's let him down. Didn't read the small print. Says it's nothing to worry about, though we may have to pull our horns in a bit further. So I said, 'All hands to the pumps. With all Daddy's contacts in the City why don't I start up a little catering business, executive lunches and the like? Good nursery food and lashings of it.' Giles not sure. Thought these days they wanted something a bit more nouvelle. I laughed, I said, 'Don't you believe it. Men are overgrown schoolboys, always were. Preached salad at Ralph for years and what good did it do?' Giles said, 'Small detail, Mum: what are you going to use for capital?' So that put the tin hat on that one. It's this bloody liquidity thing. It's funny I never heard Ralph mention it.



GO TO BLACK.

*Come up on Muriel in a bare unfurnished room. A suitcase open. A tea-chest. Afternoon.*

Job sorting out the one or two things I want to keep, though quite honestly I'm not sorry to see the back of most of it. I feel it puts me more in the same boat as Ralph. Lay not up for yourself treasures on earth type thing. The lilies of the field syndrome. Said this to the vicar who was looking round. He thought this was a healthy attitude and how much did

I think the walnut sidetable might fetch, it would go so well in their hall. Huge marquee on the lawn. People trooping through the house, and Angela Gillespie never away. Said how horrid it must be to see people poking about among one's prized possessions. I said, 'Yes,' but it isn't really. The person I do feel sorry for is Mabel, who's had it to polish all these years. Still, she was getting on like a house on fire with the auctioneer's men, who were all so careful and polite I'd have married any one of them on the spot. Angela beefing on about all the dealers being here, putting up the prices, I thought good job. Still, however much it all fetches it will only be a drop in the ocean.

At one point Angela got the Duttons in a corner and started telling the tale. Said Giles had always been a wrong 'un. I turned round and said she didn't know what she was talking about, it had been a genuine mistake. She said, 'Mistake? Hundreds of people losing their life savings a mistake?' I said, 'So why do you think I'm selling up?' She said, 'It wasn't your fault. Why should you suffer? That's what worries me, Muriel, it's not fair on you.' Fair on me or not it didn't stop her buying the corner cupboard. She's had her eye on it for years.





I suppose Giles has been a scamp. But I don't think he's been wicked. Just not very bright that's all. Still, Sloane Street is in Pippa's name so that's a blessing, and the school fees were covenanted for years ago so it's not all gloom. I sat under the chestnut tree while the sale was going on, and thought how none of this would have happened if Ralph hadn't died. Then I heard him say, 'Buck up, old girl,' and went and gave a hand with the tea. I haven't told Margaret yet. Her fourteen-year-old psychiatrist thinks this may not be the moment. Sees some signs of improvement. Margaret brought him some tulips last week. Picked them from one of the hospital flowerbeds. I apologised and said I could give them some of our bulbs. He said not at all, it was a sign she was becoming more outgoing. Wanted to know about Ralph and Margaret. I said, 'In what way?' He said, 'No particular way. When she was little.' I said, 'Ralph was fond of her: she was his little girl.' He said, 'Yes.'

Took the dogs up the hill later on. They're next I suppose. Bloody psychiatrist.

GO TO BLACK.

*Come up on Muriel in a plain boarding-house room. Evening.*

Crack of dawn this morning I routed out my trusty green cossy and spent a happy half-hour breasting the billows. The old cossy's seen better days and the moth has got into the bust but as the only people about were one or two brave souls walking the dog I didn't frighten the troops.

Came back hungry as a hunter so boiled myself an egg on the ring and had it with a slice of Ryvita, sitting in the window. Sun just catches it for an hour then, lovely. I tidied the room, did one or two jobs, and then toddled along to the library and had a walk round Boots by which time it was getting on for lunchtime, it's surprising how time does go. When I think of the things I used to get through in the old days I wonder how I did it.

Been here about a month now. Got onto it via an advert in *The Lady*. Sledmere it's called, 'Holiday flatlets'. Off season, of course, and quite reasonable. I haven't quite got the town sorted out yet. I feel sure there must be a community here if only I can put my finger on it. I had a word with a young woman at the Town Hall. Blue fingernails but civil enough otherwise. Said was I interested in Meals On Wheels. I said, 'Rather. I was 2 i/c Meals on Wheels for the whole of Sudbury,' a fund of experience. Brawn not too good but brains available to be picked at any time. She looked a bit blank. Turns out she meant did I want to be on the receiving end. I said, 'Not on your life.' But message received and understood. The old girl's past it. Hence the swim, I suppose.

Still, I soldier on and it's not quite orphans of the storm time. I look round the shops quite a bit and if I'm lucky I run into Angela Gillespie who's got her mother in a home here and comes over from time to time. We have coffee and a natter about the old days. Though I can't do that too often. Morning coffee these days seems to cost a king's ransom. And with me there doesn't have to be coffee. I can talk to anybody. The other morning I got chatting to one of these young men in orange who bang their tambourines in the precinct. Came up to me rattling his bowl, shaven head but otherwise quite sensible. His view is that life is some kind of prep. Trial run. Thinks we're being buffed up for a better role next time. As sensible as anything else I suppose. I said, 'Well, I just hope it's not in Hunstanton.' (*She laughs.*)

The big bright spot on the horizon is Margaret. Heaps better, lost a lot of weight, got rid of that terrible cardigan and now is quite a good-looking young woman. In a hostel up to pres. but planning on getting a small flat. Came down last week and says next time it could be under her own steam, takes her driving test in ten days. Miracle. She took me out to lunch just like a normal girl. Talked about Ralph etc. Doesn't blame him, wishes he were alive. I don't know what I think. Sorry for him, I suppose.

She paid the bill and left a tip, just as if she'd been doing it all her life. Of course she'll be nicely off now, Ralph tied it all up so tight even Giles couldn't get his hands on it, the rascal.

Don't see him and Pippa much, not a peep out of them for over a month now. Doesn't like to come down, says it upsets him. Don't know why. Doesn't upset me. Miss the tinies. Not so tiny, Lucy'll be twelve now. And twelve is like fifteen. Married next. I'd seen myself as a model grandmother, taking them to *Peter Pan* and the Science Museum. Not to be. Another dream bites the dust.

My big passion now is the telly box. Never bothered with it before. These days I watch it all the time. And I'm not the discerning viewer. No fear. Rubbish. Australian series in the afternoons, everything. Glued to it all. Fan.

*The dialogue is more broken up now.*

I sometimes wonder if I killed Ralph. All those death-dealing breakfasts.

We haven't had much weather to speak of. Eat less now. A buttered scone goes a long way.

*She picks up a Walkman and headphones.*

This is my new toy. Seen children with them, never appreciated what they were. Asked a young man for a listen in the precinct. Revelation. Saved up and bought one. Get the cassettes out of the library. Worth its weight in gold. Marvellous.

*She puts it on and henceforth speaks in bursts and too loudly.*

I wouldn't want you to think this was a tragic story.



*Pause.*

I'm not a tragic woman.

*Pause.*

I'm not that type.



FADE OUT *to the faint sound of the music, possibly Johann Strauss.*

# A **Cream Cracker** under the Settee

**Doris:** Thora Hird
**Policeman:** Steven Beard

PRODUCED BY **INNES LLOYD** DIRECTED BY **STUART BURGE**
DESIGNED BY **TONY BURROUGH** MUSIC BY **GEORGE FENTON**

DORIS IS IN HER SEVENTIES AND THE PLAY IS SET IN THE LIVING-ROOM AND HALLWAY OF HER SEMI-DETACHED HOUSE. SHE IS SITTING SLIGHTLY AWKWARDLY ON A LOW CHAIR AND RUBBING HER LEG. MORNING.

It's such a silly thing to have done.

*Pause.*

I should never have tried to dust. Zulema says to me every time she comes, 'Doris. Do not attempt to dust. The dusting is my department. That's what the council pay me for. You are now a lady of leisure. Your dusting days are over.' Which would be all right provided she did dust. But Zulema doesn't dust. She half-dusts. I know when a place isn't clean.



When she's going she says, 'Doris. I don't want to hear that you've been touching the Ewbank. The Ewbank is out of bounds.' I said, 'I could just run round with it now and again.' She said, 'You can't run anywhere. You're on trial here.' I said, 'What for?' She said, 'For being on your own. For not behaving sensibly. For not acting like a woman of seventy-five who has a pacemaker and dizzy spells and doesn't have the sense she was born with.' I said, 'Yes, Zulema.'



She says, 'What you don't understand, Doris, is that I am the only person that stands between you and Stafford House. I have to report on you. The Welfare say to me every time, "Well, Zulema, how is she coping? Wouldn't she be better off in Stafford House?"' I said, 'They don't put people in Stafford House just for running round with the Ewbank.' 'No,' she says. 'They bend over backwards to keep you in your own home. But, Doris, you've got to meet them halfway. You're seventy-five. Pull your horns in. You don't have to swill the flags. You don't have to clean the bath. Let the dirt wait. It won't kill you. I'm here every week.'

I was glad when she'd gone, dictating. I sat for a bit looking up at me and Wilfred on the wedding photo. And I thought, 'Well, Zulema, I bet you haven't dusted the top of that.' I used to be able to reach only I can't now. So I got the buffet and climbed up. And she hadn't. Thick with dust. Home help. Home hindrance. You're better off doing it yourself. And I was just wiping it over when, oh hell, the flaming buffet went over.

*Pause.*

You feel such a fool. I can just hear Zulema. 'Well, Doris, I did tell you.' Only I think I'm all right. My leg's a bit numb but I've managed to get back on the chair. I'm just going to sit and come round a bit. Shakes you up, a fall.

*Pause.*

Shan't let on I was dusting.

*She shoves the duster down the side of the chair.*

Dusting is forbidden.

*She looks down at the wedding photo on the floor.*

Cracked the photo. We're cracked, Wilfred.



*Pause.*



The gate's open again. I thought it had blown shut, only now it's blown open. Bang bang bang all morning, it'll be bang bang bang all afternoon.

Dogs coming in, all sorts. You see Zulema should have closed that, only she didn't.

*Pause.*

The sneck's loose, that's the root cause of it. It's wanted doing for years. I kept saying to Wilfred, 'When are you going to get round to that gate?' But oh no. It was always the same refrain. 'Don't worry, Mother. I've got it on my list.' I never saw no list. He had no list. I was the one with the list. He'd no system at all, Wilfred. 'When I get a minute, Doris.' Well, he's got a minute now, bless him.

*Pause.*

Feels funny this leg. Not there.

*Pause*

Some leaves coming down now. I could do with trees if they didn't have leaves, going up and down the path. Zulema won't touch them. Says if I want leaves swept I've to contact the Parks Department.

I wouldn't care if they were my leaves. They're not my leaves. They're next-door's leaves. We don't have any leaves. I know that for a fact. We've only got the one little bush and it's an evergreen, so I'm certain they're not my leaves. Only other folks won't know that. They see the bush and they see the path and they think, 'Them's her leaves.' Well, they're not.

I ought to put a note on the gate. 'Not my leaves.' Not my leg either, the way it feels. Gone to sleep.

*Pause.*

I didn't even want the bush, to be quite honest. We debated it for long enough. I said, 'Dad. Is it a bush that will make a mess?' He said, 'Doris. Rest assured. This type of bush is very easy to follow,' and fetches out the catalogue. '"This labour-saving variety is much favoured by retired people." Anyway,' he says, 'the garden is my department.' Garden! It's only the size of a tablecloth. I said, 'Given a choice, Wilfred, I'd have preferred concrete.' He said, 'Doris. Concrete has no character.' I said, 'Never mind character, Wilfred, where does hygiene come on the agenda?' With concrete you can feel easy in your mind. But no. He had to have his little garden even if it was only a bush. Well, he's got his little garden now. Only I bet that's covered in leaves. Graves, gardens, everything's to follow.

I'll make a move in a minute. See if I can't put the kettle on. Come on leg. Wake up.

GO TO BLACK.

*Come up on Doris sitting on the floor with her back to the wall. The edge of a tiled fireplace also in shot.*

Fancy, there's a cream cracker under the settee. How long has that been there? I can't think when I last had cream crackers. She's not half done this place, Zulema.

I'm going to save that cream cracker and show it her next time she starts going on about Stafford House. I'll say, 'Don't Stafford House me, lady. This cream cracker was under the settee. I've only got to send this cream cracker to the Director of Social Services and you'll be on the carpet. Same as the cream cracker. I'll be in Stafford House, Zulema, but you'll be in the Unemployment Exchange.'

I'm en route for the window only I'm not making much headway. I'll bang on it. Alert somebody. Don't know who. Don't know anybody round here now. Folks opposite, I don't know them. Used to be the Marsdens. Mr and Mrs Marsden and Yvonne, the funny daughter. There for years. Here before we were, the Marsdens. Then he died, and she died, and Yvonne went away somewhere. A home, I expect.

Smartish woman after them. Worked at Wheatley and Whiteley, had a three-quarter-length coat. Used to fetch the envelopes round for the blind. Then she went and folks started to come and go. You lose track. I don't think they're married, half of them. You see all sorts. They come in the garden and behave like animals. I find the evidence in a morning.

*She picks up the photograph that has fallen from the wall.*

Now, Wilfred.



*Pause.*

I can nip this leg and nothing.

*Pause.*

Ought to have had a dog. Then it could have been barking of someone. Wilfred was always hankering after a dog. I wasn't keen. Hairs all up and down, then having to take it outside every five minutes. Wilfred said he would be prepared to undertake that responsibility. The dog would be his province. I said, 'Yes, and whose province would all the little hairs be?' I gave in in the finish, only I said it had to be on the small side. I didn't want one of them great lolloping, lamppost-smelling articles. And we never got one either. It was the growing mushrooms in the cellar saga all over again. He never got round to it. A kiddy'd've solved all that. Getting mad ideas. Like the fretwork, making toys and forts and whatnot. No end of money he was going to make. Then there was his phantom allotment. Oh, he was going to be coming home with leeks and spring cabbage and I don't know what. 'We can be self-sufficient in the vegetable department, Doris.' Never materialised. I was glad. It'd've meant muck somehow.

Hello. Somebody coming. Salvation.

*She cranes up towards the window.*

Young lad. Hello. Hello.

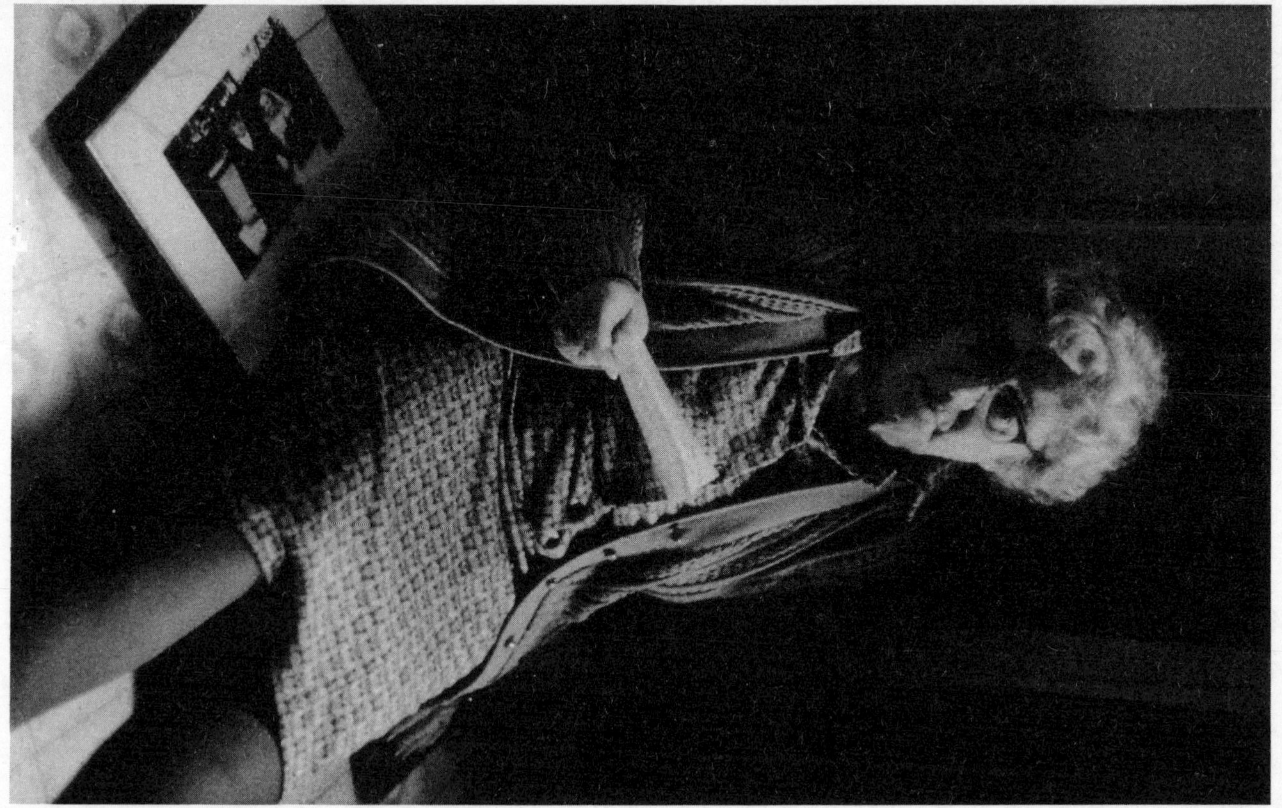

*She begins to wave.*

The cheeky monkey. He's spending a penny. Hey.

*She shouts.*

Hey. Get out. Go on. Clear off. You little demon. Would you credit it? Inside our gate. Broad daylight. The place'll stink.

*A pause as she realises what she has done.*

He wouldn't have known what to do anyway. Only a kiddy. The policeman comes past now and again. If I can catch him. Maybe the door's a better bet. If I can get there I can open it and wait while somebody comes past.





*She starts to heave herself up.*

This must be what they give them them frame things for.

GO TO BLACK.

*Come up on Doris sitting on the floor in the hall, her back against the front door, the letter-box above her head.*

This is where we had the pram. You couldn't get past for it. Proper prams then, springs and hoods. Big wheels. More like cars than prams. Not these fold-up jobs. You were proud of your pram. Wilfred spotted it in the *Evening Post*. I said, 'Don't let's jump the gun, Wilfred.' He said, 'At that price, Doris? This is the chance of a lifetime.'

*Pause.*

Comes under this door like a knife. I can't reach the lock. That's part of the Zulema regime. 'Lock it and put it on the chain, Doris. You never know who comes. It may not be a bona fide caller.' It never is a bona fide caller. I never get a bona fide caller.

Couple came round last week. Braying on the door. They weren't bona fide callers, they had a Bible. I didn't go. Only they opened the letter-box and started shouting about Jesus. 'Good news,' they kept shouting. 'Good news.' They left the gate open, never mind good news.

They ought to get their priorities right. They want learning that on their instruction course. Shouting about Jesus and leaving gates open. It's hypocrisy is that. It is in my book anyway. 'Love God and close all gates.'

*She closes her eyes. We hear some swift steps up the path and the letter-box opens as a leaflet comes through. Swift steps away again as she opens her eyes.*

Hello, hello.

*She bangs on the door behind her.*

Help. Help. Oh stink.



*She tries to reach the leaflet.*

What is it? Minicabs? 'Your roof repaired'?

*She gets the leaflet.*



'Grand carpet sale.' Carpet sales in chapels now. Else Sikhs.

*She looks at the place where the pram was.*

I wanted him called John. The midwife said he wasn't fit to be called anything and had we any newspaper? Wilfred said, 'Oh yes. She saves newspaper. She saves shoeboxes as well.' I must have fallen asleep because when I woke up she'd gone. I wanted to see to him. Wrapping him in newspaper as if he was dirty. He wasn't dirty, little thing. I don't think Wilfred minded. A kiddy. It was the same as the allotment and the fretwork. Just a craze. He said, 'We're better off, Doris. Just the two of us.' It was then he started talking about getting a dog.

If it had lived I might have had grandchildren now. Wouldn't have been in this fix. Daughters are best. They don't migrate.

*Pause.*

I'm going to have to migrate or I'll catch my death.

*She nips her other leg.*

This one's going numb now.

*She picks up the photo.*

Come on, Dad. Come on, numby leg.

GO TO BLACK.

*Come up on Doris sitting with her back against the settee under which she spotted the cream cracker. It is getting dark.*

I've had this frock for years. A lame woman ran it up for me that lived down Tong Road. She made me a little jersey costume I used to wear with my tan court shoes. I think I've still got it somewhere. Upstairs. Put away. I've got umpteen pillowcases, some we got given when we were first married. Never used. And the blanket I knitted for the cot. All its little coats and hats.





*She puts her hand down.*

Here's this cream cracker.

*She rubs it.*

Naught wrong with it.

*She eats it.*

Making a lot of crumbs. Have to have a surreptitious go with the Ewbank. 'Doris. The Ewbank is out of bounds.' Out of bounds to her too, by the looks of it. A cream cracker under the settee. She wants reporting. Can't report her now. I've destroyed the evidence.

*Pause.*

I could put another one under, they'd never know. Except they might say it was me. 'Squatting biscuits under the settee, Doris. You're not fit to be on your own. You'd be better off in Stafford House.'

*Pause.*

We were always on our own, me and Wilfred. We weren't gregarious. We just weren't the gregarious type. He thought he was, but he wasn't.

Mix. I don't want to mix. Comes to the finish and they suddenly think you want to mix. I don't want to be stuck with a lot of old lasses. And they all smell of pee. And daft half of them, banging tambourines. You go daft there, there's nowhere else for you to go but daft. Wearing somebody else's frock. They even mix up your teeth. I am H.A.P.P.Y. I am not H.A.P.P.Y. I am un-H.A.P.P.Y. Or I would be.

And Zulema says, 'You don't understand, Doris. You're not up to date. They have lockers, now. Flowerbeds. They have their hair done. They go on trips to Wharfedale.' I said, 'Yes. Smelling of pee.' She said, 'You're prejudiced, you.' I said, 'I am, where hygiene's concerned.'



When people were clean and the streets were clean and it was all clean and you could walk down the street and folks smiled and passed the time of day, I'd leave the door on the latch and go on to the end for some toffee, and when I came back Dad was home and the cloth was on and the plates out and we'd have our tea. Then we'd side the pots and I'd wash up while he read the paper and we'd eat the toffees and listen to the wireless all them years ago when we were first married and I was having the baby.



Doris and Wilfred. They don't get called Doris now. They don't get called Wilfred. Museum, names like that. That's what they're all called in Stafford House. Alice and Doris. Mabel and Gladys. Antiques. Keep them under lock and key. 'What's your name? Doris? Right. Pack your case. You belong in Stafford House.'

A home. Not me. No fear.

*She closes her eyes. A pause.*

POLICEMAN'S VOICE. Hello. Hello.

*Doris opens her eyes but doesn't speak.*

Are you all right?

*Pause.*

DORIS. No. I'm all right.
POLICEMAN. Are you sure?
DORIS. Yes.
POLICEMAN. Your light was off.
DORIS. I was having a nap.
POLICEMAN. Sorry. Take care.

*He goes.*

DORIS. Thank you.

*She calls again.*

Thank you.

*Long pause.*

You've done it now, Doris. Done it now, Wilfred.

*Pause.*

I wish I was ready for bed. All washed and in a clean nightie and the bottle in, all sweet and crisp and clean like when I was little on Baking Night, sat in front of the fire with my long hair still.

*Her eyes close and she sings a little to herself. The song, which she only half remembers, is My Alice Blue Gown.*

*Pause.*

Never mind. It's done with now, anyway.

LIGHT FADES.

# Introduction to *Talking Heads 2*

These six monologues have been a long time coming: I've been intermittently trying to write them since 1988 when the first series went out. Had I not stopped at six then, I think I could have gone on and written another half dozen without too much trouble, but seeing the first lot produced with a measure of success made the next batch harder to do. I've kept putting them aside and even when they were, in effect, finished I left them in a drawer for a year as I felt they were too gloomy to visit on the public.

This gloom is not deliberate: it is just the way they have turned out. Nor is it that, as I grow older, I take a grimmer view of the world. It's simply that, though I may sit down with the intention of writing something funny, it seldom comes out that way any more. I don't feel called upon to offer any further explanation, though I shall doubtless be asked to account for it, if only by students.





A few years after the televising of the first series of *Talking Heads* they were made part of the A Level syllabus. While I was not unflattered by this it did land me with dozens of letters from candidates wanting a low-down on the text. Some of them, it was plain, thought that writing to the author was a useful way of getting their homework done for them; others were more serious, genuinely feeling that I could give them some clues as to the inner meaning of what I had written. I fell in with very few of these requests, generally sending a postcard saying that their ideas about the monologues were as good as mine and they should treat me like a dead author, who was thus unavailable for comment.

This was not entirely facetious. A playwright is not the best person to talk about his own work for the simple reason that he is often unaware of what he has written. Someone (I think, Tom Stoppard) has compared the playwright confronted by his critics to a passage through Customs. Under the impression he has nothing to declare the playwright heads confidently for the Green exit. Alerted (and irritated) by this air of confidence an official of the Customs and Excise steps forward and asks our writer formally 'Have you any contraband?' 'No,' smiles the playwright. 'Very well,' says the officer, 'kindly open your suitcase.' Happy to comply (he has nothing to be ashamed of, after all) the playwright throws back the lid. Whereupon to his horror there lie revealed a pair of disgustingly dirty underpants and some extremely pungent socks. The playwright is covered in confusion; for though these underpants are undoubtedly his and the socks too, nevertheless he has no recollection of having packed them, still less of giving them pride of place on top of his belongings. The customs officer sniffs (as well he might). However, since there is as yet no law against the import of dirty underpants or smelly socks, the officer gingerly puts them on one side and delves further into the playwright's case.

The next revelation is some photographs. These too take the playwright by surprise. Had he packed them? Surely not. But they are most certainly his: this is a photograph of his father and here are three photographs of his mother and at least half a dozen of himself. 'Rather fond of ourselves, aren't we sir?' murmurs the customs man insolently. The playwright stammers some excuse, only thankful that the snaps are after all quite decent. But his relief is premature because, after sifting through yet more soiled clothing, the customs man now unearths another photograph: it is the playwright again, only this time he has his trousers down, he is smiling and with every appearance of pride he is showing his bottom to the camera. Now not only does the playwright not remember packing this photograph, he doesn't even remember it being taken. But this is him; those are his trousers; that is his smile and, yes, that, without question, is his bottom. 'One of our holiday snaps is it, sir?' sneers the customs officer. 'I should keep that covered up if I were you. We all have one, you know.'

And so the embarrassing examination goes on, the searcher uncovering ever more outrageous items – ideas the playwright thought he had long since discarded, an old marriage, a dead teacher and even a body or two locked in a long forgotten embrace, none of which the playwright ever dreamed of packing but which somehow have found their way into this commodious suitcase, his play.

So there is not much point in my telling you or the A Level students what *Talking Heads* is about or what I have put into my particular suitcase. All I can do is list some of the contents, note some of the themes (or at any rate recurrences), trace the origins of some of these pieces (insofar as I am aware of them) and link them occasionally with other stuff that I've written, always remembering that the relationship between life and art is never as straightforward as the reader or the audience tend to imagine.

That fictional characters are not drawn directly from life is a truism. Evelyn Waugh's epigraph to *Brideshead Revisited* puts it succinctly: 'I am not I; thou are not he or she; they are not they.' But such a straightforward disavowal is misleading, because characters *are* taken from life: it's just that they are seldom yanked out of it quite so unceremoniously as the public imagines. They aren't hi-jacked unchanged into art or shoved just as they are onto the page or in front of the camera:

the playwright or novelist has to take them to Costume or Make-up in order to alter their appearance and sometimes he even takes them to a surgeon to change their sex. So that when the writer has finished with them they come on as someone far removed from the character they started off as, yet still, as in dreams, sharing his or her original identity.

And as it is with characters so it is with places. I hope no one ever tries to construct an exact topography of these or any of my other plays because I use street names at random, generally picking out the names I remember from my childhood in Leeds regardless of their geographical location. The posh suburbs then were Lawnswood and Alwoodley, and that still holds good, but otherwise the place I have in my head is only distantly related to Leeds as it is now and as in dreams, again, one landscape adjoins another without logic or possibility. In *Playing Sandwiches*, for instance, Wilfred has been an attendant at the Derby Baths, but of course the Derby Baths aren't in Leeds they're in Blackpool, as I'm sure many viewers will write and tell me. I imagine that in my cavalier (or slipshod) attitude to topography I'm not untypical which leads me to suppose that handbooks to Proust, say, or keys to Dickens, tell only a fraction of the truth.



I note the recurrences, which may indicate preoccupations, though they may equally well betray the poverty of my imagination: there are two dogs, for instance, one a chow with an arthritic hip that gets to run along the Scarborough sands in *Miss Fozzard Finds Her Feet*, the other a noisy alsatian which gets its owner acquitted in *The Outside Dog*. It was only when the monologues were being edited that I realised I had called both dogs Tina, which in *A Woman of No Importance* is also the name of Mr Cressell and Mr Rudyard's Jack Russell.

Two characters have strokes; two receive counselling; one husband is a murderer, another character is said to be a murderer (by virtue of being a tobacconist); and another husband gets murdered. The murders mystify me, the strokes less so as I am getting to the age when that sort of thing begins to nag, though that isn't really why they figure here. What can or cannot be said is a staple of the drama and it's in this regard rather than attempting an accurate depiction of the condition that I've written about strokes. Or 'cerebral incidents' as neurologists tend to call them nowadays, doctors as inhibited in their own speech as some of the stricken patients whom they are treating.

That Violet's account of the last visit of her sweetheart should be flawless is perhaps a romanticised view of aphasia, owing something to the occasional dispensation from their symptoms enjoyed by Parkinsonian patients rather than stroke victims. Violet's remark that if she could sing everything then she wouldn't forget, is more true of sufferers from Parkinson's than it is of those incapacitated by a stroke, Parkinsonians sometimes being able to dance through a door when they are incapable of walking through it.

The press are several times unkindly noticed though not, I think, unfairly. Having on several occasions had to put up with their intrusions myself, I find I now make no distinction between reporters from the *Daily Mail* or journalists from the *Guardian*: they are more like each other than they are ordinary human beings.

Though neither the *Mail* nor the *Guardian* is a Murdoch paper, Murdoch is certainly to blame for pushing down standards not merely, as Dennis Potter said in his final interview, in journalism but in politics too and other areas of the nation's life. The danger with Mr Murdoch is that he has been around now for long enough to have mellowed into a familiar villain whose unscrupulous behaviour no longer surprises; because he is so routinely self-seeking we have begun to take it with a shrug if not a smile. So it would have been with Hitler had he lived, *Desert Island Discs* the English reward for a long life, however ill-spent.

I note the absence of children. Nearly all these women are childless, only ninety-five-year-old Violet having a son but whom she doesn't recognise as such because, with his 'big wristwatch, attaché case and one of those green raincoaty-things they shoot in', he looks more like a father than a son. No one else has children, not even in Australia where I've sometimes posted inconvenient offspring much as they did in the nineteenth century. I suppose I feel that children blur the picture and mitigate the sadness and, bringing their own problems with them, they demand to be attended to, and want to put their spoke in and are every bit as awkward in the drama as they are in life but with none of the compensations. One thing at a time is my motto and keep children out of it.

There's no sense in Wilfred having a child in *Playing Sandwiches* because the audience would just be waiting for him to interfere with it. Miss Fozzard is unmarried and past child-bearing anyway: I suspect, though, she wouldn't care for children particularly in the context of soft furnishings. Nor would Celia, the owner of the antique shop in *The Hand of God*. With her philosophy of,

'Lovely to look at, nice to hold,
but if you break it I say Sold!'

she wouldn't want small hands picking up her bibelots. I was once in an antique shop which a (not very unruly) child had just left. 'No,' said the woman behind the counter, 'I don't care for children, and that was a particularly bad example of the genre.'

On the other hand a child might have helped both Marjory in *The Outside Dog* and Rosemary in *Nights in the Gardens of Spain*, taking Marjory's mind off housework and Rosemary's off the garden. But it would also have meant there would have been no story to tell.

Another omission is, of course, the television set, which one would expect to be chattering away in the corner of many of these rooms but which must invariably be censored by playwrights protective of their dialogue. These are not naturalistic pieces but even plays that claim to be faithful accounts of ordinary life can seldom accommodate this garrulous intruder. The world of everything that is the case is not the world of drama.





*Miss Fozzard Finds Her Feet* is my second stab at chiropody, the first being *A Private Function* in 1985. I have no idea why chiropodists should strike such a chord, though when my mother was getting on and I had to sit in on a visit by the local chiropodist the situation did feel quite comic. Bernard's reference to 'your foot feller' is taken from another visit by the same chiropodist: finding my parents out, he left the time of their appointment with a neighbour, who, unable to spell chiropodist, put a note through the door saying, 'Foot Feller, Tuesday 3.30'. Finding the note my father claimed he thought it was a racing tip.

Feet did figure in my childhood as one of my aunties worked in Manfield's shoe shop on Commercial Street in Leeds and when she came round to see us in the evening she would regale us with all the events of her day, told in Proustian detail. When the door eventually closed behind her Dad would burst out, 'I wouldn't care but you're no further on when she's done.'

The names of shoes, the 'fur-lined Gibson bruised look' which Mr Dunderdale has Miss Fozzard try on, comes from twenty years ago when I was filming in an old-fashioned shoe shop in West Hartlepool. Feeling this was what proper writers did I took down a selection of names of shoes from the boxes stacked on the high shelves. I am sure the ankle-hugging bootee in Bengal bronze that Mr Dunderdale gives to Miss Fozzard is not a 'fur-lined Gibson bruised look' and I suppose I could verify this by walking down the road to Camden High Street where, to the detriment of the street as a decent shopping centre, every other shop is a shoe shop. But perhaps not, the expertise of the assistants in Camden stretching to the knowledge that shoes go on the feet but not much beyond that.

The department store where Miss Fozzard presides over Soft Furnishings is called Matthias Robinson's, which was indeed a department store on Briggate in Leeds and which closed early in the sixties. The name itself is sufficient to stamp it as an old-fashioned emporium of which there were many in Leeds: Wheatley and Whiteley, Marsh Jones and Cribb, Marshall and Snelgrove and in Bradford, memorably, Brown Muff's. Marshall and Snelgrove was a smarter store than Matthias Robinson's but both had the same hushed, carpeted elegance, soft lighting and snooty assistants (like Miss Fozzard) who called my mother 'madam' and so got her all flustered. Near where Matthias Robinson's stood is now Harvey Nichols which aspires, I suppose, to be the smartest store in Leeds though nowhere quite captures the elegance of those grander stores or their seductive smell, a blend of perfume, leather, warm carpet and (in Bradford particularly) fur coats.



When the Sistine Chapel was being restored in the 1980s, anyone with influence in the art world would be taken up in the lift to watch the restorers at work. Thus it was that several people I came across claimed to have reached out and touched either the hand of God or the finger of Adam. Easy-going as the Italians are I would be surprised if these accounts were altogether true but they gave me the idea for the beginning of a film script, *The Hand of God*, which I wrote but never managed to get produced. The script centred round a priceless drawing by Michelangelo of the hand of God wearing the ring of Michelangelo's patron, Julius II, and it's this drawing which (never having made it into a film script) turns up in the box of odds and ends grudgingly given to Celia on the death of Miss Ventriss.



'If you love beautiful things,' says Celia, 'which is why I came into this business in the first place, it breaks your heart.' I detect here a thirty-year-old echo of the only TV comedy series I ever did, *On the Margin*. The first programme featured an antique shop, with myself as the camp proprietor:

DEALER If you don't see what you want you've only got to ask. I don't put everything in the shop window.
CUSTOMER Could I just sórt of nose around?
DEALER Feel free. You must excuse my hands but I've just been stripping a tallboy.
[All this seemed quite daring in 1966.]
Mind you I'm not in this business to make money. I'm in this business because I like beautiful things and I like beautiful people to have

beautiful things. Which is why I'm very anxious to sell something to you. You see, I believe, perhaps wrongly, that if only all the beautiful people in the world had all the beautiful things there would be No More War. Don't you agree?

There is some irony in the fact that this blueprint for world peace was addressed to the young John Sergeant, who played the Customer but who is now the doyen of the BBC's political correspondents.

Nowadays antique shops are getting thin on the ground, most selling done not through shops but at antique fairs and car boot sales. It's an altogether more knowing business than it was, Sotheby's and Christie's having started the process and shaken down the country in quest of anything saleable. Celia remarks that Sotheby's and Christie's are no better than barrow boys: rather worse, in my view, as barrow boys don't charge a percentage to both buyer and seller and make them feel socially inferior into the bargain. Then there's the *Antiques Road Show* which has set everyone scouring their attics and fetching out their cherished heirlooms. Despite their eagerness to know the value of their precious possessions I have never seen anyone on the programme admit to wanting to sell the objects in question. It's a cosy contribution to our national hypocrisy.

I imagine Celia's shop as bare and uninviting, full of big furniture with not much in it in the way of bric-a-brac, the kind of shop I'd think twice about going into. Such establishments, though, are no longer the norm. Antique shops, as Celia would be the first to point out, have come down in the world. Typical stock nowadays might be a lace doyley; a napkin ring; a Penguin Special from the forties; an empty scent spray from a thirties' dressing table, redolent of long-dead 4711, and an old Oxo tin. Not antiques at all, of course, but 'collectables'.

And collectables that tread hard on the heels of the present so one is nowadays regularly confronted by items classified as antiques which one remembers in common use. Milk was brought round from door to door when I was a boy by Mr Keen the milkman with his horse and cart – and this in suburban Armley. The milk was ladled out of his lidded oval pail in gill measures, both pail and measure now regularly on offer in antique shops, the pewter buffed, the brass polished and both, I suppose, serving ultimately as receptacles for flowers or the ubiquitous pot-pourri. The history of popular taste in the eighties and nineties could be charted via the march of pot-pourri; in the twenties scenting Ottoline Morrell's lacquered rooms at Garsington, today, as Celia points out, on sale at any garage.

I miss the old-fashioned antique shops: Slee's on the upper floors of premises on Boar Lane in Leeds, where the stock was so shabby and slow-moving it seemed as if it had been aged on the premises; Taylor's in Harrogate which had in its window photographs of that famous magpie, Queen Mary, emerging from the shop in her toque and parasol, with some hapless lady-in-waiting bringing up the rear with the articles Her Majesty had admired and which etiquette demanded she must forthwith be given. Another classy establishment was Frank Williams' in Burford in Oxfordshire where I remember first going forty years ago as an undergraduate and which is now reduced to selling shirts, though at least it doesn't sell the 'pictures of mice in pinnies-type-thing' that Celia groans about (though there's no shortage of that in Burford either). And I know all this is snobbish and strikes the *lacrimae rerum* note; I should leave Celia, though a far from sympathetic character, to voice my regrets and reminiscences for me.



I realise, incidentally, as I write that the finger of God which is Celia's downfall is (and it was entirely unintentional) the finger that singles out the winners of the National Lottery.



Just as in the first series of *Talking Heads* there is only one male monologue and five by women. After that series a viewer wrote to me suggesting that if I wrote a series wholly for men I could call it *Talking Balls*. Which, had I been able to write six male monologues, I would happily have done. That I can't, I put down to the fact that when I was a child the women did most of the talking so that I've been more attuned to the discourse of women than to that of men, and though such real life monologues I come across nowadays are generally in the mouths of men I don't find male talk easy to reproduce; though it's easier when the men are damaged as Wilfred is in *Playing Sandwiches* and Graham in *A Chip in the Sugar*.

*Playing Sandwiches* dates back twenty years and is linked to a very different play, *The Old Country*, in which the main character, Hilary, is, or has been, a Soviet spy working in the Foreign Office. Accustomed to rendezvous with his Russian opposite number at various locations in London's outer suburbs he recalls how by sheer chance he nearly came to grief:

> It's quite hard to be absolutely alone. I never have. Though I have seen it. One particular afternoon I had been on one of my little jaunts, kept my appointment. Nothing unusual had occurred or was in the least likely to occur. It was a routine Thursday and I strolled back to the

station across a piece of waste ground that I knew made a nice short cut. I must have seemed a slightly incongruous figure in my city clothes. I never dressed the part, even to the extent of an old raincoat. At which point I came over the brow of the hill and found myself facing a line of policemen, advancing slowly through the undergrowth, poking in ditches with long sticks, hunting for something. It appeared there was a child missing, believed dead. Clothes had been found; a shoe. It was a bad moment. I had no reason at all for being there. I was a senior official in the Foreign Office. What was I doing on a spring afternoon, with documents in my briefcase, crossing a common where a child had been murdered? As it was no one thought to ask me any questions at all. I looked too respectable. And indeed they already had a suspect waiting handcuffed in the police car. I joined in the search and was with them when they found the child about half an hour later, lying in a heap at the foot of a wall. I just got a glimpse of her legs, white, like mushrooms, before they threw a blanket over her. She had been dead a week. I saw the man as the police car drew away through lines of jeering housewives and people cycling home from work. Then they threw a blanket over him too. The handy blanket. And I have a feeling he was eventually hanged. Anyway it was in those days. I came back, replaced the documents, had my tea by the fire in the Foreign Office. I took in some parliamentary questions for the minister, had dinner at the Garrick and walked home across the park. And in a tiled room at Uxbridge Police Station there would have been that young man waiting. Alone in a cell. Alone in custody. Alone at large. A man without home or haven. That is what you have to do to be cast out. Murder children. Nothing else quite does the trick, because any other crime will always find you friends. Rape them, kill them and be caught.
(*The Old Country, pp. 52–3*)





The young man has had to wait twenty years for his case to be considered so he is no longer quite so young or living in the metropolitan suburbs but two hundred miles north near a municipal park. But it is the same man.

I am repelled by the self-righteous morality of gaols and their hierarchy of offences whereby murder and grievous bodily harm are thought of as respectable crimes and sexual offences are not. I also feel that the press hysteria over paedophilia, and in particular over offences that occurred long in the past, has reached dangerous proportions and the availability of monetary compensation for the possible psychological effects of these injuries has made the situation more fraught with difficulties. But such is the atmosphere surrounding the subject that one thinks twice before setting out any opinions one might have on the matter.

Murder is a messy business and for Marjory in *The Outside Dog* one feels it's just another skirmish in her continuing campaign against dirt. Even a more balanced character like Rosemary in *Nights in the Gardens of Spain* shares some of the same concerns so her first thought in seeing Mr McCorquodale's blood on the sheepskin rug is what a job it's going to be getting it off.

Somewhere Proust says that no matter how sad the occasion with women it will eventually resolve itself into a question of trying on. It could, more charitably, be said to turn into a question of cleaning down, though that's a side of life Proust didn't see much of.



Keeping dirt at bay in the way that Marjory does used to take up a substantial part of every housewife's day: there was the shaking of the rugs, the blackleading of the range, having a run round with the Ewbank, not to mention putting mountains of washing through the wringer. This was the lot of every self-respecting housewife in Leeds in my childhood, where in addition to the soot there was a continuous rain of fine grit from Kirkstall Power Station.



For a woman to adhere to such a routine (and the assumptions behind it) today seems wilful or neurotic, a deliberate narrowing of the scope and satisfactions of her sex. In those days keeping a clean house was the be-all and end-all, every day the occasion for the ceremony of purification, the successive stages of which culminated around the middle of the afternoon with the celebrant sinking into a chair before making the solemn declaration, 'This is the first time I've sat down all day.' There would then be a brief interval before the children came home from school and the men from work and the place was turned upside down again.

I see my mother sitting by the newly blackleaded range, her leg nearest the grate mottled blue-black by the fire as women's legs often were then, and saying imploringly, 'I've just got the place straight. Don't upset.'

This is not the first time I have written about it:

*1 May 1978, Hartlepool (Afternoon Off)*

We film in the sluice room of the cottage hospital. Racks of stainless-steel bottles and bedpans, a sink that flushes and a hideously stained drum on which the bedpans are sluiced out. This room would be my mother's nightmare. Conditions are cramped and I crouch behind the camera tripod in order to see the action. I am kneeling on the floor under the bedpan sluice. If my Mam saw this she would want to throw away trousers, raincoat, every particle of clothing that might have been touched and polluted. This has got into the film. Thora Hird plays a patient in the hospital being visited by her husband.

'I bet the house is upside down,' she says to him.

'It never is,' says her husband. 'I did the kitchen floor this morning.'

'Which bucket did you use?'

'The red one.'

She is outraged. 'That's the outside bucket. I shall have it all to do again.'

I am assuming this is common ground and that the tortuous boundary between the clean and the dirty is a frontier most households share. It was very marked in ours. My mother maintained an intricate hierarchy of cloths, buckets and dusters, to the Byzantine differentiations of which she alone was privy. Some cloths were dish cloths but not sink cloths; some were for the sink but not for the floor. There were dirty buckets and clean buckets, brushes for indoors, brushes for the flags. One mop had a universal application while another had a unique and terrible purpose and had to be kept outside, hung on the wall. And however rinsed and clean these utensils were they remained tainted by their awful function. Left to himself my Dad would violate these taboos, using the first thing that came to hand to clean the hearth or wash the floor. 'It's all nowt,' he'd mutter, but if Mam was around he knew it saved time and temper to observe her order of things. Latterly, disposable cloths and kitchen rolls tended to blur these ancient distinctions but the basic structure remained, perhaps the firmest part of the framework of her world. When she was ill with depression the order broke down: the house became dirty. Spotless though Dad kept it, she saw it as 'upside down', dust an unstemmable tide and the house's (imagined) squalor a talking point for the neighbours. So that when she came home from the hospital, bright and better, her first comment was always how clean the house looked. And not merely the house. It was as if the whole world and her existence in it had been rinsed clean.

(*Writing Home, pp. 277–8*)

As a child I had a recurring dream, imperfectly dramatised in my play *Intensive Care*, in which my mother and I were sitting in a spotless house when suddenly the coalman burst through the door and trailed muck throughout the house. Though the dream owed something to the then adverts for Walpamur in which a child covered an immaculate wall with dirty hand prints, looking back I see that this intrusive coalman was probably my father, which accounts for the fact that, despite my alarm, my mother took this intrusion quite calmly. I can see that *The Outside Dog* is another version of this dream; not that that is much help to the viewer or the reader, though it may be useful fodder for the A Level candidates.

The Vale of York, where the open prison is located in *Nights in the Gardens of Spain* and where Rosemary and Mrs McCorquodale go on some of their jaunts, was just out of biking range when I was a boy and so seldom visited. Pre-prairified and dotted with ancient villages, duck ponds and grand country houses, it was a distant sunlit idyll and seemed to me a foretaste of what life must be like Down South. It was England as it was written about in children's books, and because I go there seldom still, it has retained some of this enchantment. Visiting country churches, which I used to do as a boy, is something I've rediscovered in middle age so in that sense I identify with Rosemary though not where gardening is concerned. I am no gardener, never managing to take a long enough view of things, finding the whole business not unstressful; I see the battle against weeds (ground elder in particular) as a fight against evil and one which invariably puts me in a bad temper.

Prison for Mrs McCorquodale is a kind of release just as it was for Miss Ruddock in *A Lady of Letters* in the first *Talking Heads*. This is a romanticised view, I'm sure, and having occasionally had to speak in men's prisons it is not a view I would so glibly advance on their behalf. I tend to regard women's prisons as women's institutes with bars on the windows, a prison sentence an ideal opportunity to brush up on the rug-making or learn French. If it were ever so it is not so now, education and vocational training in both men's and women's prisons the first victims of cut-backs.

I was put off writing *Waiting for the Telegram* for a long time because of the purely practical consideration that Violet would have to be impossibly old (nearly a hundred) to have had a sweetheart killed in the First War. And, of course, the longer I delayed writing the script the more acute the problem became. Eventually I decided that the time factor didn't really matter: in an old people's home time goes at a trickle anyway, what year it is is not of much consequence, least of all to the residents whose own age is often something of a mystery as it certainly is to Violet.

I see her living as a girl up Tong Road in Leeds, the route traversed by the No. 16 tram, the tram Violet feels she should have told Spencer about. It was a neighbourhood close-packed with red brick back-to-backs, including 'The Avenues', a run of eighteen streets named by their number, First Avenue, Second Avenue and so on. This was instanced in some sociological account I read as an example of the soullessness of nineteenth-century slum development but it wasn't quite like that. Each avenue had an atmosphere of its own, some certainly better (more genteel), others rougher or dirtier but far from being components in a featureless urban desert that the bare numbers might suggest.

Tong Road, with Sleights the greengrocers, Burras Peake's the outfitters, Gallons the grocers, and Hustwitt's the sheet music and gramophone shop, has long since gone – all that is left the unchanging black silhouette of St Bartholomew's and, a few streets over, Armley Gaol, twin bulwarks of church and state. Nowadays, with flimsy new houses clustered around the gaol, Tong Road seems bleaker than it ever was and certainly with less character, though doubtless a child brought up there today would be able to discriminate between its seemingly identical streets as effortlessly as we did then.





Some question arose during the rehearsing of the piece about the nature of a vanilla slice. It is, I suppose, a downmarket version of a millefeuille, with confectioner's custard sandwiched between layers of flaky pastry and topped off with white icing. Someone bringing vanilla slices home from the confectioner's, fancies too, and certainly fruit pies, would bear the bag like the priest the host, held high on the flat of the hand lest the fruit leak out or the icing adhere to the paper bag. It's a sight – a rite almost – that I associate with Saturday dinner-time when we would be sent 'on to the end' to McDade's, the confectioner's on the corner of Tong Road and Gilpin Place, to get something 'to finish off with'.

Violet keeps being told she will soon be getting a telegram from the Queen, though whether that custom persists and whether it is a telegram I am not sure, though doubtless I shall be told. Telegraph boys still rode the streets on their high bicycles when I was a boy, in their uniform of blue serge with red piping and a little pill-box hat. The telegram itself came in an orange envelope, smaller than the average letter, the message in capital letters on ticker tape stuck on a half sheet of rather mealy paper.

In our family one did not send telegrams lightly, partly because they were expensive but more because one was fearful of the initial shock when the door opened on the telegraph boy, the immediate assumption always being that he brought bad news. This was a legacy of the First War when telegraph boys were over-employed. Bumping over the setts on their high bicycles, every day they brought news of deaths in the trenches so that a single boy in four years of war might tell the fate of thousands. Seeing him go by women would stand at their doors to see which house he stopped at, this pageboy of death. And the same, presumably, in Germany: *Der Todeskavalier*.

I thought once of writing a TV play about such a boy, who, with men being called up, heard in the autumn of 1914 that 'they were taking on down at the Post Office' and so goes and gets his first job. He becomes a telegraph boy for the two years before he himself is old enough to enlist, thus every day bringing tidings of the fate of others that he knows may one day be his own.

And finally, an apology. How dramatists use (and invariably sanitise) illness for their own purposes is an interesting subject. The illnesses change: a hundred years ago if a character needed to fade away it was with TB or 'consumption'. When fifty years or so ago TB ceased to be incurable it lost its popularity as a dramatic disease to be replaced very often by leukaemia, another condition with which a character could make a slow and dignified exit. That neither disease was as tidy or as well-mannered as dramatists chose to imagine seems insulting to the victims and now I am conscious that I have treated Francis's death in much the same way, deaths from AIDS seldom so quick or so clean as I have made his departure, my only excuse being that it is Violet's story more than his.

The six monologues were each rehearsed for just over a week and generally taped over one day at Twickenham Studios. I am grateful to all the performers, the directors and the production team whose names are separately listed and they will know that it is no reflection on them when I say that at every stage of the production process I never ceased to miss the presence of my long-time producer and friend, Innes Lloyd, who produced the first series of *Talking Heads* and who died in 1991. It is to him these monologues are dedicated.

# The **Hand** Of God

**Celia:** Eileen Atkins

PRODUCED BY **MARK SHIVAS** DIRECTED BY **STUART BURGE**
DESIGNED BY **STUART WALKER** MUSIC BY **GEORGE FENTON**

CELIA, A MIDDLE-AGED WOMAN, SITS AT THE END OF A REFECTORY TABLE. THERE ARE ODD PLATES ON THE WALL, A GRANDFATHER CLOCK: THE CORNER OF AN ANTIQUE SHOP. IN THE COURSE OF THE MONOLOGUE CELIA SITS IN VARIOUS PARTS OF THE SHOP, OFTEN BY AN OIL RADIATOR.

I won't touch pictures. I make it a rule. I've seen too many fingers burned.

Woman comes in this morning starts rooting in her shopping bag saying she has something I might be interested in, been in the attic etcetera etcetera. The usual rigmarole. Hadn't thought anything about it, apparently, until she saw something similar on (and I knew what was coming) that television programme about antiques and that someone on the programme from Christie's…



I said, 'Barrow boys.' She said, 'Come again?' I said, 'Sotheby's, Christie's. Barrow boys. Nicely spoken, lovely suits, finger-nails immaculate. But barrow boys.' She said, 'Well anyway, he said £2000.'

I said, 'Well, he would. He doesn't have to get up at four in the morning and flog his ageing Volvo halfway across England just to sit all day in a freezing marquee and come away with two trivets and an umbrella-stand.' £2000! It was one step up from Highland cattle.

She said, 'It's a genuine oil painting. Look at the work that's gone into it.' I said, 'Madam, if you'll forgive me, could I point you along the street in the direction of A Tisket A Tasket? Basically a café it doubles as a bric-a-brac shop and Yvonne does pictures on the side…' though what I didn't say was that they tend to be mice in pinnies-type thing.

I popped over the road to tell Derek and Cyril. They'd just had a buyer in from Stockholm who'd practically cleared them out. Staffordshire mostly, which is their big thing. Doesn't do anything for me but Derek and Cyril love it; chunky, I suppose. Actually I don't have a particular line. Good cottage furniture sums it up, elm, fruitwood and anything painted. And clocks, of course, when I can get hold of them. Plus pots of the period.

Some things I won't sell. Teddy bears, for instance. Teddy bears are a minefield. I was at a sale in Suffolk and saw a teddy bear actually torn apart between two bidders, one of them a vicar.

These days they're all going in for little sidelines. Eking the job out with jam and little pots of chutney. Woman came in the other day, said, Did I have any chutney? I said, 'I shall start doing chutney, madam, when Tesco start doing gateleg tables.' But the garage sells pot-pourri so what do you expect?

I think of Lawrence. 'Christ, old girl, I didn't sink my gratuity in this place to start selling bloody condiments.' He was in bomb disposal which was why to begin with we went in for clocks. Though of course there were clocks then. There was everything then. Furniture. Pottery. Stock no problem. And if one had the eye, which I do, one could pick and choose.

Not any more. Take what you can get. And money, money, money. If you love beautiful things, which is why I came into this business in the first place, it just breaks your heart.

And everybody's an expert now, up to all the tricks of the trade. You'll see something catch their eye and they don't ask about it straightaway; they enquire about something else, pretend they're not interested then it's, 'Oh…incidentally, how much is this little thing?' It's the oldest dodge in the world and they expect you to be taken in by it. Of course they've picked all that up off the television. I won't have one. I said to Nancy Barnard, I refuse to watch. She said, 'Well, we only have it because of Fay.' Fay! They're both glued to it!

Wish I could shift this refectory table. It was a real snip when I got it but I've had it a year now and not a nibble. Lovely top. Elm.

*She gives a little smile as someone obviously looks in the window.*

Old Miss Ventriss seeing what there is. Took two Crown Derby plates off her once, just as a favour, one of them chipped.

Looking a bit frail. Going on.

Lovely cameo brooch.

FADE.

They talk as if you're not in the room.

Couple just now, looking at the Asiatic Pheasant tureen. '£60!' she said, 'I gave £2.10 for mine.' 'Yes, but when?' I wanted to say, '1955?'

And some of them so careless they practically hurl things to the floor. I've got a notice up now:

'Lovely to look at, nice to hold,
but if you break it
I say Sold!'

Somebody looking in. Goldfish bowl.

No. You can't see the price, however far you bend. You're going to dislocate your neck and you still won't see it, because I've carefully arranged the ticket so that if you want to see the price you'll have to come into the shop. Which you're not doing.

Even if they could see the price they wouldn't understand it because I've got my little code.

*She looks at the ticket on the refectory table, at the end of which she's sitting.*

I could take £1300 for this at a pinch. I've had it a year. Too long. Lawrence would be reading me the Riot Act. 'Keep your stock ticking over, old girl. Move it on.' And he did, even if it meant not making much.

'It's like Scrabble, my dear. Start saving up for the big one, the seven letter word, and you're done for. Get your letters down. £5 here. £10 there. Buy for x one week, sell for y the next. That's how you make your money.' Look well in a boardroom. Or one of these loft conversion things. I'd even consider £1150.

I kept wondering about Miss Ventriss. So what with not having seen her for a bit I thought I'd just knock on her door, see how she was.

She lives in one of the double-fronted houses on The Mount, original fanlight over the door and a lovely knocker, hand grasping a ball, which can't be later than 1820 though the house I'd have said was Victorian. But of course it's stucco which can cover a multitude of sins, and once I get inside I realise it's seventeenth century and seemingly never been touched. And I'm right, of course she isn't well, been in bed a fortnight and it's Mabel, the home help who answers the door. Now I know Mabel of old because she's been in from time to time with odd bits of stuff, little things…a silver vinaigrette, a jet brooch, spoons and whatnot, stuff I've found homes for straightaway. They all come from Newcastle, apparently, where her aunt's had to go into a home. Anyway Mabel takes me upstairs to see Miss Ventriss, who tells me she's had all sorts of tests and they still don't know what's wrong. Which probably means they do.

Thin little hand. Like dried leaves. Tragic.

Lovely bedside table with piecrust moulding. District Nurse comes while I'm there, plonks a bottle of medicine straight down on it. Criminal. I help give her some Benger's food only she fetches it straight back.

The spoon's silver and while they're cleaning her up I look at the hallmark. Provincial, Bristol, about 1830.

Same sort that Mabel brought in.

FADE.

I love a nice finish...maple, rosewood, and walnut particularly. What I can't abide is stripped pine. I don't see the point, quite frankly. And they're fanatics about it, some dealers. I mean still. They'll strip everything. Five minutes in the caustic tank and it's one hundred years of loving care down the drain. All the character gone.

I was thinking about this at Miss Ventriss's because there's polish everywhere. Walnut, elm, fruitwood. It's like a jewel box. I've been popping round on a regular basis lately, just to relieve Mabel a bit because the old girl's scarcely conscious now, doesn't know I'm there half the time. I sit by the bed with the clock ticking...carriage clock, tortoiseshell veneer, fluted, about 1750. Made me think of Lawrence. Lovely.

Of course, everywhere you look there's something. It's like houses used to be in the fifties, and most of it museum quality practically. It's from her grandfather, he was a great collector apparently.



I said to Mabel, 'What's going to happen to all this?' She said, Well she didn't think there were any relations. There'd been a niece in Canada but she had a feeling she was in an airline crash.

I couldn't get her to take me round at first. Said she was under strict instructions from the solicitors. I said, 'What solicitors are those?' She said, 'Paterson, Beatty and Brown.' I said, 'Well, there's no problem there because I took a kneehole desk off Mr Paterson and gave him a very good price.'



She was still a bit reluctant so I said, 'Mabel, I can well understand why you have to be careful. It's so easy for little things to go walkabout, particularly with old people. Silver, little brooches, you know the sort of thing?' She went a bit quiet so I said, 'Shall we start with upstairs?'

I couldn't believe it. Every room a treasure trove. Amazing.

When I was going Mabel said, 'I'll try and steer some of it your way if I can.' I said, 'Yes, well there'd be a nice little margin on most of this even running to the two of us. If the worst comes to the worst, of course.' Mabel says 'Yes. Though she seems a bit better today. Kept more of her dinner down anyway. Still, you've only to look at her under that nightdress and there's nothing there.' I said, 'Yes. Where did that nightdress come from?' She said 'Her grandmother, I think. It's all hand done. There's half a dozen of them in the linen cupboard, some of them never worn. Tragic.'

Of course the sharks are beginning to gather. I'm sitting by the bed this afternoon when Derek knocks at the door bearing one of Cyril's wizened egg custards. Mabel didn't let him get his foot round the door only then Nancy Barnard rolls up in her terrible beetroot slacks, says that she and Fay swear by some tincture from the swamps of Paraguay that they'd bought in Chelmsford, should she get her some? I said to Mabel, 'They're so transparent.'

Miss Ventriss is asleep so I have a little look at her bed. It's a country piece. About 1830 I'd have said, painted (which always gets my vote) and in such good condition. The doorbell goes again so while Mabel's downstairs I lift up the mattress and where the paint isn't worn it's as good as new.

I'm just tucking the sheet back when I see her little eyes are open and she's watching me. I think she said, 'Happy?' Only Mabel came in just then.

Of course you can't tell when it gets to this stage, it goes to the brain.

The visitor's the priest, come to anoint her and whatnot, just to be on the safe side, as the doctor says she could go any time. Mabel and I left him to it, just stood respectfully in the background. Had a little embroidered cloth that he covered the chalice with, Arts and Crafts by the look of it and a beautiful thing. Pity it can't be used for something.

*Pause.*

Of course, when she said 'Happy?', what she probably meant was that *she* was happy.

FADE.

I said to Nancy Barnard, 'Am I a person?' She said, 'Come again, love?' I said, 'Am I a person? Or am I simply a professional bargain hunter?'

Because that was what she was implying. I said, 'I've been coming here as a friend.' She said, 'I know that.' Bright red cardigan, carmine lipstick and, at the funeral, leather trousers. Even Nancy had managed to find a skirt. Niece…she'd never even met Miss Ventriss, went to Canada at the age of six. Mabel had given me to understand she'd died in an airline crash. Turns out what she'd had was a hairline fracture, no crash at all.

And of course she comes in for everything. Which is understandable, except that no sooner does she see the place than she announces that aside from one or two of the choicest pieces which she'd be keeping for herself, she'd be sending the rest to Phillips.

I said, 'Mrs O'Rourke, I'm sure there are several local concerns who'd give you a very good price and you wouldn't be landed with the vendor's commission.' Turns out she's not paying much commission anyway as the stuff is of such good quality she'd come to an arrangement.

It was then she offered me this box of odds and ends from the desk drawer…I'd been very kind to her aunt, she said, and she wanted to give me a bit of something in return.

I said, 'Thank you very much but I don't want to be given anything.' She said, 'That's good because with the solicitors being such sticklers I probably ought to charge you a nominal price anyway then it's all legal and above board. Shall we say £5? I said, 'I don't sell bric-a-brac.' She said, 'Well, if you give me £5 and it fetches more than that you can give the rest to Oxfam.' I said, 'What do you do in Canada?' She said, 'Public relations.' I said 'Oh' pointedly. 'You must be on holiday then,' gave her £5, took the box and went.

Of course being Canadian she probably thought I was being nice.



I haven't been able to face unpacking the box. In fact, I've only just done it now. Much as I expected. One or two pressed glass ashtrays that I can get £2 or £3 a piece for. A little gunmetal cigarette case and a serviette ring. All of them items for the oddments box. The only thing of any interest at all is a rather smudgy drawing of a finger (I think it's a drawing, it may be a print) but the frame is very distinctive. Quite small but with little doors that open so it looks a bit like an altar, nineteenth century probably.



When I've got a minute I'm going to take the drawing out and put something a bit more conventional in, a flower print or something. Smarten it up a bit. Might fetch £30 or so, you never know.

*Pause.*

Funny thing to put in a frame, a finger.

FADE.

I think the refectory table's gone. Came in this morning. Only young. Curly hair. Can't have been much more than twenty. I said, Was he looking for anything in particular? He said, Well, he did want a little present for his girlfriend but he was interested in the refectory table. Didn't begin by asking the price, which is always a good sign, just said could I measure it for him?

While I'm rooting about looking for a tape measure he picks up one or two bits and pieces. I'd brought Miss Ventriss's little drawing out thinking I could spend the afternoon taking it out of the frame, and I'd just popped it down on the refectory table where he picks it up, then puts it on one side so's he could look more closely at the table top.

When I'd measured it he got underneath and had a proper look; there was a bit of worm but in a piece that age it would be unusual if there wasn't and anyway we both thought it was dead. So he said, what was the best I could do? I'd given £1100 for it a year ago so I said, 'Well, I can't do much under £1700. Say £1650. It's elm.' He said, 'I know. It's beautiful. If it will fit, it's just what we're looking for.' So I give him my card and he writes down the measurements and he's going to ring back this afternoon.

Just as he's going he picks up the drawing again and says 'What is this?' I said, 'Well, it's a finger, isn't it?' He said, 'Yes. I'm not sure I like that, though it's a nice frame. How much is it?'



I thought, Well, it's an educated voice, I'll take a chance. I said, 'I can't really do it much under £100.' He put it down pretty smartish. I said, 'The frame alone's worth more than that.' He said, 'Yes, it's the frame I'm really interested in.'



I reckoned to look at my book. I said, 'Well, I can do it for £90 and if you're not particular for the drawing I can take it out.' He said, 'No, don't bother, I can do that.' And just then somebody comes in and he writes me out a cheque really quickly. I wrapped it up and said, 'And you'll let me know about the table?' He said, 'What?' I said, 'The table.' He said, 'Oh yes. I'll phone you this afternoon. I think it'll be just right.'

I've just popped along to the bank and put the cheque in and now I'm waiting for him to call. It's funny I'd come down to £90 but he was in such a rush he'd still made it out for £100.

FADE.

I said, No, I wasn't the sort of person who is resentful. I'd made my profit and they had made theirs. Selling on, everybody makes something, that's what the antique business is all about.

They'd posed me outside the shop and this young woman stood by the camera and I had to look at her and not at it.

She said, Would I be asking them to give me an ex gratia payment? I said, I didn't think I would be asking and I was sure they wouldn't be offering. Of course it would be nice if they did. I think I would…in the circumstances.

I'd actually forgotten all about it. It was six months ago at least (apparently they had a lot of tests to do on the paper and whatnot). Then

Nancy Barnard comes banging on the window one morning before I'd even opened, holding up a copy of the *Telegraph* and pointing to this photograph on the front page. And there's the young man, and a blow-up of the finger.

Which, so all (or anyway some) of the experts say is by Michelangelo, a study (one of the few apparently) of the hand of God on the Sistine Chapel ceiling.

'I knew I'd seen it before,' Nancy says, 'only it was Fay who pointed it out. Glued to the telly box as usual she said it's like the finger they have at the start of the *South Bank Show*. Such a shame! If you watched the telly you might have known.'

What makes it special apparently is the ring. God doesn't have a ring on his finger on the ceiling, I mean why should he...but the ring on my...on the finger has, very faintly, the arms of the Pope who commissioned it...Julius something or other, who was Michelangelo's patron. Very satirical apparently on Michelangelo's part, though I don't see the joke.



But all of which, needless to say, bumps up the estimated price. Not been sold yet but could fetch anything...£5 million, £10 million... unique.



A finger. That size.

'Poor you,' said Nancy. 'Oh,' I said, 'it happens.' Only when she'd gone I was physically sick.

The young man who bought it, whom I thought looked quite classy, turns out to be some young blood from Christie's. Says in the paper he picked it up in a junk shop. Junk shop.

Of course the person who ought to feel really sick is the niece, Mrs O'Rourke. I don't think she can ever have looked in the box so she'll have had no idea. So I've dropped her a line. Wipe the smile off her face.

Been quite busy. Mostly people just wanting a look. At me, chiefly.

Still, they've bought the odd thing. Sold a couple of lemonade bottles yesterday. Only my stock's low. Can't face going to sales yet. And I've still got this bloody refectory table.

Knee deep in tomatoes so I made some chutney. Frilly top. Italic label. 95p a bottle. Sold three this afternoon.

FADE.

# Miss Fozzard Finds Her Feet

**Miss Fozzard:**
Patricia Routledge

PRODUCED BY **MARK SHIVAS** DIRECTED BY **PATRICK GARLAND**
DESIGNED BY **STUART WALKER** MUSIC BY **GEORGE FENTON**

NONDESCRIPT SUBURBAN SITTING ROOM. IN THE COURSE OF THE MONOLOGUE MISS FOZZARD SITS ON VARIOUS CHAIRS OR STANDS BY THE FIREPLACE BUT THE SETTING IS THE SAME THROUGHOUT.

Bit of a bombshell today. I'm just pegging up my stocking when Mr Suddaby says, 'I'm afraid, Miss Fozzard, this is going to have to be our last encounter.' Apparently this latest burglary has put the tin hat on things and what with Mrs Suddaby's mother finally going into a home and their TV reception always being so poor there's not much to keep them in Leeds so they're making a bolt for it and heading off to Scarborough. Added to which Tina, their chow, has a touch of arthritis so the sands may help and the upshot is they've gone in for a little semi near Peasholme Park.



'But,' Mr Suddaby says, 'none of that is of any consequence. What is important, Miss Fozzard, is what are we going to do about your feet? You've been coming to me for so long I don't like to think of your feet falling into the wrong hands.'



I said, 'Well, Mr Suddaby, I shall count myself very lucky if I find someone as accomplished as yourself and, if I may say so, with your sense of humour.' Because it's very seldom we have a session in which laughter doesn't figure somewhere.

He said, 'Well, Miss Fozzard, chiropody is a small world and I've taken the liberty of making a few phone calls and come up with two possibilities. One is a young lady over in Roundhay, who, I understand is very reasonable.'

'A woman?' I said, 'In chiropody? Isn't that unusual?' 'No,' he said, 'not nowadays. The barriers are coming down in chiropody as in everything else. It's progress Miss Fozzard, the march of, and Cindy Bickerton has her own salon.' I said, 'Cindy? That doesn't inspire confidence. She sounds as if she should be painting nails not cutting them.'

'Well,' he said, 'in that case the alternative might be more up your street. I don't know him personally but Mr Dunderdale has got all the right letters after his name. He's actually retired but he still likes to take on a few selected clients, just to keep his hand in. However he does live out at Lawnswood and unless I'm very much mistaken you're not motorised?' I said, 'No problem. I can just bob on the 17. It's a bus I like. No, if it's all the same to you and the Equal Opportunities Board I'll opt for Mr Dunderdale.' He said, 'I think it's a wise decision. Allow me,' (and he winked) 'Allow me,' he said, 'to shake hands with your feet.'

I've been going to Mr Suddaby for years. I think it's an investment, particularly if you're like me and go in for slim-fitting court shoes (squeeze, squeeze). Mr Suddaby reads me the riot act, of course, but as he says, 'It's a free country, Miss Fozzard. If you want to open the door to a lifetime of hard skin, I can't stop you.' What view this Mr Dunderdale will take remains to be seen.

When I get back Mrs Beevers has her hat and coat on, can't wait to get off. Says Bernard has been propped up in a chair staring at the TV all evening. She helps me get him upstairs and then I sit by the bed and, as per the recovery programme, give him a run-down on my day.

Mr Clarkson-Hall down at the Unit says that when somebody has had a cerebral accident, 'In lay terms, a stroke, Miss Fozzard, we must take care not to treat them like a child. If your brother is going to recover his faculties, dear lady, the more language one can throw at him the better.'

I was just recounting my conversation with Mr Suddaby and how they're decamping to Scarborough when Bernard suddenly throws back his head and yawns.



I rang Mr Clarkson-Hall this morning. He says that's progress.

*Pause.*

I do miss work.

FADE.



I'm just getting my things on to go up to Mr Dunderdale's this evening, when Bernard has a little accident and manages to broadcast the entire contents of his bladder all the way down the stairs. Mrs Beevers is taking her time coming and it's only when I've got him all cleaned up and sitting on the throne that the doorbell eventually goes. Except even then it's not her, just a couple from church about Rwanda. I said, 'Never mind Rwanda, can we deal with the matter in hand and get a middle-aged gentleman off the lavatory?' So we get him downstairs and manoeuvre him onto his chosen chair five inches from the TV screen.

After they've gone I said, 'You can work the remote; it's about time you remembered how to wipe your own bottom.' Not a flicker. Of course, that's where they have you with a stroke: you never know what goes in and what doesn't.

When Mrs Beevers eventually does roll up she's half an hour late which means I've missed the ten past and have to run all the way up Dyneley Road so by the time I'm ringing Mr Dunderdale's doorbell I'm all flustered and very conscious that my feet may be perspiring. He said, 'Well if that is what is troubling you, Miss Fozzard, I can straightaway put paid to the problem because I always kick off the proceedings by applying a mild astringent.'

Refined-looking feller, seventy-odd but with a lovely head of hair, one of the double-fronted houses that look over the cricket field. Rests my foot on a large silk handkerchief which I thought was a civilised touch; Mr Suddaby just used to use yesterday's *Evening Post*.

He said, 'Well, Miss Fozzard, I take one look at these and I say to myself here is someone who is on her feet a good deal. Am I right?' I said, 'You are. I'm in charge of the soft furnishing department at Matthias Robinson's, or was until my brother was taken ill. Anything you want in cretonne you know where to come.' He said, 'I might hold you to that but meanwhile could I compliment you on your choice of shoe.' I said, 'Well, as a rule I steer clear of suede because as a shoe it's a bit high maintenance, but sometimes I think the effort with the texturiser pays dividends.' He said, 'I can see we share a philosophy. If I may, I'll just begin by clipping your toenails.'





He said, 'Of course as soon as you walked in I picked you out as a professional woman.' I said, 'How?' He said, 'By your discreet choice of accessories.' I said, 'Well I favour a conservative approach to fashion, peppy but classic if you know what I mean.' He said, 'I do. There's been a verruca here, but it's extinct. Do you know why I chose the profession of chiropody?' I said, 'No.' He said, 'It's so that I could kneel at the feet of thousands of women and my wife would never turn a hair.' I said, 'Oh. Is there a Mrs Dunderdale?' He said, 'There was. She passed over.'

When he'd finished he rubbed in some mentholated oil (Moroccan apparently) and said I'd just feel a mild tingling effect which wasn't unpleasant and said my feet were in tip top condition, the only possible cloud on the horizon a pre-fungal condition between two of my toes that he wanted to keep a watchful eye on.

Had on a lovely cardigan. I said, 'I hope you'll excuse me asking but is that cardigan cashmere?' He said, 'Well spotted, Miss Fozzard. This may be the first time you've seen it but it won't be the last, could I offer you a glass of sweet sherry?'

Churchwarden at St Wilfred's apparently, past president of the Inner Wheel and nicely off by the looks of it, a pillar of the community. When he's at the door he says, 'Next time, if you're very good, I shall initiate you into the mysteries of the metatarsal arch.'

I thought about it on the bus and when I gave Mrs Beevers her money I told her that with my wanting to get back to work she'd no need to come again as I was going to advertise for someone permanent. Bernard's got a bit put by and if this isn't a rainy day I don't know what is.

He was watching TV so I switched it off and took him through my evening as Mr Clarkson-Hall said I should. He looked a bit snotty but I said 'Bernard, nobody ever learned to talk again by watching the snooker.' Told him about Mr Dunderdale and the pre-fungal condition between my toes, his cashmere cardigan and whatnot.

As Mr Clarkson-Hall says, 'Miss Fozzard, it doesn't matter what you say so long as it's language: language is balls coming at you from every angle.' And it's working. I'd got him into bed and was just closing the door when I heard him say his first word. I think it was 'cow'.

When I rang Mr Clarkson-Hall to tell him he said, 'Why cow?' I said, 'Probably an advert on TV.'



Still he agreed: it's a breakthrough.

FADE.



It was just that bit warmer today so I thought if I went along in my mustard Dannimac I could team it with my ancient peep-toe sandals that haven't had an airing since last summer when I had a little run over to Whitby with Joy Poyser.

Well, Mr Dunderdale couldn't get over them. Said he'd not seen a pair like them in fifteen years and that in the support they gave to the instep plus the unimpeded circulation of air via the toe no more sensible shoe had ever been devised. Made me parade up and down the room in them and would have taken a photograph only he couldn't put his hands on his Polaroid. Anyway I'm taking them along so that we can do it next time.

Wants me to go fortnightly until my *tinea pedis* yields to treatment but he's going to do it for the same fee and now that I'm back at work and we've got Miss Molloy coming in to see to Bernard there's no problem.

She said, 'Call me Mallory.' I said, 'Mallory? What sort of name is that? I wouldn't be able to put a sex to it.' She says, 'Well, I'm Australian.' Strong girl, very capable. And a qualified physiotherapist with a diploma in caring. It's Australian caring but I suppose it'll be the same as ours only minus the bugbear of hypothermia.

Ideally I would have preferred someone older, or someone less young anyway only we weren't exactly inundated with applicants which surprised me because I'd have thought it would have been a nice little sideline for a pensioner, though they'd have to be able-bodied. She chucks Bernard about as if he's two ha-porth of copper. Hails from Hobart, Tasmania, originally; I suppose England offers more scope for caring than the bush. And she and Bernard seem to hit it off, says she likes his sense of humour. I said to Joy Poyser, 'News to me. I didn't know he had one.'

Mind you, it's bearing fruit as movement's certainly coming back, he can hop up and down stairs now, more or less under his own steam. Speech too, because of course with him having company all day he gets the practice.

I was telling the whole saga of the stroke to Mr Dunderdale as he was tackling a patch of hard skin. He said, 'What did Bernard do, Miss Fozzard? I said, 'Not to put too fine a point on it, Mr Dunderdale, he was a murderer. He said, 'Oh. That's unusual.' I said, 'Well, he was a tobacconist which comes to the same thing. Sweets and tobacco, a little kiosk in Headingley.' He said, 'Yes, well sweets and tobacco…it's a lethal combination.' I said, 'He smoked, he was overweight and he certainly liked a drink. Worry is another cause, I know, but as I said to Mr Clarkson-Hall that is something he never did. But now, of course he's paying for it. Only what seems unfair is that I'm paying for it too.'





Mr Dunderdale looked up and he said, 'Yes' (and he had my foot in his hand). He said, 'Yes. If there had been thirteen disciples instead of twelve, the other one would have been you Miss Fozzard'.

Green silk handkerchief this time. Last week it was red.

The words are beginning to come back, though, no doubt about it and when he can't manage a word I get him to do what Mr Clarkson-Hall suggested, namely describe what he means and skirt a path round it. Miss Molloy makes him do it as well and she says one way and another they get along. Bathes him every day, rubs him with baby oil, says that where bedsores are concerned prevention is better than cure.

I still go in on a night and give him all my news. Mr Dunderdale had been saying that it was a pity evolution had taken the turn that it did because if it hadn't we might have found ourselves making as much use of our feet as we do our hands, which in the present economic climate might have been just what's needed to tip the balance. Miss Molloy said, 'That's interesting,' only Bernard just groans.

Personally I'm surprised she can put up with him but she says that by Australian standards he's a gentleman.

I hear them laughing.

FADE.

Soft Furnishings, we're always a bit slack first thing so I'll generally do a little wander over into Floor Coverings and have a word with Estelle Metcalf. I wish it was Housewares we were next to as that would make it Joy Poyser because Estelle's all right but she's a bit on the young side, big glasses, boy friend's one of these who dress up as cavaliers at the weekend.

I said to her this morning, 'Shiatsu.' She said, 'Come again?' I said, 'Shiatsu, what is it?' She said, 'Is it a tropical fish?' I said, 'No.' She said, 'Is it a mushroom?' I said, 'No.' She said, 'Is it Mr Dunderdale?' I said, 'Why should it be Mr Dunderdale?' She said, 'Because most things are with you these days.' I said, 'I shall ignore that, Estelle. Suffice it to say it's a form of massage involving various pressure points on the body that was invented by the Japanese.' She said, 'That's all very well but it didn't stop them doing Pearl Harbour, did it?' Neville's besieging York on Sunday, trying out his new breastplate. Estelle's going along as an imploring housewife who comes out under a flag of truce.



Just then a customer comes in wanting some seersucker slipovers so we had to cut it short. I don't talk about Mr Dunderdale. And if I do she talks about Oliver Cromwell.



I go weekly now, though Mr Dunderdale won't charge me any more. I was sat on the sofa afterwards while he put away his instruments and he said, 'Good news, Miss Fozzard. We seem to have cracked the *tinea pedis*, not a trace of it left. I think that calls for a sherry refill. Are you in a hurry to get off?' I said, 'No. Why?' He said, 'Well, we still have a little time in hand and I wonder if I might prevail upon you to try on a pair of bootees?' I said, 'Bootees?'

He said, 'Well, I'm using the term loosely. They're technically what we would call a fur-lined Gibson bruised look but bootees is a convenient shorthand. The shade is Bengal bronze.' I said, 'Well, they're a lovely shoe.' He said, 'Yes. Cosy, ankle-hugging they make a beautiful ending to the leg. They're a present, of course.' I said, 'Oh, Mr Dunderdale, I couldn't.' He said, 'Miss Fozzard, please. My contacts in the world of footwear procure me a considerable discount. Besides there is a little something you can do for me in return.' I said, 'Oh?' He said, 'My years in bending over ladies' feet have resulted in an intermittently painful condition of the lower back which, if you are amenable you have it in your power to alleviate.' I said, 'I do, Mr Dunderdale?' He said, 'You do, Miss Fozzard. I'm going to put one cushion on the hearthrug here for my head and the other here for my abdomen and now I'm going to lie down and what I want you to do is to step on my lower back.' I said, 'Should I take the bootees off?' He said, 'No, no. Keep the bootees on – their texture makes them ideal for the purpose. That's it. Steady yourself by holding onto the edge of the mantelpiece if you want.'

Then he said something I couldn't hear because his face was pressed into the carpet. 'What was that, Mr Dunderdale?' 'I said, "Excellent," Miss Fozzard. You may move about a little if you would care to.' I said, 'I'm anxious not to hurt you, Mr Dunderdale.' He said, 'Have no fears on that score, Miss Fozzard. Trample away.' I said, 'I feel like one of those French peasants treading the grapes.' He said, 'Yes. Yes, yes.' I said, 'Do you feel the benefit?' He said, 'Yes, yes, I do. Thank you. If you don't mind, Miss Fozzard I'll just lie here for a little while. Perhaps you could see yourself out.'

So I just left him on the hearthrug.

When I got back Bernard is sitting on the sofa with Miss Molloy, both of them looking a bit red in the face. 'We were just laughing,' Miss Molloy says, 'because Bernard couldn't think of a word.' 'Well,' I said, 'he must learn to skirt round it.' 'Oh, he did that all right,' she said. 'You're an expert at that, aren't you Bernard?' And they both burst out laughing.

Mr Clarkson-Hall's very pleased with him. Says he's never known a recovery so quick. Says he didn't have the privilege of knowing Bernard before but he imagines he's now quite like his old self. I said, 'Yes. He is.'

After Miss Molloy had gone he comes in here while I'm having my hot drink and says he's thinking of opening the kiosk again and that Mallory is going to help him. I said, 'Does Miss Molloy have any experience of sweets and tobacco?' He said, 'No, but she's a fun-loving girl with a welcoming whatever it's called and that's half the battle.'

Note from Mr Dunderdale this morning saying his back is much better and that he was looking forward to seeing me next week.

Estelle suffers in the back department, the legacy from once having had to wield a spare pike at the Battle of Naseby. So I was telling her all about me helping Mr Dunderdale with his, only she wasn't grateful. Just giggles and says, 'Ooh, still waters!'

Floor coverings, they ought to have somebody more mature. She really belongs in Cosmetics.

FADE.

I don't know what's got into people at work. I come in this morning and the commissionaire with the moustache who's on the staff door says, 'Have a good day, my duck.' I said, 'You may only have one arm, Mr Capstick, but that doesn't entitle you to pat me on the bottom. Next thing is I'm

invoicing some loose covers in Despatch when one of the work experience youths who can't be more than sixteen gives me a silly wink.

I said to Estelle, 'My Viyella two-piece doesn't normally have this effect.' She said, 'Well they're just wanting to be friendly.' I said, 'Friendly? Estelle, I may not be a feminist (though I did spearhead the provision of pot-pourri in the ladies toilets) but people are not going to pat my bottom with impunity.' Estelle says, 'No. The boot's on the other foot,' and starts giggling. I said to Joy Poyser, 'How ever she manages to interest anyone in serious vinyl flooring I do not understand.'

House dark when I got in. I imagine they're in the sitting room, the pair of them only I call out and there's no sound. So I get my tea and read the *Evening Post*, nice to have the place to myself for a change.

Then I go into the sitting room and there's Bernard sitting there in the dark. I put the light on and he's got the atlas open. I said, 'What are you doing in the dark?' He said, 'Looking up the Maldive Islands.' 'Why,' I said, 'you're not going on holiday?' He said, 'No, I'm not. How can I go on bloody holiday? What with?' And he shoves a bank statement at me.

I've a feeling he's been crying and I'm not sure where to put myself so I go put the kettle on while I look at his statement. There's practically nothing in it, money taken out nearly every day. I said, 'What's this?' He said, 'It's that tart from Hobart.' I said, 'Miss Molloy? But she's a qualified physiotherapist.' He said, 'Yes and she's something else…she's a – what do you call it – female dog.'

I said, 'Did you sign these cheques?' He said, 'Of course I signed them.' I said, 'What were you doing, practising writing?' He said, 'No.' I said, 'Where is she?' He said, 'The Maldive Islands, where I was going to be.' I said, 'Well we must contact the police. It's fraud is this.' He said, 'No it isn't.' I said, 'What did you think these cheques were for?' He said, 'I knew what they were for. For services rendered. And I don't mean lifting me on and off the what's it called. It's stuff she did for me.' I said, 'What stuff?' He said, 'You know.'



I said, 'Remember what Mr Clarkson-Hall says, Bernard. Trace a path round the word.' He said, 'I don't have to trace a path round the bloody word. I know the word. It's you that doesn't. You don't know bloody nothing.' I said, 'Well one thing is plain. Despite your cerebral accident your capacity for foul language remains unimpaired.' He said, 'You're right. It bloody does.'



I made him some tea. I said, 'She's made a fool of you.' Bernard said, 'You can speak.' I said, 'You mean talk. I know I can speak. The expression is, you can talk. Anyway why?' He said, 'Monkeying about with your foot feller.' I said, 'Mr Dunderdale? What's he got to do with it?' He said, 'Little games and whatnot. He's obviously a…a…' I said, 'A what?' He said, 'A…thing.' I said, 'Skirt a path round the word, Bernard. A what?' He said, 'Skirt it yourself you stupid…four legs, two horns, where you get milk.' I said, 'Cow. You normally remember that.'

I was telling Joy Poyser about it and she said, 'Well, why did you tell him about the chiropodist?' I said, 'Mr Clarkson-Hall said that I should talk to him, it's part of the therapy.' She said, 'It's not part of the therapy for Estelle Metcalf, is it? You told her. She's not had a stroke.' Apparently she's spread it all over the store.'

Anyway I came upstairs, left him crying over the atlas, when suddenly I hear a crash. I said, 'Bernard? Bernard?'

*Pause.*

'Bernard!'

FADE.

Estelle ventured into Soft Furnishings yesterday, first time for a week. Testing the water, I suppose. Said Neville was taking part in the battle of Marston Moor on Sunday. She's going along as a camp follower but they're short of one or two dishevelled Roundhead matrons and was I interested? I said, 'It's kind of you to offer, Estelle, but I think from now I'd be well advised to keep a low profile.'

People don't like to think you have a proper life, that's what I've decided. Or any more of a life than they know about. Then when they find out they think it's shocking. Else funny. I never thought I had a life. It was always Bernard who had the life.

He's worse this time than the last. Eyes used to follow you then. Not now. Log. Same rigmarole, though. Talk to him. Treat him like a person. Not that he ever treated me like a person. Meanwhile Madam is laid out on the beach in the Maldives. He was on the rug when I found him. Two inches the other way and he'd have hit his head on the fender. Lucky escape.



I'd written to Mr Dunderdale, cancelling any further appointments. I didn't say why, just that with Bernard being poorly again it wasn't practical anyway. Which it wasn't.



So it was back to normal, sitting with Bernard, doing a few little jobs. I'd forgotten how long an evening could be.

Anyway, I was coming away from work one night and a big browny-coloured car draws up beside me, the window comes down and blow me if it isn't Mr Dunderdale.

He said, 'Good evening, Miss Fozzard. Could I tempt you up to Lawnswood? I'd like a little chat.' I said, 'Could we not talk here?' He said, 'Not in the way I'd like. I'm on a double yellow line.' So I get in and he runs me up there and whatever else you can say about him he's a very accomplished driver.

Anyway he sits me down in his study and gives me a glass of sherry and says why did I not want to come and see him any more. Well, I didn't know what to say. I said, 'It isn't as if I don't look forward to my appointments.' He said, 'Well, dear lady, I look forward to them too.' I said, 'But now that I have to get help in for Bernard again I can't afford to pay you.'

He said, 'Well, may I make a suggestion? Why don't we reverse the arrangement?' I said, 'Come again.' He said, 'Do it vice versa. I pay you.' I said, 'Well, it's very unusual.' He said, 'You're a very unusual woman.' I said, 'I am? Why?' He said, 'Because you're a free spirit, Miss Fozzard. You make your own rules.' I said, 'Well, I like to think so.' He said, 'I'm the

same. We're two of a kind, you and I, Miss Fozzard. Mavericks. Have you ever had any champagne?' I said, 'No, but I've seen it at the conclusion of motor races.' He said, 'Allow me. To the future?'

It's all very decorous. Quite often he'll make us a hot drink and we'll just sit and turn over the pages of one of his many books on the subject, or converse on matters related. I remarked the other day how I'd read that Imelda Marcos had a lot of shoes. He said, 'She did…and she suffered for it at the bar of world opinion, in my view, Miss Fozzard, unjustly.'

Little envelope on the hall table as I go out, never mentioned, and if there's been anything beyond the call of duty there'll be that little bit extra. Buys me no end of shoes, footwear generally. I keep thinking where's it all going to end but we'll walk that plank when we come to it.

I've never had the knack of making things happen. I thought things happened or they didn't. Which is to say they didn't. Only now they have…sort of.

Bernard gets an attendance allowance now and what with that and the envelopes from Mr Dunderdale I can stay on at work and still have someone in to look after him. Man this time. Mr Albright. Pensioner, so he's glad of a job. Classy little feller, keen on railways and reckons to be instigating Bernard into the mysteries of chess. Though Mr Albright has to play both sides of course.

At one point I said to Mr Dunderdale, 'People might think this rather peculiar particularly in Lawnswood.' He said, 'Well, people would be wrong. We are just enthusiasts, Miss Fozzard, you and I and there's not enough enthusiasm in the world these days. Now if those Wellingtons are comfy I just want you in your own time and as slowly as you like very gently to mark time on my bottom.'

Occasionally he'll have some music on. I said once, 'I suppose that makes this the same as aerobics.' He said, 'If you like.'

It's droll but the only casualty in all this is my feet, because nowadays the actual chiropody gets pushed to one side a bit. If I want an MOT I really have to nail him down.

We're still Mr Dunderdale and Miss Fozzard and I've not said anything to anybody at work. Learned my lesson there.

Anyway, people keep saying how well I look.

*Pause.*

I suppose there's a word for what I'm doing but...I skirt round it.

FADE.

# Playing
## **Sandwiches**

**Wilfred:** David Haig

PRODUCED BY **MARK SHIVAS** DIRECTED BY **UDAYAN PRASAD**
DESIGNED BY **STUART WALKER** MUSIC BY **GEORGE FENTON**

A MIDDLE-AGED MAN IN THE BASIC UNIFORM (DONKEY JACKET, NAVY BLUE OVERALLS) OF A PARKS ATTENDANT. HE SITS AGAINST THE PLANKS OF A PARK SHELTER, PAINTED BUT WORN AND COVERED WITH GRAFFITI.

I was in the paper shop this dinnertime getting some licorice allsorts. Man serving me said, 'I wish I was like you.' Shouted out to the woman, 'I wish I was him. Always buying sweets, never gets fat.' I said, 'Yes, I'm lucky. Only I cycle.' She said, 'Yes, I've seen you. You work for the Parks Department.' He said, 'Weren't you a lollipop man once?' I said, 'No.' He said, 'I thought I'd seen you, stood at the crossing.' Racks and racks of magazines. Always men in there, looking.

Janet was dressmaking, doing the twins' christening frocks. I said, 'They put on you, Janet. Before these frocks there's been no word for long enough.' She said, 'Well, whose fault is that?' Apricot satin, little buttons down the front.





Mr Trickett nosing round this afternoon at what he calls 'grassroots level' ordains a blitz on the bushes behind the playground. Privet mostly, all stinking of urine and clogged up with every sort of filth...sheaths; jamrags; a shoe; some tights; sick; dog muck. They come over the wall on a night after The Woodman's turned out, lie down drunk in all that filth and stench and do it. They do it in the playground too, laid down over one end of the slide where the kiddies slide along with their bottoms, then just chuck the evidence down anywhere.

I'm nearly finished when Mr Kumar stops with his barrow and brushes and we walk back to the yard together. He's from Bombay so he takes all this filth in his stride. Born a street sweeper, apparently, what they call an untouchable, though he's very neat, you'd never think it. Going on about getting his wife over from India. Got some decent digs in the Brudenells only a person from Liverpool comes and kicks the door in in the middle of the night. Thinks the English don't like the Indians; says the only Indians the English like are the Gurkhas. The Gurkhas cut people's heads off so that makes them the salt of the earth.

As we're going by the office Mr Parlane calls me in and says he's heard from Wakefield but they still can't trace my records. Foreman, dinner supervisor, lollipop man, I must have left some trace, was I sure I'd got all the digits right? I reeled the number off again and he said, 'Well, I'll try Pontefract, Wilfred, but it's been six months now.'

I went the long way round, pushing the bike. Just one kiddy by herself on the swings. Kiddy black. Mother, white, having a cig, watching.

FADE.

*Against anonymous wallpaper; a bedroom, say.*

I don't like a cargo of relations; I never have. I wasn't particular to go to the christening only Janet wanted to see what her frocks looked like on and anyway, as she said, who are Barry and Yvonne to look down their nose, their Martin's been had up twice for drunken driving.

Slight hiccup round the font because, since Martin hasn't actually managed to turn up they're short of a godfather. Yvonne wants to go ahead without but the young lad who's in charge says that though he personally is very relaxed about it, the church does tend to insist on there being a full complement of godparents.



We're all standing round looking a bit stumped when little Rosalie, who's seven, pipes up and says, 'Why can't Uncle Wilfred be it, he's my godfather.' Barry straight off clouts her only the priest who doesn't look much more than seventeen and new to the parish says, 'Would Uncle Wilfred be a possible solution?' I don't say anything at all only Yvonne gets in quick, 'No, Wilfred wouldn't be a possible solution because…' and Janet looks at her '...because they're not currently motorised.' The priest lad looks as if he's about to say that wheels aren't part of the job description when Yvonne spots Grandpa Greenwood who's just been out to spend a penny and says, 'He'll do'. The priest says, 'Isn't he a bit on the old side?' Yvonne says, 'No he isn't. He still goes ballroom dancing.' So it ends up being him. I said to Janet, 'At least baby Lorraine won't have any problems with the Military Twostep.'



Afterwards we adjourn to Sherwood Road where Pete and Gloria had laid something on, beer chiefly by the looks of it, one of those dos where the women end up in one room and the men in another. There are kiddies all over the place, though, and what with Pete's alsatian plunging around, sheer bedlam. That's irresponsible in my view, a dog that size when there are kiddies about. One snap and they're scarred for life. A lot of larking about with the children, Barry throwing their two up in the air till they screamed then pretends to throw one to me but doesn't. Ginger tash. Big fingers. Does a bit of decorating now and again, was in a remand home when he was young.

Then Pete starts telling his so-called jokes. 'Now then, which would you rather have, Wilf, a thousand women with one pound or one woman with a thousand pound?' 'Else neither,' says Barry and I saw him wink but I didn't take on. I thought I'd go and help wash up only no sooner were all the women in the kitchen when Janet has to embark on the saga of her womb, how we could have had children only the angle of it was wrong. So Yvonne chips in, 'It's not your angle, love, it's his that matters.' So there's a lot of smutty laughter and I go out and sit on the back step.

Little Rosalie's playing in the yard, throwing her ball against the wall, clapping her hands and lifting her leg to throw the ball under, all that. When she stops she comes and sits on the step and I say, 'I think that deserves a sweet, Rosalie,' and give her a licorice allsort. Suddenly there's a banging in the window and Yvonne bursts through the door and gets hold of the kiddy 'I told you, madam,' starts laying into her, and clawing the sweet out of her mouth. The dog's barking, the kiddy's crying, the old man has an accident and they're all shouting. So anyway we came away.



Janet doesn't say anything. Only when we're at the bus stop she says 'I don't want to have to be flitting again. If you made a decision never to buy any more licorice allsorts it would be a step in the right direction.'

So anyway, I promised.



FADE.

*The edge of a bandstand, some wrought iron, but scribbled over and defaced.*

Anybody that wants to make a fortune should invent something that'll erase the stuff they write up. There's a plaque on the wall by the fountain:

> This park was opened on July 17 1936 by the
> Rt. Honourable the Earl of Harewood KG. TD.

'So eat shit' some bright spark has sprayed across it, with the result I'm down there all morning with the Brasso and a wire brush.

'Think of it as a labour of love, Mr Paterson,' Parlane said. 'The present one's the music-lover.' 'Who?' 'The Earl of Harewood. Father married the old Princess Royal.' He hangs about for a bit then eventually says, Had I got a minute and he hoped I wouldn't take it amiss but had I been in prison? I said, 'No. What would I have been in prison for?' He said, He'd no idea, it was just that when records go walkabout as mine plainly had that was often the case.

I said, Well, it's not the case in this case, thank you very much and was my work unsatisfactory? He said, 'Far from it, the place has never been

so tidy. You, Mr Paterson are a textbook example of why we went performance related. But you're also an example of somebody who has eluded all the fielders and ended up in the long grass, bureaucratically speaking. Well, don't worry. Gordon Parlane is going to make it his personal mission to retrieve you.'

It started spitting this afternoon so I thought I'd keep out of the rain and sweep up the bandstand. Young woman there again, the kiddy; I've seen them once or twice now, poor-looking, eating chips out of a carton.

She says, 'Are we all right sitting here?' I said, 'That's what it's for, visitors.' She said, 'We often come. The council's put us in bed and breakfast only the hotel's got proper people too and they don't like us around during the day. Samantha hates it, don't you Samantha?' The kiddy comes over and offers me a chip. 'You're privileged,' the mother says, 'she's frightened of men generally. Won't go near her father. Mind you, neither will I.'

Bonny little thing, only her mother's put her some earrings in, stud things. And one in her little nose and she can't be more than seven.

I wonder the law lets them do it, because that's interference in my view, ornamenting your kiddies, hanging stuff on them as if they were Christmas trees.

I'm sweeping up the rubbish and pretend to sweep up the kiddy too so she starts screaming with laughter. 'Oh,' her mother says, 'I think you've clicked. What is this place?' I said, 'What place?' 'This. This shelter thing.' I said, 'It's a bandstand. The band used to play here once upon a time.' She said, 'What band? You mean like a group?'

The kiddy came and stood by my knee. 'Yes,' I said. She said, 'Where did the fans go then? In the bushes?' She laughed and the kiddy laughed and put her hand on my leg. I said, 'It's stopped raining, I'd better get on.' She threw the chip carton down. She said, 'We'll see you. Wave to the man, Samantha. Wave.'



As I'm pushing the barrow back there's a policeman hanging about the fountain. Said he was just showing the flag and he'd be obliged if I'd keep my eye open for any undesirable elements. I said, 'Drugs, you mean?'



He said, 'Drugs or whatever. Men sitting too long on the benches type thing. Parks make for crime. This beat's a bugger.' As he was going he said, 'Pardon my asking but didn't you use to work at the Derby Baths?' I said, 'No, why?' He said, 'Nothing, the face is familiar. My two both got their bronze medal there. Well, I won't detain you, particularly since our Asian friend appears to be waiting.'

Pushing his barrow back Mr Kumar's all smiles because his wife has arrived. 'They took all her clothes off at the airport but otherwise,' he says, 'it was all as easy as falling off a log. I am a very happy man.'

'They're sly,' Janet said. 'Probably wants your job.' I said, 'What for?' 'His brother, his uncle, his nephew. They're all the same. Anyway I got my promotion. Same grade now as I was before. Keep this up a bit longer, Wilfred, and we might be able to run to a car again soon.'

FADE.

*Planks again or municipal bricks. An outside wall, say.*

Bit of excitement this morning. Body in the bushes. Little lad found it looking for his ball. Old man, one of the winos probably. Two police cars, an ambulance and more fuss made of him dead than there ever was alive. The child not worried at all, the mother hysterical. All over by half past ten and we were soon back in go mode, drizzle included.

I was heading for the tennis courts, trying to steer clear of the bandstand only Trickett shouts after me, 'Paterson. I don't want you skulking back there. The bandstand's in a disgusting state.'

Somebody'd thrown up all over the seat and I'd just about got it cleared up when the girl's calling out and the kiddy comes running in waving her little pink plastic handbag thing. 'Samantha's got you a present, haven't you Samantha. Give it to Mr...what's your name?' The child was putting her arms out to be lifted up.

'Hargreaves,' I said. 'My name's Hargreaves.' 'Give it to him Samantha,' and she takes out a daffodil from her little handbag and we put it in my buttonhole. 'She picked it herself,' the mother said. 'My name's Debbie.'

They sit watching while I go on cleaning up. She said, 'You're a bit too nice for this job aren't you? You look as if you should be doing something more up-market, a traffic warden or something.'



I said I liked being outside. The kiddy was pretending to help me sweep up again. 'It didn't used to be like this,' I said, 'all scribbled over and stuff written up.' 'Oh,' she says, 'I like the lived in look. Cans and litter and all that. You don't want it too clinical. Anyway it's all litter basically isn't it...Leaves is litter. Soil. We like it, don't we Samantha?'



I said, 'Why did you put them earring things in?' She said 'Her studs? Well, I don't see why she shouldn't have all the advantages other kids have. She's as good as anybody else. Don't you like them?' I said, 'No, Debbie. I do like them.'

After a bit the mother says Did I like her. I said Why? She said, 'Well we keep running into one another.' I said, 'You won't have Samantha tattooed, will you?' 'Oh no,' she said, 'not until she's old enough to make her own decisions. It's part of her life choices isn't it? Did the fountain used to go?' I said, 'Yes. When I was a boy. The fountain went. The band played. People kept off the grass. It was lovely.'

Mr Kumar comes by and says I have to call in at the office when it's convenient. He smiles at the girl but she doesn't take on. 'I don't care for Asians,' she said when he's gone. 'Neither one thing nor the other in my opinion.'

I went along to the office straightaway only it turns out to be nothing. Parlane has got some new idea about chasing me up on the computer. He said, 'I'm going to fax all your details over to Thorpe Arch, tell them Wakefield has been playing silly buggers (which they're always happy to hear) and get them as a personal favour to me to beam you up nationally. And if that doesn't work even Gordon Parlane is going to have to admit defeat.'

Coming out I ran into Mr Trickett. 'Oh,' he said spotting my buttonhole, 'Picking flowers now, Paterson?' I said somebody'd broken it off. He said, 'I don't know why we bother. They don't want gardens, they want their hands chopping off. I'd decapitate them let alone the bloody daffodils.' 'Anyway,' he said, 'Get rid of it. It sends the wrong message.'

They were still hanging about when I went back. 'Mr Hargreaves has lost his buttonhole,' Debbie said and the kiddy starts crying only when I pick her up she stops.

On the way home I called in at the sweetshop.

FADE.

*Some sort of institutional background, half green, half cream. Wilfred is unshaven, with no tie on.*

Janet's just been down, apparently. Left a clean vest and stuff at the desk. They said she wasn't allowed to speak to me at this stage; she said she didn't want to anyway.

It was the rain that did it because I'd given the bandstand a wide berth all week only Trickett comes into the yard this morning saying it was all flooded and wasn't that typical, one drop of rain and the place grinds to a halt. Tells me to get some rods and try and locate the problem. So I trundle over there and it's one of the grates that's stopped up. And I'm just getting my arm down to feel what the stoppage was when Samantha comes running along by the railings and puts her little face through the bars.

I said, 'Hello. Are you in prison?' She said, 'No. I've got an umbrella.' And she shows me her baby umbrella.

Her mother's all cross, pulls her away from the puddle and says, 'Are you going to be here long? I've got to go and see my social worker woman. Can I leave her with you for half an hour? She likes you. She won't be any bother.' I said, 'Why can't she go with you?' She said, 'Because her dad'll be there and if he sees her he'll want to keep her. Go on.'



I was going to say no, only I didn't have to because just then Mr Parlane appears and wants a word so they clear off, leaving me with my arm still down the drain. I suddenly feel the culprit and it's two or three condoms all mixed up with leaves plugging up the pipe so I pull the lot out and all the dammed up water just empties away.



'Success,' I say to Mr Parlane and show him the bundle, 'Problem solved.' He said, 'No, not entirely. Would you step along to the office for a minute or two. And bring your barrow.'

It was Trickett who gave me my cards, with one week's pay in lieu, said I'd made several false statements so I'd better not have any silly ideas about wrongful dismissal and had I thought about bringing the Parks Department into disrepute let alone anything else.

Parlane hung about outside and when I came out said what about working in an old people's home or even a mortuary, somewhere out of harm's way, where I couldn't do any damage. 'Because you're a good worker, Wilfred, you really are.'

I went out the playground way, empty with it being wet, just a woman and a baby. I think she's a child minder. Only suddenly Samantha comes running out from behind the see-saw and gets hold of my hand. I said, 'Where's her mother?' The woman said, 'Gone over to the social. She said she'd be back by now. I've got to go, can I leave her with you?' I said, 'No.' 'Debbie said I could. She'll be back any minute. Let her go on the slide. She likes the slide.'

She wouldn't go on the slide because it was all wet, so we went and sat in the shelter. I put my hand on my knee and she put hers on top of it, then I put mine on and she topped it off with her hand. And we played that game for a bit. Sandwiches she called it.

Then I pretended to go to sleep, only she got on the seat and tried to open my eyes with her little fingers. She kept wanting to hold my hand but I wouldn't. Her little hand kept pecking at my hand, like a little bird trying to get in. Only my hand was a fist, honestly. Tight, she couldn't get in.

'There's nothing in there for you,' I said, 'I don't have anything for little girls. My shop's closed.' 'No it's not,' she says and slips her little finger in between my fingers and wiggles it about and looks at me and laughs.

She laughs again. She knew what she was doing. She must have known what she was doing.

So I took her in the bushes.



FADE.

*White tiles. Wilfred is in prison clothes; eye swollen; bandage on his hand.*



I said, 'She wanted to show me her dance.' Her mother said, 'What dance? She doesn't have a dance.' Somebody shouts out, 'You'll dance.'

They fetched me in and out the back way under a blanket. Women there shouting. Something hit me on the head. Said in the van it was a packet of cornflakes. Coins as well. Aught they have in their shopping bags.

They have to ravel it all out in words. 'Then what did you do? Then what?' As if there was a plan. As if I meant to go from A to B. 'Well,' says the counsel, 'you bought the sweets, didn't you? You gave the wrong name.' I said to the young policewoman, 'It's what I thought she wanted.' 'That's what men always say,' she said, 'choose how old you are.'

Perhaps it would be easier, said the judge, if Samantha came up here. So she went and stood by his knee and held his hand. I thought, 'Well, that's what I'm here for.'

I asked for a number of other offences to be taken into consideration, some of them in Huddersfield where I've never even been. The police said it didn't matter as it meant they could close the book on lots of cases and it would go in my favour. It didn't. They just said my record proved that I was a hopeless case.

The judge said I would be given treatment. I haven't been given any treatment. They've put me by myself to stop the others giving me the treatment. The getting scalded in the kitchen treatment. The piss in your porridge treatment.

The doctor said, 'Did anyone touch you when you were little?' I said I didn't want any of that stuff. 'No, they didn't. And if they did, it's done. Anyway, they tell you to touch people now. They run courses in it.' 'Not like that,' he said.

Janet's been. Usual tack. Blames the mothers, says if they can't look after them they don't deserve kiddies in the first place. All her daffodils have been rooted up, plant pots broken. Next stop Newcastle, probably.

Mr Kumar. Says, I miss you Mr Paterson. I miss our walks with our barrows and brushes. You are the untouchable now. And he pats my hand. Says he's gone up one rung on the ladder now, is an attendant at the Art Gallery. 'No condoms to speak of,' he says. 'No sick on the floor. And on the walls the beautiful ladies and landscapes of Leeds. I tell you, Mr Paterson, it is a cushy number.'



When they put me away last time I used to think when I got out I'd go somewhere right away, a shed in the middle of a moor. And I'd fence it round with railway sleepers and get myself a bad dog and be a recluse.

Only kids would come. They'd know.



The prison must be near the station. I hear the trains on a night. And a school somewhere. There's a playtime at a quarter to eleven. And they come out at four. It's the one bit of my life that feels right and it's that bit that's wrong.

Men groan and cry out. Shout and scream in the night. It's like a tropical forest. Wild beasts.

I didn't foist them off like grown-ups do. I looked at them. I listened to them.

Sometimes there's a plane crosses the top left hand corner of my window. I think of the 'No Smoking' sign going on, the seats put back in the upright position, the pilot beginning his descent to Leeds and Bradford airport.

I used to go hiking when I was a boy. Over Nidderdale Moors. A reservoir. That would be the place. Nobody there at all.

FADE, *and in the black a long drawn-out howl.*

# The **Outside** Dog

**Marjory:** Julie Walters

PRODUCED BY **MARK SHIVAS** DIRECTED BY **GAVIN MILLAR**
DESIGNED BY **STUART WALKER** MUSIC BY **GEORGE FENTON**

Afternoon. The kitchen. Against a blank, wallpapered wall.
One chair. Possibly some artificial flowers.
Similar settings throughout.

I'd be the same if it was a cat. Because they make as much mess as dogs. Only cats you can be allergic to, so people make allowances. And flowers, of course, some people. Only we don't have flowers. Well, we do but they're all washable. I just think it spies on me, that tongue lolling out.

He took the van over to Rawdon last night. Said it was Rawdon anyway. Doing something or other, fly-tipping probably. Takes Tina which was a relief from the woof-woofing plus it gave me a chance to swill.

I'd had Mrs Catchpole opposite banging on the door in the afternoon saying she was going to the council because it wanted putting down. I said, 'I agree.' She said, 'I'm getting a petition up.' I said, 'Well, when you do, fetch it across because I'll be the first signatory.' I hate the flaming dog. Of course she doesn't do it with him. Never makes a muff when he's around.





He comes in after midnight, puts his clothes in the washer. I said to him last week, 'Why don't you do your washing at a cultivated hour?' He said, 'You're lucky I do it at all.' Still, at least the washer's in the shed. I shouted down, 'That dog's not inside is she?' He said, 'No. Get to sleep.' Which I was doing only when he comes up he has nothing on. He leaves it a bit then slides over to my side and starts carrying on.

Found a dog hair or two on the carpet this morning so that meant another shampooing job. I only did it last week. This shampoo's got air-freshener in, plus a disinfectant apparently.

Non-stop down at the yard since they started killing off the cows, so when he comes in this dinner-time he wants to eat straight off. Swills his boots under the outside tap and he's coming in like that. I said, 'Stuart. You know the rules. Take them off.' He said, 'There's no time.' So I said, 'Well, if there's not time you'll have it on the step.' Sits there eating and feeding Tina. She licks his boots. Literally. I suppose it's with him coming straight from the slaughterhouse.

Seems to have lost another anorak, this one fur-lined.

Fade.

She comes up this afternoon, his mother, all dolled up. Says, 'You've got this place nice. How do you manage with our Stuart?' I said, 'I've got him trained.' She said 'He's not trained when he comes down our house.' 'Well,' I said, 'perhaps he doesn't get the encouragement.' She said, 'I don't like it when they're too tidy. It's not natural.'

Not natural at their house. They've no culture at all. First time I went down there they were having their dinner and there was a pan stuck on the table. When it comes to evolution they're scarcely above pig-sty level. And she must be sixty, still dyes her hair, fag in her mouth, big ear-rings. She said, 'You don't mind if I smoke? Or do you want me to sit on the step?'

I gave her a saucer only it didn't do much good, ash all over the shop. She does it on purpose. It had gone five, she said, 'Where is he?' I said, 'Where he generally is at this time of day: slitting some defenceless creature's throat. They're on overtime.'

She went before it got dark. Said she was nervous what with this feller on the loose. Made a fuss of Tina. Remembered her when she was a puppy running round their house. I remember it an' all. Doing its business all up and down, the place stank. It was me that trained Stuart. Me that trained the dog.





Except for the din. Can't train that. Leaves off, of course when he appears. He doesn't believe she does it. I said to him, 'Is it safe for me to go on to the library?' He said, 'Why?' I said, 'There's a lass dead in Wakefield now.' He said, 'You don't cross any waste ground. Take Tina.'

Anyway I didn't go and when he's changed out of his muck and swilled everything off he put on his navy shirt, little chain round his neck and the tan slacks we bought him in Marbella. I brought him a beer in a glass while I had a sherry. Him sat on one side of the fire, me on the other, watching TV with the sound down. I said, 'This is a nice civilised evening.'

Except of course madam gets wind of the fact that we're having a nice time and starts whimpering and whatnot and jumping up outside the window and carries on and carries on until he has to take her out. Gone two hours so I was in bed when he got back.

Comes upstairs without his trousers on. I said, 'What've you done with your slacks?' He said, 'The dog jumped up and got mud on. Anyway it's quite handy isn't it?' I said, 'Why?' He said, 'Why do you think? Move up.'

Lots of shouting and whatnot. I thought in the middle of it, it's a blessing we're detached. 'Sorry about that,' he said when he'd done. 'I get carried away.'

Loudspeaker van came round this afternoon saying the police were going to be coming round. House to house. I was just getting some stuff ready to take to the dry cleaners while it was light still.

Couldn't find his slacks.

FADE.

She said, 'Have you any suspicions of anyone in your family?' I said, 'What family? There's only me and him.' He said, 'We can't talk with this dog carrying on. Can't we come inside?' I said, 'You've told people not to open their doors.' She said, 'But we're the police.' I said, 'Well, take your shoes off.'

She's in uniform, he's got a raincoat on. She said, 'We've had complaints about the dog. It's in your print-out.' I said, 'Oh it's the dog, is it? I thought it was the killer you were after.' She said, 'Your hubby says it never barks.' I said, 'When did you talk to him?' She said, 'At his place of employment. These are the dates of the murders. Look at them and tell me whether you can remember where your husband was on any of these dates.' I said, 'He was at home. He's always at home.' She said, 'Our information is he'll sometimes go out.' I said, 'Yes. With the dog. Do you know dogs? They occasionally want to have a jimmy riddle.' She said, 'What about this fly-tipping? His van's been seen.' I said, 'The van's not my province. Though I've shared the back seat with a beast head before now.'

Meanwhile the one in the raincoat's been sitting there saying nothing, looking round, sizing the place up. Suddenly he stands up. 'Can I use the toilet?' I said, 'Now? Well, you'll have to wait while I put a paper down.'

I took him upstairs and waited outside. He says, 'I can't do it with you listening.' So I came downstairs again. And she says, 'He's got a funny bladder.'

'One last question. Have you noticed anything out of the ordinary about your husband stroke boy friend stroke father stroke son…well, that's husband in your case…over the last six months?' 'Like what?' 'Blood on his clothes?' I said, 'There's always blood. He's a slaughterman. Only you won't find any in here. And you won't find any outside. He swills it off.' I said, 'Your friend's taking his time.' She said, 'Men have problems with their water. I've an idea he has an appliance.'

When eventually he comes down he says, 'You keep the place tidy.' I said, 'I used to be a teacher.' He said, 'What did you teach?' I said, 'Children.' He said, 'Do you have any?' I said, 'Does it look like it?'

As they're going Mother Catchpole opposite is stood in the road

and shouts across, 'I've got something to tell you.' So the girl goes over and has a word. Comes back. 'Nothing,' she says. 'Just the flaming dog.' 'Nobody listens to me,' she's shouting, 'I've had a depression with that dog.'

I shut the door. When I went upstairs to wipe round the toilet I saw he'd moved one or two ornaments. Nothing else that I could see.

When his lordship came in I said, 'You never told me they'd been to your work.' He said, 'It was routine. I've tipped on one of the sites where they found one of them.' I said, 'Did you find that ticket?' He said, 'What ticket?' 'For the dry cleaners. The tan slacks.' He said, 'Oh yes. They're at work.' I said, 'You're not wearing them for work. They're good slacks are them.' He said, 'They're shit-coloured. What do I want with shit-coloured trousers?'

He was in the yard swilling his boots when he was saying all this. Outside. He's started being much more careful about all that. I don't know what's got into him.

FADE.

Lad opposite just delivering four pizzas to No. 17. She's a widow, living on her own with a son in New Zealand and a heart condition, what's she wanting with four pizzas? I bet she's never had a pizza in her life. They must think I'm stupid. The doctor said, 'Why can't you sleep?' I said, 'The police are bugging my home.' She said, 'Yes. There's a lot of it about.' Asian too. They're normally a bit more civil.

We went out in the van the other night and he stopped it somewhere and said, 'Do you think it's me?' I said, 'No.' He said, 'Well, my mam does. It was her that went to the police.' 'And what did they say?' 'Told her she wasn't the only one. Mothers queuing up apparently.' I said, 'Well, she might cut a bit more ice if she didn't wear that leopard-skin coat thing. Legacy from when she was at it herself.' 'At what?' 'Soliciting.' He said, 'Who told you that?' I said, 'You did. You said she was hard up.' He said, 'It was years ago. I was still at school.'





Went out with Tina later on and comes in all worked up again. Sets to. Thought he was going to go through the bed. And saying stuff out loud again. I thought of them across the road, listening, so I put my hand over his mouth at one point, which he seemed to like.

I waited to see if there was anything in the papers only there wasn't. Been nothing for about a week now. You can get things out of proportion, I think.

I found where they'd put their listening thing this morning. Little hole in the skirting board. Did it when he was reckoning to go to the lavatory. Must have been quick because he'd managed to colour it white so it didn't show only some fluff got stuck to the paint so that's how I spotted it.

*Sound of a newspaper coming through the door. She picks it up.*

They've found another one, it looks like. This time on a skip. Been there...about a week.

FADE.

One of them leaps over the wall, quite unnecessarily in my opinion because the gate's wide open. They get it off the TV. Five police cars. Batter on the door and when he opens it bowl him over and put handcuffs on him and take him off with a jacket over his head.

Tina, of course is going mad and they've got a dog of their own which doesn't help. I said, 'You're not fetching that thing in here.' He said,

'We've got a warrant.' I said, 'His dog's not been in here so I don't see why your dog should.' He said, 'This is an instrument of law enforcement.' I said, 'Yes, and it's an instrument of urinating against lampposts and leaving parcels on pavements. I don't want it sniffing round my stuff.' He says, 'You've got no choice, love,' and shoves me out of the way.

One of them's upstairs going through the airing cupboard. I said, 'What are you looking for? Maybe I can help?' He said, 'If you must know we're looking for the murder weapon.' I said, 'Oh, I can show you that. This is the murder weapon (*Points to her tongue*). This is always the murder weapon. You want to drag the canal for that.'

He said, 'You sound sicker than he does. I don't think you realise the seriousness of your situation. If we find you know what's been going on you'll be in the dock yourself.' I said, 'Don't put those sheets back. I shall have them all to wash now you've been handling them.' He said, 'We shall want all his clothes and other selected items,' and produces a roll of bin bags. 'Is everything here? He hasn't got anything at the dry cleaners?' I said, 'No.' I said, 'How do I know we'll get all this stuff back?' He said, 'That's the least of your worries.'





When eventually they go the handler reckons to take charge of Tina, except that he can't get her to go in the car with them. Then when they do force her in they all pile out sharpish because she's straightaway done her business in the car. I laughed.

It was suddenly quiet when they'd gone, just Mother Catchpole at her gate shouting. 'The doctor says I'm clinically depressed. That dog wants putting down.'

The police said not to touch anything but I wasn't having the place left upset like that so I set to and cleaned down and repaired the ravages a bit. One or two folks outside the house looking in and the phone rings now and again but I don't answer.

Dark by the time I'd finished but I didn't turn the lights on, just sat there. They must have charged him around six because suddenly there's cars drawing up and the phone's going like mad and reporters banging on the door and shouting through the letter-box and whatnot.

I just sit there in the dark and don't take on.

FADE.

Another parcel of excrement through the letter-box this morning. Postmarked Selby. Pleasant place. We had a little run there once in the van. Saw the cathedral, abbey, whatever it is. Shop with booklets and teatowels

the way they do. Had a cup of coffee at a café down a street. The postman whanged it through that hard it split on the doormat.

It's probably deliberate. I'd got some plastic down from the previous times but still I'd to set to again. Spend a fortune on Dettol.

The trial's in Manchester for some reason. Out of the area. They can't call me unless I choose. Which I don't. Woman spat at me in Sainsbury's so I shop at the Asian shops now. Everywhere else they stare. Have to go thirty miles to get a perm. Go by minicab. Asians again. Never liked them much before. Don't ask questions. Godsend.

Reporter comes ringing the doorbell this afternoon. I think they must take it in turns. Shouts through the letter-box. I said, 'You want to be careful with that letter-box. You don't know what's been through it.' Says I'm sitting on a gold mine. Talks about £10,000. My side of the story.

Final speeches today. It rests on the dog, apparently, the rest is circumstantial. The van seen where the murders were, stopped once even but nothing else. Nothing on his tools. Nothing on his clothes. Only they found some blood belonging to the last one on the dog. The defence says it could have rolled in the blood because with the dog being fastened up all day when they went off he let it roam all over. So it doesn't mean he was with her, or anywhere near as the dog was off the lead.

The judge likes dogs. Has a dog of his own apparently. I don't know that'll make any difference.

I saw him before the trial started. Looked thinner. I was disappointed not to see him wearing a tie. I thought a tie would have made a good impression only they use them to commit suicide apparently.

I wish I'd something to do. I've cleaned down twice already. The yard wants doing only I can't do it with folks and reporters hanging about.

*Pause.*

He's lying, of course. Our Tina hasn't been seen to, so when he takes her out he never lets her off the lead. Ever.



FADE.

'Marjory! Marjory!'

They still shout over the gate now and again, one of them there this morning. Most of them have gone only they leave a couple of young ones here just in case I go shopping. Jury's been out two days now and they think it might be a week.



Anyway I thought while the heat was off I might be able to sneak out into the yard and give the kennel a good going over. The forensics took away her blanket so that's a blessing. I said to the feller, 'Don't bother to fetch it back. I'd have wuthered it long since if he'd let me.'

I peeped out of the gate to see if it's safe to swill and there's just a couple of the young reporters sat on Mrs C's doorstep having a cup of tea. I don't know what she's going to do when it's all over. She's had the time of her life.

Anyway I chucked a bucket of water under the kennel and then another only it didn't seem to be coming out the other side. I thought it was muck that had built up or something so I went in and got a wire coat hanger and started scraping about underneath and there's something there.

It was his tan slacks, all mucky and plastered up with something. I sneaked in and got a bin bag and fetched them inside.

Thinking back the police had been round with the dog but I suppose it couldn't smell anything except Tina. I sit there staring at this bag wondering whether there's anybody I should ring up. Suddenly there's a banging at the door and a voice through the letter-box.

'Marjory! Marjory!'

I didn't listen I ran with the bag and put it in the cupboard under the stairs. More clattering at the door.

'Marjory! Marjory! They've come back, the jury. He's been acquitted. He's got off. Can we have a picture?'

FADE.

The young woman says, 'Did I want any assistance with costume or styling? There'll be a lot of photographers.' I said, 'What's the matter with what I've got on?' She said, 'I could arrange for someone to come round and give you a shampoo and set.' I said, 'Yes, I could arrange for someone to come round and give you a kick up the arse.'



Though come to think of it I couldn't actually. She said, 'The paper's got a lot of money invested in you.' I said, 'Well, that's your funeral.'

Picture of him and the dog on the front page this morning, dog licking his face, ears up, paws on his shoulder, loving every minute of it. Spent the night in a hotel, five star, paid for by the newspaper. Article 'These nightmare months.' I stood by him, apparently. Says the longed-for reunion with his wife Marjory is scheduled for sometime this afternoon.



Police furious. The inspector in charge of the investigation said, 'Put it this way. We are not looking for anybody else.'

Sat waiting all afternoon. Photographers standing on the wall opposite, and on chairs and kitchen stools, two of them on top of a car. One up a tree. Police keeping the crowds back.

Getting dark when a big car draws up. Pandemonium.

Policeman bangs on the door, and Stuart's stood there on the doorstep and all the cameras going and them shouting, 'Stuart, Marjory. Over here. Over here please.' They want pictures of us with the dog, only the fellow from the newspaper says, No. They're going to be exclusive, apparently.

I said, 'Well, I've washed her kennel.' He says, 'She's not staying in there.' I said, 'You're not fetching her inside.' He said, 'I bloody am.' I said, 'Well, she'll have to stay on her paper.'

Later on when we're going to bed I wanted to shut her downstairs in the kitchen but he wouldn't have that either, keeps kissing her and whatnot and says she has to come upstairs.

When we're in bed he starts on straightaway and keeps asking Tina if she's taking it all in.

Afterwards he said, 'Are you surprised I'm not guilty?' I said, 'I'm surprised you got off.' He said, 'Don't you think I'm not guilty?' I said, 'I don't know, do I?' He said, 'You bloody do. You'd better bloody know. You're as bad as my mam.' I said, 'I'm not your mam.' He said, 'No, you're bloody not' and laughs.

I must have fallen asleep because when I wake up he's sleeping and the dog's off its paper, sat on his side of the bed watching him.

I get up and go downstairs and get the bin bag from under the stairs only I don't put any lights on. Then I get the poker and go out into the yard and push the slacks back under the kennel.

It's a bit moonlight and when I look over the gate they've all gone, just a broken chair on the pavement opposite.

I get back into bed and in a bit he wakes up and he has another go.

FADE.

# Nights in the **Gardens** of Spain

**Rosemary:** Penelope Wilton

PRODUCED BY **MARK SHIVAS** DIRECTED BY **TRISTRAM POWELL**
DESIGNED BY **STUART WALKER** MUSIC BY **GEORGE FENTON**

A PLAIN SUBURBAN DRAWING ROOM WALL. ROSEMARY IS A MIDDLE-AGED, MIDDLE-CLASS WOMAN, SITTING ON A CHAIR.

Nobody normally gets killed round here; they're mostly detached houses and you never even hear shouting. So it took me a minute to tipple to what she was saying.

I said, 'Dead? Is it a heart attack?' She said, 'Oh no. Nothing like that. Just look at me, I'm in my bare feet.'

I really only know her to nod to but they have a lovely magnolia so once when she was in the garden I called out, 'You've had more luck with your magnolia grandiflora than I have.' But she just smiled and said, 'Yes.' And since I didn't have another remark up my sleeve ready, that was the end of that. I do that all the time, start a conversation but can't keep it going.



Blondish woman, a bit washed-out looking. Nice, tired sort of face. Anyway she comes out into the road and waits for me to get to their gate and says, 'I know I don't really know you, only there's something wrong with Mr McCorquodale.'



I was actually rushing because I'd planned on getting the five to nine and going into Sainsbury's but anyway I went in. I said, 'Has he been poorly?' She said, 'No. I've a feeling he's dead. Come through…only Mrs Horrocks…he doesn't have any trousers on.' I said, 'Well, I do a stint at the hospice twice a week, that's not a problem.' Only to be fair I just take the trolley round I've never actually been there when anybody's been going and they think I'm not really ready to administer the consolation yet.

She had a nice linen dress on, very simple. I think she might have been drinking.

He was lying on his back on the rug, one of those fleecy hairy things with blood and whatnot coming from somewhere behind his head. And it's awful because the first thing I thought was, Well, she'll never get that out.

He had on these green Y-fronty things which I'd have thought were a bit young for someone who's retired, but Henry's the same, suddenly takes it into his head to go in for something he thinks is a bit more dashing. Little Terylene socks. I said, 'Should I touch him?' She said, 'Well, you can if you want but he is dead. I've been sitting here looking at him for an hour.' I said, 'His pants are on back to front.' She said, 'Oh that's me. I thought I'd better put them on before I fetched somebody in.'

He had a little tattoo not far from his belly button and I remember when they moved in Henry said he thought he had something to do with vending machines.

I said, 'Did he bang his head, do you think?' She said, 'Oh no. I shot him. I've put the gun away.' And she opens the sideboard drawer and there it is with the tablemats and playing cards. He had a gun because he'd been in Malaya apparently.

My first thought was to ring Henry and ask what to do but I couldn't face the fuss. I was still a bit nervous of calling 999 because I'm never sure what constitutes an emergency. Anyway I thought if she'd waited an hour already I might as well get her a cup of tea first, and as I was running the tap I called out, 'The police haven't already been, have they?' She said, 'No. Why?' I said, 'Nothing.'

Only there was a pair of handcuffs on the draining board.

FADE.

*Another wall.*

The policeman had some difficulty writing. Big boy, nice ears, spelling all over the place.

When I asked him what he thought had happened he said, 'Well, it's marriage isn't it, the stresses and strains of. Though we don't normally expect it with oldish people, they've generally got it out of their system by then. And it's a bit early in the day. People seem to like to get breakfast out of the way before the shooting starts.'

I'm just signing my statement when Henry arrives back and of course prolongs the process. 'I don't know that Mrs Horrocks quite means this, officer. What you said to me on the phone, young lady was…' I said, 'Henry. You weren't there.' The policeman winks and says, 'Now then, we don't want another shooting match do we?'

I mean at first Henry didn't even know who they were. He said, 'Not the chow?' I said, 'No. That's the Broadbents.' Anyway he sits about for a bit, whistling under his breath, then goes upstairs and attacks his computer.

After the policeman had gone I went up and apologised and asked Henry whether he thought anything had been going on. He said, 'Why?' I said, 'Well, she didn't have anything on under that linen dress.' Of course any suggestion of that embarrasses Henry, he's such an innocent. He said, 'Rosemary, I don't know what sort of world you think you're living in but there's probably some perfectly reasonable explanation. In the meantime let's just remember that somebody has died. I'm only sorry that you had to be the one who was passing, because I'd have preferred you not to have been involved.'

I went out later to get some milk at the garage and there were still one or two reporters outside number 17, a whole branch of the magnolia broken off. One of them said, 'Are you a neighbour? Did you know the McCorquodales?' I shook my head and didn't say anything so one of them shouts after me, 'You owe it to the community.' So I turned round and said, 'Yes, and you owe it to the community not to break branches off people's magnolia trees.' And of course that's just the point where the photographer takes a picture and it's in the paper this morning with me looking like a mad woman and the caption 'The real face of suburbia.' Whereas the real face of suburbia was Henry's when he saw it.

I woke up in the night and I could hear him whistling under his breath. I said, 'Are you thinking about Mrs McCorquodale?' He said, 'No, I was thinking about the house. Prices are down as it is and something like this isn't going to help matters.' He reached over from his bed and took my hand. 'You must try not to be upset, but if we don't get at least 175 we shall have to kiss goodbye to Marbella.'

I keep wondering if I ought to have told somebody about the handcuffs.

FADE.

*Rosemary is in the conservatory.*

I'd put on my little greeny-coloured costume, which is at least tried and tested, only when I came down Henry said, 'Oh, are you going in that?' So I went and changed into the black. No need, because it was all very casual, the policeman in his shirt sleeves, and some barrister taking me through what I'd said, scarcely interested at all. I gave her a little smile; they let her sit down most of the time, she did look pale.

Pleaded not guilty, which you have to do apparently even when they know you did it, only then her lawyer reads out a list of stuff they'd found wrong with Mrs McCorquodale when she'd been arrested, old fractures, new cigarette burns and one of her teeth loose. Another lawyer then jumps up and said, 'Were other people involved?' And she said, 'No,' and he said he wouldn't pursue that at this stage. The upshot is she was sent for trial.

I said to Henry, 'Does that mean they'll have to go through it all again?' He said, 'Oh yes. This is just the beginning.'

Policewoman came round this afternoon, said Did I want any counselling? I'm entitled to it, apparently, through having seen a body and

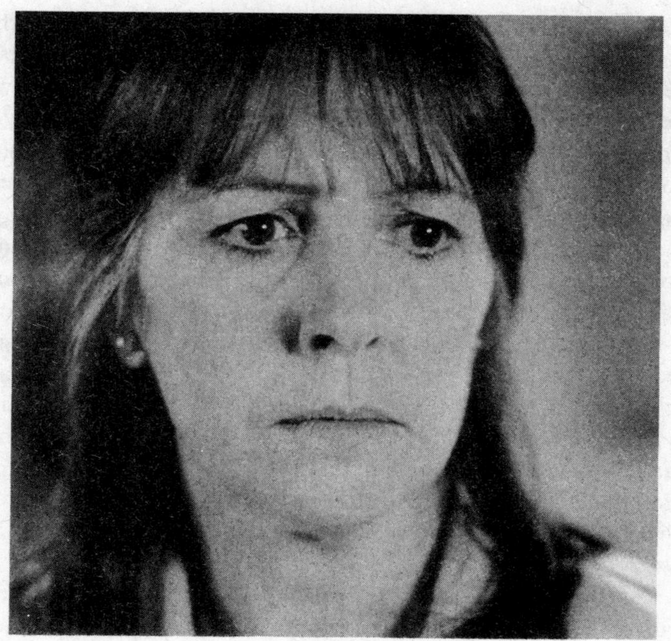





should have had it earlier only they had a charabanc run off the road so they've had a bit of a backlog.

Pleasant enough girl, though she would go on about all the terrible dreadful things she'd seen, accidents and violence and whatnot, so my seeing just one body seemed pretty ordinary really. But maybe that's part of the counselling. We sat in the garden having some tea. Heavy on the biscuits; polished off half a dozen sandwich creams. She said, It was nice it was so civilised, had I seen a naked corpse before?

She was just going when she turns back and she says, 'Mrs Horrocks, when I went on the counselling course one of the things they teach you is that it helps to look things in the face right from the start.' I said, 'Well, I did look at the body; I actually touched it.' She said, 'Yes, but when the police start digging, which they have to do, there is a potential for distress.' I said, 'Digging?' She said, 'Metaphorically.' I said, 'Why should it affect me?' She said, 'All the indications are that it won't. But the potential is there. Things come out and I want you to know I'm here for you. I'm on a bleep.'

I said to Henry, 'It's nice she should be so concerned.' He said, 'It's what she's there for...unfortunately.'

Article in the *Mail* yesterday, which I'd always thought was that bit more refined but it's full of silly stuff about the case, what goes on behind the neat privet hedges-type-thing. I said to Henry, Fat lot they know. There actually isn't a privet hedge in the entire road. They're mostly beech and one or two cypresses leylandii. He said he didn't think that was quite the point and to a reporter a hedge was simply something to be peered through.

Still, talking of neat, what with her being away on remand their garden which is usually so immaculate is already beginning to look a bit… well…shaggy. She's got a herb garden outside the back door and the borage has gone berserk, bullying its way all over the border. Made me long to nip over and put it in its place.

I didn't want to ask Henry, though, as I was sure he'd think it 'Inadvisable, Rosemary, quite candidly,' but no, it turns out he's all in favour and it had in fact occurred to him, though, it has to be said, coming at it from a different angle from me, saying that if ever we're going to get anywhere near our asking price a garden going to seed in the same road is the last thing one wants.

So the upshot is I've started toddling up the road with my trusty secateurs. Thought I'd cut back the poppies now that they've flowered and give the achillea a chance to come through. Of course, I've scarcely got my kneeling pad down before Miss Lumsden's out, contriving to come by with an unconvincing bottle of Lucozade en route for the bottle bank. Wants to know if there are any sweet peas going begging. I said I'd thought of picking some and taking them down to the hospice. She said 'What a nice idea. Some people might feel a bit funny about them but I suppose they're too far gone to care.'

And lots of jokes of course. On the lines of Mr Pemberton's 'Who do I have to shoot for you to come and do my garden?' Smile got a bit fixed after a bit. Except that Sheila Blanchard did actually come in and lend a hand weeding the borders. Said she didn't blame her a bit. 'I mean husbands, Rosemary. Who needs them?' I said, 'Well, they can be a comfort.' She said, 'Can they? Reggie isn't. I'm the comfort merchant. What's Henry like?' 'Oh,' I said 'very…' and I said such a silly word 'very considerate.' I saw her smile and she's a nice woman but I know it'll be all up and down the road by tomorrow.

But he is considerate. Timid, I suppose. Always has been. Wish he wasn't sometimes.

What I haven't told Henry is that I dropped Mrs McCorquodale a note to the prison, bringing her up to date on what I've been doing. I do it every day now, in fact, even send her snaps. Told her today I was keeping an eye on the alchemilla mollis, lovely plant but you have to read it the riot act occasionally.

She rang this afternoon to thank me. I didn't know you could do that in prison, ring up. Her name's Fran.

'Dear Fran…'

FADE.

*The conservatory.*

I've misjudged Henry. Got him quite wrong. Thirty years of marriage and you think you've got somebody all weighed up but no. He's lost half a stone while the case has been going on – and never set foot in the office. I thought, well, you're a better person than ever I thought you were. I said to Fran, 'He's more worried about you than he's ever been about me.' I mean the day I had my scan he went off to a golf tournament.

So as a reward I got out the brochures for Marbella and that seemed to cheer him up.

It's all come out in court, though. Turns out that Mr has led her a dog's life. Literally. The defence produced the collar and lead in evidence. Beat her. Terrorised her. 'A saga of protracted and imaginative cruelty' counsel said.

The prosecution, of course, goes after her, claiming it was all part of some game, sexually speaking, and that the cruelty was what she wanted. But she said if it had been mutual he wouldn't have been interested. Anyway how is it mutual to have your arm broken?

A lot of lurid details, how he sometimes used to put a hood over her head so's she couldn't see and bring in other people to watch. Business associates, she thought. Leading lights in the world of vending machines, probably.

Henry says she was lucky because there was another case going on the same week up in Liverpool, a man had up for killing a child, and that pushed her out of the limelight a bit.

Of course, what Henry calls the wild and woolly feminist ladies were out in force even shouting from the gallery. 'To a degree irresponsible,' Henry said. 'However mitigating the circumstances, Rosemary, she has to be looking at a custodial sentence.' Then, when he only gave her two years, the judge gets it in the neck from the law and order brigade. But, as Sheila Blanchard said, 'Worth every minute of it, dear, if you ask me. A couple of years basket weaving and you get the bed to yourself. Cheap at the price. I just wish I had a gun. As it is I'm pinning my hopes on his prostate.'

I can't go and see her so often now she's convicted and Henry doesn't know I go at all. Well, I've never had a best friend, the sort you can tell everything to. Never had one, never been one, even when I was a girl. Not the type, I suppose. And no secrets to tell either. And with not having children I wasn't a member of that club either.

She's in Rissington, the other side of York. It's one of these modern places, looks like a business park or an out of town shopping centre. Crimes 'R' Us. She's transformed the prison garden, which used to be very utilitarian, cabbages, lettuces and whatnot.

Only now she's got them to do some interplanting, even make it a bit of a potager…and while it's never going to be Sissinghurst…the site's too windy…it's still streets ahead of what it was. She has visions of it being open to the public but that's difficult with it being a prison. We go and sit on a seat in the garden and she's started telling me about all the stuff he forced her to do. Said she wanted me to know in case it made me not want to see her any more. I said, 'Don't be silly.' But terrible things I never knew people did. And with the hood over her head and men there, watching in silence. More than watching actually.

One of them who had a funny habit…and I knew what she was going to say the second before she said it…a funny habit of whistling under his breath.

*Pause.*

Of course, a lot of people do that.

FADE.

*Kitchen.*

'I see they're selling the Murder House,' Sheila Blanchard calls out to me this morning. 'The board's gone up. Asking 160.' I didn't say I knew, or that actually it's sold already. Fran says they're an Asian family, quite well-to-do, have a chain of electrical shops. I thought, Well, that won't do Marbella any good. Poor Henry. Golf with Jimmy Tarbuck takes a knock.

I look at him a lot now, this once upon a time spectator, or maybe still, who knows, somewhere. And I think…Well, sometimes I just think,

'You dark horse.' Other times I think about Fran and get upset. He caught me staring at him the other night, said 'What are you looking at, young lady?' I said, predictably, 'Nothing.' 'You've been getting a bit broody lately,' he said. And he patted me on the knee. (*She pulls a face.*)

What I'd actually been thinking was whether all these years he'd been wanting to see me crawl round the room naked on my hands and knees. No worse than bedding out, I suppose, though if I did it nowadays I'd have to have my knee pads on, which might take the edge off things a bit.

But I think about the collar and lead, then I think Well, that's what my marriage has been like too, being jerked along. I mean, what else is Marbella?

We never settled on what to call it, that was part of the trouble. The garden's made me quite used to things having a common name and a Latin one. Only with sex neither seemed to suit Henry. Coming from me, anyway. Just got embarrassed.

He's no idea I go and see her. I tell him it's the hospice. The farm goes from strength to strength; she's put her onions in for shows and gone commercial with the tomatoes. She's there every free moment, well, I say free. Except that when I say goodbye at the gate it feels it's me that's going back to prison.

Once a month they let her out for a half day and we go off for the afternoon and do all sorts. Open gardens, obviously, auctions we've been to, car boot sales. And old churches, which I've never cared much for, only Fran knows a lot about them. One church in the middle of a field near where there'd been a battle. And we sit there in a pew while she explains all the architectural features. And sometimes I think I've never been so happy in my life.

She took my arm this last time, just as we were coming down some steps at Fountains Abbey and then, when we got to the bottom, she didn't let go. It was just like it was when I was a girl when a boy did it. Such a bold step. And so meant.

And I thought, here I am strolling arm in arm with someone who murdered her husband. I said…out loud…'I know what this is.' She said, 'What is it?' I said, 'It's life.'

She wasn't feeling all that clever today so we just went and sat in the grounds, and she held my hand again. Going into York next week for a check-up. I thought I could go along and hang about the hospital just on the off-chance I might see her but she'll be with a warder apparently so I won't.

Gave me this.

*She has a large tomato which she puts to her cheek.*

FADE.

*A patio wall. A tropical night. Crickets, etc.*

I've never had to start a garden from scratch before. There are no features at all. Flat, square, stony it's like one of the 'before' pictures in the gardening magazines. Or an exercise yard.

A lawn's pretty much out of the question in this heat and the water supply's very quixotic, though Henry says the greens at the golf club are immaculate. And he saw Sean Connery last week. So I sit and look at it and draw plans. 'Look on it as a challenge,' Henry says. 'You'll crack it, young lady,' he says. 'I know you.' (*The dialogue is now quite broken up.*)

She died, did Fran. A lot of toing and froing before they eventually tracked it down. No surprise to either of us. Doctors. It's the first thing that occurs to you and the last thing that occurs to them. By which time it's too late. 'Oh, it was always too late, Mrs Horrocks.'

She was in a hospice at the finish so I knew the drill. I used to hold her hand, kiss it. And she'd kiss mine. We'd talked about a little garden centre.

Best thing that could have happened, Henry said. Which is when I should have packed my bags. Instead of which I just went and sat in the greenhouse for a bit. Typical.

He'll sometimes wear one of these caps with the big peaks that boys wear. Reckons it's for the sun. Caught him the other day wearing it back to front. I suppose it's known as a new lease of life.

There are supposed to be lots of criminals round here. Bank robbers and such like who can't go back, play golf all day.

Of course it's just what would happen in a play. Fran shot him so she had to pay. Only this place is crawling with people who haven't paid. Unless you count just being here as paying.

The gardening books talk about the plants that are supposed to like shade. They say they prefer it.

I don't believe it. I don't believe anything likes shade. They do perfectly well in the shade, it's true. But give them even…(*and there's quite a long pause*) give them a bit of sun and suddenly they come into their own.

I sit here at night, listening to the frogs and the crickets, and Henry, whistling under his breath.

FADE.

# **Waiting** for the Telegram

**Violet:** Thora Hird

PRODUCED BY **MARK SHIVAS** DIRECTED BY **STUART BURGE**
DESIGNED BY **STUART WALKER** MUSIC BY **GEORGE FENTON**

THE SPEAKER IS AN OLD LADY IN A WHEELCHAIR. SHE HAS A RUG OVER HER KNEES. THE BACKGROUND IS PLAIN AND UNCLUTTERED. SOMETIMES SHE IS PARKED BY A RADIATOR, SOMETIMES BY A WINDOW OR THE END OF A BED. THE SHOTS NEED NOT BE CONTINUOUS AS WRITTEN BUT CAN BE BROKEN UP BY A CUTAWAY OF VIOLET'S HANDS, TWISTING HER HANDKERCHIEF, TURNING HER WEDDING-RING OR JUST FOLDED IN HER LAP. SOMETIMES WHEN SHE IS TRYING TO REMEMBER THINGS OR EXPRESS THEM SHE FILLS UP WITH TEARS BUT THESE ARE ONLY BRIEF AND SHE GENERALLY BATTLES ON.

I saw this feller's what-do-you-call-it today. Except I'm not supposed to say 'what-do-you-call-it'. Verity says, 'Violet. What-do-you-call-it is banned. When we cannot find the word we want we *describe*, we do not say 'what-do-you-call-it'. Well, you won't catch me describing that. Besides, 'what-do-you-call-it' *is* what I call it. Somebody's what-do-you-call-it. Anyway I saw it.





I didn't think anything about it only somebody must have gone and alerted the office because next thing you know Bouncing Betty poles in. She says, 'Violet, I have to ask you this. Was the penis erect?' I said, 'Nurse Bapty. That's not a word I would use.' She said, 'Erect?' I said, 'No. The other.' She said, 'Well, Violet. You've had what we call a stroke. You're sometimes funny with words.' I said, 'I'm not funny with that word.' She said, 'Things have changed now, Violet. Penis is its name. All the other names are just trying to make it more acceptable. Language is a weapon, Violet. We're at war.' I said, 'Who with?' She said, 'Men.'

He was a smartish feller, can't have been more than seventy and a lovely blue suit. He could have been a bank manager except he had no socks on. I said, 'You can put that away.' He said, 'I've got a big detached house in Harrogate.' I said, 'That's no excuse.' He said, 'It's got five bathrooms.'

*She turns her wheelchair.*

They've inaugurated this what-do-you-call (*She checks herself*)...this chair-lift thing. I think he must have come up from downstairs. There's been one or two of them trying to migrate. They get bored. Do you wonder? Anyway when he saw it wasn't cutting much ice with me he takes it over to Hilda, only she's busy braying on her tray with her spoon so it doesn't make much of an impact there either. Mary's asleep and when he wakes her up and says, 'Look at this', she says, 'Is it dinner-time?' and goes back to sleep again.

In the finish he comes back to me and says, 'I've forgotten, did I show you this?' At which point Rene rushes in, sees his lordship with his trousers down and says, 'Are you my taxi? I'm all ready.'

I said to Francis, 'And they call it a rest home.'

FADE.

They haven't given it up. We were throwing this ball about… a big, felty thing…I could never catch a ball when I was little so I know I can't do it now. Anyway Nurse Bapty comes in and wheels me to the window and says, 'Violet, having seen this penis, would you like some counselling?' I said, 'Nurse. I'm nearly 95.' She said, 'Yes, Violet, but you're a victim and choose how old you are, you're still flying the flag of gender.' I said, 'Well I think a cup of tea would do the trick, Nurse Bapty, thank you.' I call them all Nurse and she is a nurse only a lot of them aren't, they're just young lasses.

Francis is a proper nurse, though, he's got letters after his name and you can tell because he has me out of my clothes in no time. I said, 'Somebody tried to undress me once, only he wasn't a patch on you. Are you as sharp as this with your girl friend?' He said, 'You're my girl friend.'

He has some grand arms.

FADE.

I can't reckon up names. New lass on this afternoon, bonny little thing, helping Francis put me to bed for my lie down. I said, 'What's your name, love?' She says, 'Devon.' I says, 'That's never a name, it's a place.' She says, 'Yes, a very beautiful place. My mam and dad used to go on holiday there.' I said, 'Well, it's a good job they didn't go to Skegness.'

She looks right mad, only Francis laughs so she laughs an' all. I think she's got her eye on him.

I drop off and when I wake up there's a fellow by my bed. He goes, 'Hello!' I said, 'Hello' and shut my eyes again. They send these folks round to test you.

When I open them again he's still there. 'Hello!,' he goes. Fattish feller, sixty odd, gingery tash. He said, 'It's Donald, mother. I'm your son.'

He didn't look like a son, looked more like a father. Big wristwatch, attaché case, one of these green raincoaty-things they shoot in. Anyway I take no notice and he starts on the Hello! game again. Hello! Hello! Made me feel like a budgie. I said, 'Bugger off.'

Mrs…Mrs…light-coloured lady…Shah comes in, starts

squeegeeing round. He says, 'It's tragic, isn't it. She'd never had a day's illness in her life. I think it's a disease of civilisation. Does it happen in your country?' She says, 'I'm from Huddersfield.'

Then Rene comes in, ready for off as usual. She says, 'Are you my taxi? I've been waiting all morning.' 'I've just remembered,' he says, 'I'm wanted in Wakefield,' shoves his tash in my face and he's off. Mrs Shah says, 'Was that your son?' I said, 'He thinks so.' She says, 'My son's got in to do engineering. He's six foot two.'

I lay there working it out. If I had a son I must have had a...husband. So when Francis was wiping my bottom later on I said, 'Did I get married?' He said, 'Yes, can't you remember?' I said, 'I remember one young man but I don't think I took the plunge. Are you married?' He said, 'You get star treatment here, Violet. Even the Queen doesn't get her bottom wiped.'





FADE.

What's her name came round today...her that helps me with talking... (*She thinks*)...name of a cricket bat, else a gas oven...Verity. She's a nice-looking lass but makes nowt of herself, a big jumper thing...I said, I bet you've got a right nice...' She goes, 'Describe, Violet, describe...' I said, 'A right nice...them two things with pink ends that men like...Bust.'

By, she did look narked! She said, 'Things are different now, Violet. Women have control of their own bodies.' I said, 'Is that why I can't get them to take me to the toilet?'

Then we start doing these exercises, naming folks. I'm quite good at that...Rene, Mary, Hilda. And then I get stuck. She says, 'Describe, Violet. Say, the lady in the yellow frock.' I said, 'The black lady.' She said, 'No, Violet. It's better to say the lady in the yellow frock.'

I says to Francis, 'It's a complicated business talking. I never used to give it a thought.' He said, 'What?'

He wasn't listening. He was miles away. Really quiet. Not like him. He's generally so full of...them things you get in tins...beans!

He's a lovely looking lad.

FADE.

Rene gollops her food. She was sick today all down Francis's front. I said, 'You gollop your food, you.' She said, 'Well, I have to. I've got a taxi coming.' I said, 'Rene, where's this taxi taking you?' She said, 'Armley.'

I said, 'Armley where?' She said, 'My mam and dad's in 1947.' I said, 'Well, if he can take you there I bet he does a spanking trade.'

Anyway she fetches her dinner back all down Francis. So he says, 'You'll have to excuse me, ladies' and he takes his...tunicky thing...right off. And by, he's a grand-looking lad! Not a mark on him and right big (*She mimes shoulders*)...here. It made you want to...(*She mimes a kiss*)...do that, whatever it's called. Lovely. Devon came in I saw her having a look.

When he's finished cleaning up he says, 'Well, Violet you've seen something today.' I said, 'I've seen it before.' He just has a little bit of this (*She touches her hair*)...starting here (*She touches her chest*). Like they do at that age. (*She starts to cry.*) I said, 'Don't go get yourself...' He said, 'What?' I said, 'Like when you don't come back. Khaki...poppies.' He said, 'Nay, that's all done with now. They don't die like that.' And he looked right...(*She touches her cheeks meaning tears*)...what's it called?

FADE.

I saw my legs today. I didn't own them. They didn't look like my legs at all. That Devon was giving me a bath. I said, 'Them's never my legs.' She said, 'Whose legs do you think they are?' I said, 'Well, you never know in this place. I've had somebody else's teeth before now. And this frock isn't mine. Tangerine doesn't suit me. Where's that green little frock?' She said, 'Hilda kept wetting herself in it and it's gone funny.' Francis wouldn't have put me in this frock. Only he wasn't there.

She's putting me back on the bed and I said, 'Well I've learned one thing. I'm not Betty Grable.' She says, 'Who's she?' No wonder your talking goes…even when you get it right they think you're barmy. Francis knows all the old film stars…Betty Grable…her that sings and that one with the cig and her hair up…bit of a madam…Bette Davis.

Anyway I'm sitting up in bed when they all waltz in with this cake. Turns out it's my birthday. I'm ninety something…I don't know, they



did tell me. Candles. Tasted like candles did the cake. Anyway I had to reckon to be… pleased (*She pretends to smile*)…Kept saying a few years more and I'll be getting the…now then…lad comes on a bike…folks stood at the door, weeping…telegram. Her on the horse at the end of the pictures, she sends it you apparently. Queen.



No Francis though. I said to Nurse Bapty, 'Where is he?' She said, 'He's gone for a check-up.' I said, 'Check-up for what?' She said, 'Oh, they do that now.'

*Pause.*

I hate tangerine.

FADE.

Verity fetches a young lad in this morning. She says to him, 'You're privileged. Violet is our oldest resident.' She says, 'Spencer's going to ask you one or two questions for his school project. It's about the past.'

Poor-looking lad, bonny face. Floppy clothes, shirt-tail out. I said, 'Is that your big brother's jumper?' He says, 'No. It's dead smart is this.' Gets out his exercise book, and says, 'What was it like then?' I said, 'Well…' He said, 'Were things better or worse?' I said, 'Well, my legs were better.' He said he didn't mean that. Verity comes back and he says, 'She doesn't seem to know what I'm talking about.' Verity says, 'Well, she's had a stroke. Come on, I'll find you another one.' (*Violet is a bit upset.*)

I said to Francis, 'He'd mean trams and whatnot. Strikes. Tin-baths. The war.' Francis says, 'Which war?' I said, 'The proper war when all the young lads got killed. "Never again." That war.' He looked right sad and said, 'Hold my hand.' So I did. Then he said, 'Did you have a young man?' I said, 'Yes.' He said, 'What was he like?' I said, 'His name was Edward. They had a little confectioner's down Tong Road. He used to fetch my mam a vanilla slice. Every time he came round, a vanilla slice.'

I still had hold of his hand. I said, 'When you were courting then, it was a kind of...where you fight...' He said, 'Struggle.' I said, 'Ay. He'd manage to get one button undone one night, and another the next. And lasses weren't supposed to do much in them days, just lie back and get ready to draw the line. And because I'd let him get so far one night, he'd know where the front line was, so the next night he'd get there a bit quicker and push on a bit further...another button, you know. It was that...grudging somehow. But it was the way you felt you had to be then.



Anyway he was going off to France next day; he was in camp over at Church Fenton and they'd given him a pass for his last night. My mam...oh she was a good 'un...she put some anemones in a vase...I love anemones...and put a fire in the front room and then she reckoned she had to stay at my Aunt Florence's that night. Ordinary folks then were better than they're ever given credit for, for all they were so straitlaced.



I gave him his tea and then we went and sat in the front room and he started on like, undoing my buttons and kissing and whatnot. Only I'd wanted to look nice so I'd put on my best frock and he couldn't fathom how it unfastened. I should just have taken it off but I didn't and, poor lamb, he got so fed up with these flaming buttons, in the finish he gave up.

He'd taken his leggings...his puttees off because they were hot and he was in his shirtsleeves; they were right rough khaki shirts then, really cheap and itchy. Anyway in the finish he gets up off the sofa and says, 'Hang this lot,' and he takes his shirt off and everything else besides. Doesn't say a word, just takes it all off and stands there on the hearthrug. Oh and he looked a picture, with the fire and that. Not a mark on him. Then he says, 'Take your clothes off now.'

*She covers her face with her hands.*

And I didn't. I didn't. And I wanted him so much. I don't know...it was just the way I'd been brought up. And he stands there looking down at me...and then he just picks his clothes up and goes next door and after a bit I heard the front door bang.

They look old in photographs compared with what they look now. Only they weren't. They were lads, same as you. And just as grand.

*Pause.*

I saw the yellow thing the boy on the bike brings…his sister fetches it round…telegram. And a vanilla slice for mam. Then later on they had a letter reckoning to be from the King, same as everybody did who'd lost somebody. They keep saying I'll be getting a telegram soon…for my birthday.'

Francis says, 'Do you know something Violet? In all that, you never said, "What do you call it?" or "What's its name?" Not once. You knew all the words.'

'Only I should have let him, shouldn't I? I've never forgiven myself.' 'Well,' Francis says, 'how can you know?' Still holding my hand.



*Pause.*

Poor lad, he looks right washed out.

FADE.



I thought they'd got pneumonia beat. A big strapping lad like Francis. Devon said it was a blessing, he'd have died anyway. I said, 'A blessing? A young feller like that?'

And he was such a gentle soul. She was doing my legs, plastering me up with stuff and right hard hands, not a patch on Francis. I said, 'He'd have made some lass a grand husband.' She said, 'It wasn't lasses; it was lads.' I said, I knew it was lads. She said, 'Well I wish you'd told me.' Right nasty.

*Pause.*

I didn't know it was lads but I wasn't having her telling me. Lads or lasses, he was a love.

Rene's gone an' all.

*Violet looks towards the empty bed.*

Went in the night. They thought I was asleep so they didn't bother to put the screens round. Saw it all. Putting the white socks on. Bit of giggling. Right as rain when she came to bed. Made me promise to wake her up if her taxi came. Well, it came in the finish. I said to Francis…no, I didn't.

*Pause.*

My arm seems to have gone to sleep this morning and this hand.

*She looks at her hand.*

Now then I'll have another one of these somewhere.

*She locates her other hand, lifts it onto her lap and sits with her hands folded. She sings.*

I've got sixpence
Jolly jolly sixpence
I've got sixpence
To last me all my life
I've got twopence to spend
And twopence to lend
And twopence to send home to my wife.

If we sang everything I shouldn't forget.

*All this very broken up with pauses.*

Pets is what you want in this place. Else babies. Summat you can… (*She makes a stroking movement*) do this with. Not have to talk to.

*Pause.*

It's no game is this.

*Pause.*

We're the pets. Fed and cleaned out every day. It's a kennels is this.

*Pause.*

Pedigree Chum. Pedigree Chum.

FADE.

# The Cast

Alan Bennett plays Graham in *A Chip in the Sugar*

Patricia Routledge plays Peggy in *A Woman of No Importance*

Maggie Smith plays Susan in *Bed Among the Lentils*

Julie Walters plays Lesley in *Her Big Chance*

Patricia Routledge plays Irene Ruddock in *A Lady of Letters*

Stephanie Cole plays Muriel in *Soldiering On*

Thora Hird plays Doris in *A Cream Cracker Under the Settee*

Eileen Atkins plays Celia in *The Hand of God*

David Haig plays Wilfred in *Playing Sandwiches*

Patricia Routledge plays Miss Fozzard in *Miss Fozzard Finds Her Feet*

Julie Walters plays Marjory in *The Outside Dog*

Thora Hird plays Violet in *Waiting for the Telegram*

Penelope Wilton plays Rosemary in *Nights in the Gardens of Spain*